"Ace director John Badham's handbook, *John Badham on Directing*, is a mercifully non-academic, extremely practical and very entertaining look at the task of making pictures, covering just about every aspect of the director's job. It is not in the least didactic, and includes a multitude of quotes from other filmmakers that are also most illuminating. The book is quite charming as well, and should become a standard text."

— Peter Bogdanovich

"I've been directing for a lot of years, but I wish this book had been around when I first started. It would have made my life a lot easier as a director. One hell of a good read!"

— Richard Donner, Director, *Lethal Weapon*, *Superman*, *The Omen*, *Goonies*

"What a gift this book is for the novice and not-so-novice filmmaker. John Badham shares his vast experience and knowledge of every important aspect of directing, with clarity and precision. As he dissects even the most complex issues, he achieves the most precious quality: simplicity. Truly a must-read."

— Dezso Magyar, Master Teacher and former Artistic Director of The American Film Institute, Canadian Film Center, and Chapman University's Dodge College

"It's said there are ten easy steps to directing movies but unfortunately no one knows what they are. John Badham comes as close as anyone ever has to demystifying the art of directing while still managing to offer a thoughtful, fun, and engaging read. It's a book for filmmakers and film lovers alike."

— Edward Zwick, Director, *Glory*, *Blood Diamond*

"This book is a no-nonsense guide to directing and John talks it as good as he walks it. His take on working with actors and navigating their demons is both searingly honest and immensely entertaining."

— Emilio Estevez, Actor, Filmmaker

"Whether you're a veteran director, a film student, or someone interested in the process of filmmaking, *John Badham on Directing* is essential reading for anyone seeking how to do that delicate dance that is directing the actor."

— Daniel Sackheim, Director, *The Walking Dead, House M.D.*;
Emmy winner for *NYPD Blue*

"This book is packed with useful tools and nuggets of hard-won wisdom, from a real industry veteran. If anyone's qualified to do a nuts-and-bolts book about directing, John Badham is your guy."

— Alex Epstein, Screenwriter, *Bon Cop, Bad Cop*; Director, *You Are So Undead*

"Through generous quotes and wonderful stories, Badham takes the reader through the trials and tribulations of directing, opening up a world few have ever seen. Both highly enjoyable and highly informative."

— Matthew Terry, Filmmaker, Screenwriter, Teacher

"*John Badham on Directing* is a marvelous and memorable book, which should be required reading for every aspiring film and television director, actor, or screenwriter. This is a beautifully curated spectrum of practical advice from a master craftsman and teacher, combined with extraordinary wisdom assembled from industry leaders: one of a handful of truly useful books in a crowded field."

— James Bundy, Dean/Artistic Director, Yale School of Drama/Yale Repertory Theatre

"You don't need to be a movie director, or even want to become one, to enjoy John Badham's informative, witty, no-nonsense treatise on the hoops that must often be jumped through to make a movie or TV show. Larded with savvy tips from over thirty of his peers, *John Badham on Directing* mines his wealth of experience behind the camera to provide a fascinating journey through the evolving realities of an ever-changing business."

— Joe Dante, Director

John Badham
on Directing

Notes from the Sets of
Saturday Night Fever, WarGames,
and More

John Badham

MICHAEL WIESE PRODUCTIONS

Published by Michael Wiese Productions
12400 Ventura Blvd. #1111
Studio City, CA 91604
(818) 379-8799, (818) 986-3408 (FAX)
mw@mwp.com
www.mwp.com

Cover photo by Joe Lederer
Copyedited by Gary Sunshine
Interior layout by William Morosi

Printed by McNaughton & Gunn

Manufactured in the United States of America

Library of Congress Cataloging-in-Publication Data

Badham, John, 1939-
 John Badham on directing : notes from the set of Saturday night fever, War games,
and more / John Badham.
 pages cm
 ISBN 978-1-61593-138-5 (pbk.)
 1. Motion pictures--Production and direction. I. Title.
 PN1995.9.P7B2725 2013
 791.4302'33--dc23
 2013016105

Printed on Recycled Stock

FOR LEVINSON

Contents

Contributors

Allan Arkush is an Emmy-winning TV director and executive producer of the hit series *Heroes, Crossing Jordan* and *Hellcats*. His Ramones' cult classic *Rock 'n' Roll High School* is one of the top 10 rock 'n' roll DVDs ever.

Paris Barclay is a two-time Emmy Award winner and the busiest director of single-camera episodes in the DGA. He is the main director and an executive producer on FX's hit *Sons of Anarchy*. He is currently preparing a biopic of Barbara Jordan with Viola Davis in the lead role. He is the president of the Directors Guild of America.

Gary Busey was nominated for an Oscar for his star-making performance in the lead role of *The Buddy Holly Story*. He has been acting in film and TV for over forty years, including two films with Badham, *The Law* and *Drop Zone*.

D. J. Caruso began his career working with Badham on several films as 2nd unit director and producer before beginning his own feature career with *The Salton Sea*. He's gone on to direct *Disturbia* and *Eagle Eye* starring Shia LeBeouf and *Standing Up* for release in 2013. He's currently preparing the film *Invertigo*.

Gilbert Cates is the director of the Oscar-nominated films *I Never Sang for My Father* and *Summer Wishes, Winter Dreams*. He produced the Oscar telecast a record fourteen times, and served as vice president of the Academy of Motion Picture Arts and Sciences, as well as president of the Directors Guild of America.

Stephen Collins has appeared in numerous films and television series in his nearly forty-year acting career. He is best known for his role as Reverend Eric Camden on the series *7th Heaven*, and his appearance as Decker in *Star Trek: The Motion Picture*.

Martha Coolidge is a president emeritus of the Directors Guild of America and winner of a DGA award for *Meet Dorothy Dandridge*. Her works include *Rambling Rose* with Laura Dern, *Lost in Yonkers* with Richard Dreyfuss, and *Out to Sea* with Jack Lemmon and Walter Matthau. She is a professor at The Dodge College of Film and Media, Chapman University in Orange, California.

Jan DeBont gained fame as a cinematographer on films like *Basic Instinct, Hunt for Red October* and *Black Rain*. His first film as a director was the hit *Speed*, followed by *Twister* and *Lara Croft Tomb Raider*.

Richard Donner has directed the global hits *Superman, Lethal Weapon* and its three sequels, in addition to *The Goonies*, and *The Omen*. He is also a prolific producer alongside his wife, Lauren Shuler-Donner. His biography, *You're the Director... You Figure it Out* by James Christie, is available on Amazon and in bookstores.

Richard Dreyfuss won the Oscar in 1978 for his performance in *The Goodbye Girl*. His acclaimed career has taken him from *Jaws* to *Mr. Holland's Opus* and dozens of films in between. Dreyfuss worked with Badham on *Whose Life Is It Anyway?, Stakeout,* and *Another Stakeout*.

Jodie Foster won two Best Actress Academy Awards for *Silence of the Lambs* and *The Accused* in addition to forty-five other major acting awards. She is the director of three films, *Little Man Tate, Home for the Holidays* and *The Beaver*, starring herself and Mel Gibson. She worked with Badham at age eleven on an episode of the series *Kung Fu*.

John Frankenheimer cut his teeth in the heady days of live TV dramas. His acclaim in that medium led him to Hollywood where he continued this success with *The Birdman of Alcatraz, The Manchurian Candidate, French Connection II, Black Sunday* and *Ronin*.

Taylor Hackford is the former president of the Directors Guild of America and has directed thirteen features, including *An Officer and a Gentleman, Against All Odds, Dolores Claiborne* and *Ray*. He is married to Oscar-winning actress Helen Mirren.

Peter Hyams began telling stories as a journalist before becoming captivated by filmmaking. He is also one of the few directors who photographs almost all of his own films. Some of his more notable works include *2010* (the sequel to *2001: A Space Odyssey*), *Timecop, The Presidio* and *End of Days*.

Patty Jenkins directed Charlize Theron's Oscar-winning performance in *Monster*. She recently won the DGA award for her direction of the pilot of the AMC series *The Killing*.

Eriq LaSalle is an accomplished actor, director and novelist. He is best known for his long run on the hit show *ER* and his appearance in *Coming to America*. His directorial debut, *Rebound*, was executive produced by Badham.

Penelope Ann Miller was a Tony Award nominee for *Our Town*, and starred in *The Freshman* with Marlon Brando and Matthew Broderick. She also starred in *Carlito's Way* with Sean Penn, winning a Golden Globe nomination, as well *Awakenings, Chaplin* and *Other People's Money*.

Michael McMurray, the cinematographer of fifty-eight episodes of *Psych*, has directed episodes of *Soul Food, Psych* and *Warehouse 13*.

Donald Petrie began his career as an actor, segueing into directing and following in the footsteps of his father, director Daniel Petrie. He has helmed the hit comedies *Grumpy Old Men, Miss Congeniality* and *How to Lose a Guy in 10 Days*. He is on the National Board of the Directors Guild of America.

Sydney Pollack took up directing on advice from legendary actor Burt Lancaster. His prolific career as producer and director includes *Tootsie, The Way We Were, Three Days of the Condor, The Firm*, and Oscars for both directing and producing *Out of Africa*.

Brett Ratner began directing music videos for hip-hop, rap and pop artists before segueing into directing feature films with *Money Talks*. Next came the smash hit *Rush Hour* series, *X-Men 3*, and *Red Dragon*. His most recent film was *Tower Heist* with Eddie Murphy and Ben Stiller.

John Rich directed and produced some of the most well-known and loved shows in television, including *The Jeffersons, Maude, Benson,* and *Barney Miller*. He won three Emmy Awards for *The Dick Van Dyke Show* and *All in the Family*. A longtime vice president of the Directors Guild of America, he was a major force in forging creative rights for television directors.

Mark Rydell was nominated for a Best Director Oscar for *On Golden Pond*. Other films of his are *The Reivers, The Cowboys, The Rose* and *The Fox*. He received an Emmy nomination for his direction of *James Dean*.

Judge Reinhold is known for his wonderfully quirky work in *Fast Times at Ridgemont High*, the *Beverly Hills Cop* series, *Stripes, The Santa Clause 3* and John Badham's *Floating Away*.

Martin Sheen is a Golden Globe- and Emmy-winning actor, best remembered for his haunting performance in *Apocalypse Now*, and his seven-year run as President Josiah Bartlett on *The West Wing*. He is the father of actors Emilio Estevez and Charlie Sheen.

Brad Silberling made his feature debut with 1995's *Casper* after getting started directing in television. He went on to direct *City of Angels* with Meg Ryan and Nicolas Cage, *Moonlight Mile* with Susan Sarandon and Dustin Hoffman, and *10 Items or Less* with Morgan Freeman.

Steven Soderbergh burst onto the filmmaking scene with the indie sensation *Sex, Lies and Videotape* in 1989. In the years since he has successfully moved between huge studio films like the *Ocean's Eleven* series and *Erin Brockovich* to small budget projects like *Magic Mike, Bubble* and *Schizopolis*. He was national vice president of the Directors Guild of America.

Oliver Stone is an innovative writer and director of films that examine the darker side of society, past and present. He is best known as the co-writer/director of *JFK, Nixon, Platoon, Wall Street, Born on the Fourth of July*, and most recently, *Savages*.

Betty Thomas started out in improv comedy at Second City alongside Bill Murray. She later expanded into acting with a seminal role on *Hill Street Blues*. While there she began directing films like *28 Days, Doctor Dolittle*, and *Private Parts*. She won the Emmy in 1990 for her work on *Dream On*. She is a filmmaker-in-residence at The Dodge College of Film and Media, Chapman University, in Orange, California. She is a vice president of the Directors Guild of America.

Jeanne Tripplehorn became prominent starring opposite Michael Douglas in *Basic Instinct*. She continued to impress as a strong screen talent in *WaterWorld, The Firm* and *Brother's Keeper*. She appears in fifty-three episodes of *Big Love* and is a new addition to *Criminal Minds*.

David S. Ward is the Oscar-winning screenwriter of *The Sting* who is also known for directing the beloved baseball film *Major League* and its sequel. In addition to his writing and directing work, he is a professor at The Dodge College of Film and Media, Chapman University, in Orange, California.

James Woods is one of the most acclaimed character actors of our day, appearing on stage, screen and TV and working with some of the top directors in Hollywood such as Martin Scorsese, David Cronenberg, Sergio Leone, Oliver Stone and Robert Zemeckis. He starred in Badham's *The Hard Way* alongside Michael J. Fox.

Michael Zinberg is a DGA Award-winning director of such classic TV series as *The Bob Newhart Show, The Good Wife, L.A. Law, Quantum Leap, The Practice, Everybody Loves Raymond, Gilmore Girls* and *Lost*. He is a longtime member of the Western Directors Council of the Directors Guild of America.

Using This Book

irecting is often seen as part art and part craft. Like other classic hybrids, architecture and writing, the practitioners are proud of their work, and glad to share their knowledge with those eager to learn. The part of the hybrid called art falls into that inchoate ability called talent: virtually impossible to teach, difficult to describe and unmistakable when observed. When writing *I'll Be in My Trailer* I talked to many skilled and talented directors and actors who shared their personal insights, tips and stories on the complicated and challenging relationship between actors and directors. In that way I am still as much of an apprentice as a craftsman. The art will be left to others to assay.

 **Steven Soderbergh:** I imagine you'd agree that we can teach the practical stuff about directing. If we could inject people with the soul of an artist then we'd all be Stanley Kubrick. That's a personal thing — whether they have a point of view that's interesting and specific or not, you can't inject somebody with that. They grew up with it. You know? But you can teach them the craft, and it's a fun craft to teach and to learn.

In the time since that book came out, many more talented directors and actors have contributed their additions and responses to the ideas expressed in the first book.

PART ONE of this book deals more specifically with the issue of trust (or lack thereof) between actor and director. It looks at solutions and techniques for overcoming this nasty problem.

In particular it addresses some of the real differences between directing film and directing episodic television. Though most of the basic techniques of directing film and television are the same, there is a substantial difference in protocol between the two as far as a director is concerned.

PART TWO deals with techniques I've learned directing stories with elements of action and suspense in them (every type of film can contain both action and suspense) using examples from my films *Blue Thunder, WarGames,* and *Nick of Time.* I've incorporated lasting lessons from experts on the subject like Alfred Hitchcock, Joel and Ethan Coen, Adrian Lyne, and Brett Ratner as well as films like *No Country for Old Men, Rush Hour,* and *Fatal Attraction.* This section asks: What are the elements that make a successful action or suspense sequence? How important is point of view? How critical is jeopardy? How are actors best directed in action sequences? How to keep safety the main priority on an action set? How to use storyboarding to its best advantage? How much coverage is enough? How is suspense created? How is it maintained?

PART THREE of this book is The Director's Checklist. Before you start rehearsals, any rehearsals, what questions have to be asked? Teaching film students at Chapman University has been as much of an education for me as it has for them. In part, my experiences with them led to the development of twelve key questions. Whether you've directed no films or a hundred films these are the basic tools that help deconstruct a script or a scene, looking for what makes the film or the scene either work or not work. Skilled and experienced directors use these tools so intuitively they may not even be aware of using them. Others flounder about either looking for keys to unlock the scene or, what is worse, staging the scene in a manner that's quick and easy without really understanding what the scene is about. Years ago at Universal Television the series *McHale's Navy* had a huge ensemble cast. Because the shooting schedule was so brutally short the team of actors were often lined up in a row and shot in a series of close-ups. The joke at the time was that the director would call out, "OK boys, give me a nice tight '16 shot.'"

The checklist contains the tools that keep the director and actor on the right path to creating a good scene. When a scene isn't working, how can you dig down to a solution? By taking the time to fully understand and explore the scenes and theme of the script you're directing, you're not only better prepared to answer any question on set, but you'll know how to approach guiding your actors in their performances. These questions can be used in any dramatic medium: films, television, and plays.

▲ ▲ ▲

One day on the set of *Stakeout,* with Richard Dreyfuss and Emilio Estevez, we were waiting for our DP John Seale to finish lighting a complicated setup. Richard and Aidan Quinn, who was playing the crazy escaped convict, were talking about what they enjoyed about the art and craft of acting.

Of course they discussed being able to create characters and bring them to life. They talked about the fun of being able to say dialogue written by great writers. Interestingly, the subject of money never came up. I suspect that like many actors they would work for free on a film or play that they loved.

As best I can remember the conversation went something like this... only funnier:

Richard Dreyfuss came up with an idea I had never heard anyone articulate before. He said, "I love being able to solve problems." "What do you mean?" asked Aidan Quinn. Richard replied, "I'm talking about how all these things we've been discussing can also come under the heading of 'problem solving.' When we're getting ready to act, or direct, and in the process of acting or directing, we're always solving problems. Every line of dialogue, every bit of staging, every technical detail at each moment is a problem that we need to address and solve in the most creative and efficient way."

By that point Emilio Estevez had joined in and added, "What you're saying is that the thing that gets us out of bed before dawn and lets us hang around dirty old sets in weird clothes for ungodly hours is the prospect of continuous challenges. How to make things come alive, how to make things believable."

Aidan Quinn jumped in and asked, "Is it just me or does it work for you guys that even though we've all been doing this for a long time that it doesn't get old? It's the same job. Why is that?"

This seemed to stop everyone for a moment and I could hear John Seale telling the AD that he was ready for the cast. It sounded like this conversation would have to be continued after the take was finished.

When I called "Cut" and "Print" after a few takes on the scene and we had moved on to shoot the reverse coverage, Dreyfuss gathered us together and said, "I think I know the answer to Aidan's question. The reason we're all still here playing like kids in a sandbox is because each and every problem that we face here needs a new and creative solution."

"True," said Emilio. "Each line of dialogue, each moment in a scene, how we relate to other characters, what we want as characters is different."

"It better be," said Aidan. "If we just act the same old thing we did in the last scene, made the same old choices, not only would it be boring to us, but to the audience as well."

"When that happens," said Richard, "the whole thing is lost. Audiences tune out if it's no fun to watch. When it's no fun to act we just hack through it and hate coming to play. In fact, it's no longer play, now it's work!"

This conversation has stuck with me for a very long time because it seems so close to the truth of what we as actors, directors, writers, designers, cinematographers, and editors try to achieve every day. Every film we engage is different from the last and we are always trying to bring a fresh creative mind to it. Steven Spielberg once commented to an interviewer about his TV series *Amazing Stories* that he was constantly trying to avoid "xeroxing" himself.

I hope you find something in this book that will inspire you to create, or help you through a tricky situation with an actor, or give you the tools to take a good scene on the page to the next level with your contribution as a director.

I've included photos of posters from the international versions of some of my films. They're often very different from the US posters, sometimes even featuring a different title, and are fun to compare with the originals.

John Badham
September 2013

PART I

A LACK OF TRUST:
The Five Mistakes

Introduction

A Nasty Bit of Laundry

Before *I'll Be In My Trailer* was published in 2006 I was seeking as much as I could learn from other directors and actors about our mutual working relationships. After its publication I had many emails, phone calls, and conversations with actors and directors adding to the subject. The word that kept coming up was "trust."

When you've spent much time around actors you've probably heard something scurrilous whispered between them. That's in public. What actors say in private among themselves is probably worse. Here it is. You ready?

Many... most... let's say lots of actors don't trust most directors. Not a bit, not a whit, not a crumb. They have been

Japanese edition of I'll Be in My Trailer.

flogged, flayed, and betrayed by directors ever since they were told in acting class to pretend they were a fried egg that had been beaten by their Rooster Dad. Misled, misrepresented, and flat-out ignored, they have been treated like robotic pieces of meat, if you'll pardon the metaphoric succotash. Viewed as misbehaving children who live in a fantasy world of explosive egos and DUIs, actors often find themselves demeaned, devalued, and depressed.

Taylor Hackford: Well, the whole idea of trust between actors and directors is so critical, and I think it's why many actors distrust directors, because they never take the time to gain their trust and to let them feel that somebody smart is working with them. Some directors are afraid of actors. Some directors don't want to talk to them.

It's easy to understand how an actor can store up resentments over time and begin to see all directors as louche or suspect. Polite directors, talented directors, and helpful directors all get lumped in with the mediocre ones, the abusive ones, the screamers, the idiots, and the invisible directors who only shoot the same master, two shot, over shoulder, close-up, close-up time and again, no matter what they're shooting. Like Lucy and Ethel in the chocolate factory, they race through their work, if you can call it work, making a hodge-podge of all they touch.

Delia Salvi: The best-kept secret in the entertainment industry is how much actors, including award-winning performers, distrust directors, and how directors often fear or dislike actors.[1]

Exaggeration you say? Maybe. You have to look at it from the point of view of the actor who has been tortured and ignored his whole career. His resentment has built up a volcanic pressure inside that wants to explode when a director comes around with his snotty little "notes." One well-known character actor, who we'll call "Cary," told me flat-out, "Most TV directors don't have a clue about actors. They are all about lenses and angles. I protect myself thoroughly, I'm director-proof. They're not going to screw me with their incompetence." Even the famously talented directors, the Scorseses, Spielbergs, and P. T. Andersons who are great communicators often have to rehabilitate the bottle-scared... sorry, battle-scarred, shell-shocked, PTSD actor to trust his creative collaborator, the director.

---

[1] Delia Salvi. *Friendly Enemies* (New York: Billboard Books, 2003), xv.

Gilbert Cates: I understand why some actors become pricks. I get it. You go through many difficult times before you get cast in a role. You build up a heap of resentment and anxiety. Most of it is fear. Most of it is actors afraid of being asked to do something that they can't do, and being found out that they can't do it.

Little wonder that any actor who has achieved any level of respect will demand director approval, both in films and television series. They want to feel confident that their director not only knows his craft as a filmmaker but also has respect for the actor and understands the character he is playing. They want to know they will be protected from looking bad or foolish. They want to know they can rely on both help and inspiration as well. Actors want to be directed... but by people who help them do their best work.

Jodie Foster: I'm not afraid of actors, and I think sometimes directors are afraid of actors, because they don't entirely understand the process of acting. There's something very mysterious about it. It's a skill, they just don't know what the skill is.

When an actor steps on a film set he knows that he only has so much control over the elaborate process of filmmaking. It's quite different from the world of theatre where most actors are trained. There, they have much more control over their world. Every night is a different performance and can be improved, corrected, and adjusted. Bad directions can be ignored, staging can be fixed. That doesn't mean that it will be better or that it was bad initially. It does mean that the actor feels more control in a theatre environment.

Judd Nelson, one of the famous Brat Pack and star of *The Breakfast Club,* sadly reminisced that when he first started acting, "I thought all movies were going to be collaborative and have rehearsals and a director who liked us."[2]

---

[2] Susan King, "Judd Nelson Interview," *Los Angeles Times,* October 2, 2012.

Stephen Collins: I think sometimes as an actor you just know that you can trust a director. He's saying something. You think, "Oh God, I don't know." You know him well enough to say, "Oh screw it. I'm going to take a leap of faith because he's got something going here." I think actors just want to be heard. If an actor really feels that he or she has been heard, they'll give up what's on their mind. If you feel like you've been stamped down and can't put your two cents in, then you never commit to the scene.

Let's see how that worked out in practice with one of the toughest actors, and one of our best directors.

Michael Zinberg: I was doing an episode of *The Practice.* I had a huge show with James Whitmore Sr. He was a brilliant actor. I grew up watching him on television and in movies, on the stage when I could. I saw his one-man shows. I was intimidated. I was frightened. This is the right guy. This is somebody special. Now I know his son very well, James Whitmore Jr. He's a great director in his own right. I said, "I got a huge show with your dad, do you have any tips?" He thought for a beat and he said, "Well, if you have anything to say, it better be good."

So in comes Mr. Whitmore to talk with me about the script. We get to this one pivotal scene. I said, "This is how I think this scene should play." He said, "You're absolutely wrong." I said, "OK, tell me." He pitched me his idea. I said, "I don't think so. I don't think that fits within the context of the show." I said, "But I'll check. I'll check with David Kelley, the show-runner, and I'll come back to you." Kelley agreed with me how the scene should play. I came back to Whitmore, "I think you're wrong. But let's see what happens when we get to the stage."

So now we rehearse the scene. He does the scene exactly the way I asked him to do it. So at this point, I'm taking "yes" for an answer. When we roll on the first take he performs beautifully and flawlessly, exactly what I'd asked him to do. Take two, same thing, perfect. I said, "I'm good." I said, "I think that scene is exactly right." I said, "Is there anything else that you'd like to do? Would you like to do another take any way you want to do it?" Whitmore replies, "Nope." I said, "You're happy, I'm happy."

Later on that day, I went to his dressing room. I asked him, "Were we saying the same thing all along?" He said, "No, no, no, you're dead wrong." I said, "I'm dead wrong?" He said, "Yeah, you totally misinterpreted the scene." I said, "OK, but you did the scene the way I asked you to do it." He said, "You're the director." I said, "Thank you," and I walked out. He won an Emmy for that performance, having nothing to do with me, just because he's so damn good. I mean, he was brilliant.

Postscript: I run into him at a restaurant in Beverly Hills. He's having dinner with his wife, Noreen, and I'm with my wife, Leslie. I went over to him and I said hello and introduced them to Leslie. Whitmore Sr. looks up at her and says, "Well, your boy isn't much of a director but he's got good taste in women."

Isn't that fabulous?

In the film and digital environment, whether films, television, webisodes, or YouTube kitten videos, control of a film may be in the hands of the director for a time, who then has to turn it over to the producer, who gives it to the studio, who gives it to the distribution company or network, who is influenced by their idea of what the audience or sponsor wants. What remains is too often a testament to the destructive power of homogenization. Final cut, like freedom of religion, is a noble idea, greatly aspired to but more honored in the breach than the observance.

In the world of film schools where there should be innocence, a freshness, a naïveté, a collegial spirit that should be immune to many of these obstacles, there is nonetheless a gathering of students of varying degrees of talent and experience who are still learning to express themselves. There are tyro directors who don't know how to talk to actors partially because they are themselves still learning social skills and basic psychology of human behavior. There are actors who have real talent, who are genuinely interested in acting, and there are too many who just want to be "movie stars," with the looks of a Gap ad model and the talent of a tortoise.

In film school, for better or worse, everyone gets into the act. Everyone wants to do the director's job. The dolly grip, the electrician, and the prop person will each say "I'm really a director" and know how to do it better than the director *du jour*. No one is shy about showing off their superior knowledge. A simple discussion of an approach to a scene or a setup soon resembles a meeting of the Kazakhstan Parliament replete with shouting, ripped shirts, and wounded egos. It's a miracle how many good films still come out of film schools and a testament to the strength of human beings to overcome impossible odds that defy even the strongest filmmaker.

I have been asking directors and actors everywhere what are the signs and symptoms of directors who aren't trusted? What do they do that makes actors grit their teeth and wish they had gone to law school instead? We're not just talking about being popular with actors; nice but hardly the end goal. Filmmaking is not primarily a social club. What do we as craftspersons and artists do that gets in the way of making the best film possible? Many of the problems we'll discuss incubate in television or low-budget films where schedule often trumps quality and there is little time for niceties. But the truth is that they are universal problems existing at all levels of filmmaking.

For now, let's focus on the cast. Many of the ideas will apply easily to our crew who need and deserve just as much respect and attention as the cast. The difference being, the crew is usually more compliant and easier to work with.

It's enough to say for now that *Number One* on the call sheet, as the star or lead actor is code-named, is such a critical part of every equation and production decision that to ignore, demean, or take lightly their participation is a fatal mistake. Whether they are well behaved and committed to making the best film possible, just pulling down a paycheck, or on an ego trip, *Number One* must be considered at every turn. We want them to look their best, to feel their best, and enjoy giving all they can give to the film they are fronting and headlining. Being *Number One* is a huge responsibility. Directors and producers have to recognize that the film can be made or broken by their performance.

And it goes without saying that there is no "one size fits all" when it comes to actors, how they work, their temperaments, their backgrounds. It's part of the challenge and part of the fun.

D. J. Caruso: I learned, having five children, just as every one of them is totally different from the other, every actor is different. You can't have the same directorial approach to Al Pacino that you have to Shia LaBeouf or to Michelle Monaghan or to Matthew McConaughey. What I've learned is to quickly discover whether the actor is a reactive actor, or an aggressive actor.

Val Kilmer, for example, is very reactive. He knows what he wants to do, and in order for me to affect his performance, I have to use off-camera people to change his performance. He reacts to what he's getting from the other actors.

On the other hand a guy like Matthew McConaughey is just gung-ho. He just wants an action verb, like be more aggressive. If aggressive isn't enough, it's going to be, "I want you to take her clothes off when you're talking." He'll come back and say, "Give me a verb. Give me a verb."

You have to learn to adapt to every actor's style of working. Where a guy like Shia LaBeouf — and this is the truth — take one, take two, I don't have to do anything. I don't have to do anything. He's spoiled me forever.

But Shia spends preproduction with me. He goes on location scouts. He calls me and asks me questions. In rehearsal we never do the lines, but he wants to know something like, "Should I have a picture of my brother in my hand?" Everything's about his preparation and the foundation of the character. When we get to the set, I swear to God, you're prepared to do more takes because...

you always have to do more takes. But Shia nails it the first time. I think, "That can't be it, I can't be moving on already." You literally can, because in two movies I've done with him he's messed up a line once, one time. And it was a line that I changed the night before.

So I've learned to really adapt my style and figure out what kind of actor I'm working with, from the Angelina Jolies who are very cerebral, to Matthew McConaughey who is all about action.

So how do we deal with this hotbed of distrust, egos, and competition? The entire philosophy of this book is based on one simple principle: People tend to reject the influence of someone they don't like. Whether it's a disliked director, doctor, or teacher, there is tremendous resistance to following their advice or learning from them. Benedict Carey, writing for the *New York Times* about George Steinbrenner, the once-tyrannical owner of the New York Yankees, points out that even he mellowed substantially in his later years, having realized that the most effective leaders "find a way to mix some patience with their Patton, to persuade rather than intimidate, to convince people that their goals are the same as the boss's."[3]

Michael McMurray: There doesn't have to be a lot of stress. A lot of people in our industry think there has to be a lot of stress to get the job done right. If you're not stressed out to the max and if it's not mean and miserable and heavy and ugly, then how could it be good? I think people are like kids or pets — if you treat them nicely, they always want to do better for you.

And there is no need to transform oneself into Charles Dickens' obsequious hand-wringing "umble servant" Uriah Heep or a grinning ape. It's mostly about respect.

---

[3] Benedict Carey, "The Boss Unbound," *New York Times*, July 18, 2010.

D. J. Caruso: You have to be the authority figure. You can't be just buddy-buddy, because there has to be a captain. And so I've learned over the years how to try to choose an actor who's really going to be your partner.

And that you can only learn by sitting with them, by talking to other people that have worked with them so you don't step on land mines where they were sweet in the meeting and then turn into a monster on the set.

Let's look at several directors' common mistakes.

Chapter 1

Mistake #1: Directed by Anonymous

There's always plenty of sitting around on sets waiting for one task or another to be completed. A director can only do so much helping before having to get out of the crew's way. He can spend this waiting time in many ways, hopefully productive. I like to talk with the actors about the upcoming scene or anything that's concerning them. Often an actor will tell me about a film or TV episode that he acted in. "Who was the director," I often ask. This is followed often by a long pause and a bit of riffling through his mental contacts. Then I hear, "He was a tall guy, I don't remember his name" or "She had real curly hair," or "He liked to shout a lot."

At first I used to think that this was coming from some bobble-head who was only thinking about himself. Surely this couldn't be the case with actors who are playing leads or major roles. Uh... yes, it could. It's especially true in television where a series may have a dozen or more directors in a season. Every show starts to blur together and the schedule is so hectic that basic niceties and courtesies go by the boards. People barely introduce themselves; many don't try to remember names, they just nod without even hearing the name much less storing it away in their Swiss cheese memory banks. Then they work together for days or even weeks on end and may never learn each other's names.

> **Michael Zinberg:** In series television, the smart directors know the crew before they walk on the stage. Most of them get to know the crew during prep. Man, they can help you or not help you. If you're a dick, they'll find out fast and it won't be pretty.

If we're talking about the crew this kind of behavior is rude, but not necessarily damaging. Crews are inured to being treated rudely by directors. This doesn't make it right, polite, or even a good practice. Because they need the work they swallow their pride and press on. Sure it's easier, or, more accurately, lazier. But we can get a much better result from people that we treat as individuals, not cogs in the filmmaking machine.

> **John Woo:** I think if you want to work with actors, first, you have to fall in love with them. If you hate them, don't even bother.... I treat actors as though they're part of my family. Before I start shooting, I insist on spending time with my actors. We talk a lot, and I try to see how they feel about life, what kinds of ideas they have, what kinds of dreams. We talk about what they love and what they hate. I try to discover what each actor's main quality is because this is what I'll try to emphasize in the film.
>
> ...Once we start working, there are two primary things. First, of course, is communication with the actor. To achieve that, I always try to find something more trivial — we both like soccer. It's very important because often the whole communication process will rest on that. It's something you can always fall back on when conflicts arise. The other thing I pay attention to is the eyes. When an actor acts, I always stare at his or her eyes. Always. Because it tells me if he or she is being truthful or just faking it.[1]

Just by knowing someone's name and using it on a regular basis we are making personal contact with her. She becomes a person who wants to help us get the job done well. She becomes a person

---

[1] Laurent Tirard, *Moviemaker's Master Class* (New York: Faber and Faber, 2002), 148.

who looks forward to coming to work and who feels she is part of something worthwhile... even if it's just a small film or TV episode.

Martin Sheen: I had the joy of working with Steven Spielberg just last year. I couldn't believe his character on the set. He was so available to everybody. He was so personable. He shared everything about himself and wanted to know, "Where are you from, Martin? Oh really? I didn't know you were from Ohio. Isn't that something? What did your dad do?" I said, "Oh he worked in a factory." "I didn't know that. Really? How many children are in your family?" You know what I'm saying? He genuinely wanted to know who I was when I had only met him socially here and there. I was so disarmed. You watch that set and it's not just the actors who will go to any lengths for him. It's the whole set. The whole crew will break their back for this guy — anything. He sits behind that monitor. He knows exactly what he's looking for and he'll get it in the shortest amount of time but he won't leave until he gets it. Then he invites everyone involved to come and look at the replay and if someone's not happy, "All right, let's try it again."

Whenever I step on a set for the first time I make it a point to know the names of all the actors, heads of departments, and the names of their "best boys." I will know the camera operators, their assistants, and their dolly grips, all this without having met most of them. I use mnemonic tricks, rote memory, anything to be able to address them by their first names as quickly as I can. This is not to be popular, this is just good business.

Gary Busey: One thing that's very important to others is, remember their name. You have an ally. The name is so important. People don't realize how important the name is. Maybe they do, but not so much as to take two seconds to learn one. "I'm terrible with names" is just a lazy excuse for not paying attention.

Get 'Em While You've Got 'Em, Before You Get 'Em.

How does the director establish a relationship with the actors? When do we get to know them? Is it in the audition? The rehearsal? The shoot?

The truth is it gets harder and harder every year to create that relationship with the actor before the day of the shoot. At the audition the actor comes piling into the casting office after all the other things he's been doing that day. He grabs the script sides and puts all his concentration into getting a grasp of the character and how to play it. Called into the audition room he is lucky to have a word or two with the casting person about the scene. Then the camera records and he performs it with the casting assistant who may or may not read well.

What's wrong with this picture? Lots and lots. In a feature film and most television shows the director is present and able to give the actor some direction. The smart director knows this is not just time to find an actor for a role; it is a chance to experiment with the scene long before getting to the stage. You have the actor's attention cranked up full to 11. He wants that job and is focused on the director like a leopard on a steak.

Eriq La Salle: I find, as an actor, when a director gives me an idea in an audition, if a director gives me something I haven't thought about, that director has me. Even in the audition process, I'm always impressed when a director says, something like, what you are doing is fine, but let's try it this way. Whether I get it or not, I'm glad I went in and I had an interesting time.

Whenever I direct I'm always trying to find the thing that they haven't thought about that's going to give them a greater understanding of the situation, of themselves and the character. That to me is one of the marks of a good actor or director.

Even if the actor isn't quite right for the role he can be a source of ideas and will be delighted to try the scene any way the director suggests. I will often tell the actor who is auditioning, "You know this is a crazy idea that isn't in the script, but will you try playing just the opposite of what you just did? For example, instead of you celebrating getting an engagement ring at the dinner table, try making fun of the proposal. But use the same dialogue."

Now I can get an idea of what the actor is made of. Now I can see how he responds under a bit of light pressure.

Sometimes this works, sometimes not, but one thing is always true: the actor will never forget that you worked with him and asked him to access his creative juices. He will always remember you.

What can you learn from this? Plenty. You know now how much the actor can stretch and how he responds under pressure. Does he create something new or does he just repeat what he did the first time? If the latter then it probably won't get any better on the set and you should look for somebody else. It will be the infamous "office reading" that's only a robotic recitation. Like a prerecorded message, it never changes. If the actor does respond with an unusual or creative choice, the director has also learned what kind of playing the scene will allow. It's free rehearsal with no pressure.

 **Martha Coolidge:** To me the auditioning process is to search the extremes of what the part might demand and find the actors who are going to bring something beyond whatever I imagined, rather than somebody who has to beat it out of them or manipulate it out of them.

This is why it is so important the director be present at auditions. Otherwise you only get part of the information you need. Watching recorded interviews only gives you part of the information. It's like buying a car based on seeing the commercials, but never driving it. Curiously, frustratingly, maddeningly enough, many TV shows manage to skip having the director at auditions. Maybe not deliberately trying to keep the director out of the loop but dragging them off on location scouts and other things that seem more pressing. The auditions are done by the casting director and now show up online on every executive's computer. Choices get made. If the director doesn't pay attention to when auditions are happening and insist that she be present, the producer and the network subtly hijack the process.

What's the problem with this? The actor has given a reading without much of a compass to guide him beyond the writer's stage directions. When the producer and the network view the auditions on their computers, hopefully they are not taking phone calls, or chatting with associates. This would not only be disrespectful to the actor, it would also be shooting the show in the foot. Then executives send out *fatwas* and *ex-cathedra* dictates about who will play every role, right down to the Nurse #2 who only has one line, "This way, Doctor." Easy to see how directors have a hell of a time getting their choices heard. At least if the director were present at the auditions she could know the actors well enough to see beneath the surface and her recommendations would carry more weight. Besides which, the experience of working with the actor during the audition has started the creation of a bond between actor and director that will grow stronger over time.

Homework... Do It

If you're getting serious about casting someone, you want to do homework on who he is. You can say to yourself, "Oh yes, I know Brad Pitt's work." Do you? Go back, look again. Pay attention to how he does things. Where are his mannerisms, his strong points, his weak points? You need that information fresh in your mind. This is where the Internet is such a blessing. If you don't know his work beforehand you can find his films so easily. You owe it to yourself to learn all you can about what he likes and doesn't like. Call directors he has worked with in the past and get their take on the actor. Every director will return the call and share what they know. It's not only professional courtesy, they may need to call you one day.

Donald Petrie: Jack Lemmon kind of encompasses a role all around. Walter Matthau finds something that he can glean onto that is the character. One of the reasons I managed to work so well with Walter is the first day we met he said, "I don't know if I can do this. First, this is called *Grumpy Old Men,* I'm not old. See this hair? There's not a gray one in it." He was arguing that he wasn't old enough to play this role. What I said to him, and again I'd done my homework, so I said, "But Walter, you did so brilliantly in *Koch.*" Jack Lemmon had directed him in *Koch* where he played an old man. "Yeah, I just don't have a way to kind of glom onto this character. I don't know it yet. I've got this doctor that works for me and he talks like he's got cotton in his mouth all the time." I said, "Oh, that sounds great." Then I knew I had him. Sure enough, if you listen to, "Crazy drivers!" he sounds like he's got something in his mouth. He chose that thing to kind of build his character around.

They're On Board

After you, the producer, the studio, the network... and God, have discussed, argued, fought... and gone with the one God wanted in the first place. *After* the deal is made with the agent and the manager (who just made himself a producer) and you had to agree to listen to script notes from the star's ten-year-old daughter, what's the next step? (Just kidding... the daughter is really eight.) Call the actor on the telephone. Don't text, tweet, email, Facebook, or smoke signal... call the actor. They all have phones. Call him up and welcome him to the film. Tell him how delighted you are to get to work with him. Even if you are not delighted (which could happen if your casting choice was overpriced, overruled, or overlooked) *still* tell him you are delighted. Disingenuousness is not always a bad thing. On a cynical but very realistic level if you are going to have to work with him you are going to have to make the best of it. That won't happen if he thinks you didn't want him in the first place. Now get his thoughts on how he sees the character and how he likes to work.

> **Jodie Foster:** I love it when directors come to me before the first few days of shooting and say, "What do you like and what don't you like?" "Tell me how I should approach you and how I shouldn't. What happens in this circumstance? Do you like doing a lot of takes? Do you like to be first? Do you like to be second?" "Is it OK if there are lots of people surrounding you? Do you like a lot of noise?" All those questions are completely fair to the professional actor. You just set up the scenes accordingly.

When you've got your actor on the phone that's the time to ask if he has any questions or concerns about his part, wardrobe, or dialogue. Does he like several takes, or just a few, how about rehearsal on set? Obviously you are giving him the chance to open up but also you are probably asking questions he hasn't confronted yet. You don't want to put him on the spot or embarrass him in any way, you just want to get him thinking. If you didn't get to meet him in person you are putting a voice to your name. It's a critical first step in bonding with the actor who wants to know that you are looking out for him and will take care of him to get his best work. He won't feel like he's "on the floor alone" as Gary Busey says when he is getting nothing from the director. He'll come to work feeling someone is there for him.

> **Allan Arkush:** That whole sense of protecting the actor just really makes them be so much better. They end up trusting you so much that they feel they can't make a mistake, and that if they do make a mistake, you've got their back. Obviously with series regulars that's a lot.

This is the easiest phone call you will ever make and it will only take a few minutes. Of course the best is meeting in person over a meal, but I've made calls from tops of mountains, from the van during tech scouts, or at 3 a.m. to talk to Bryan Brown in Australia. Anywhere. Just get it done; you'll be glad you did.

Elia Kazan: As a director, I do one good thing right at the outset. Before I start with anybody in any important role, I talk to them for a long time. The conversations have to do with their lives and before you know it, they're telling you all about their wives, their mothers, their children, their infidelities, and anything else they feel guilty about... They're dying to tell you they tried to kill their brother once. They're eager to tell you their problems with their father.... I veil it. I make it sound like chatter. An actor will tell you anything in five minutes, if you listen.... By the time you start with an actor, you know everything about him, where to go, what to reach for, what to summon up, what associations to make for him. You have to find a riverbed, a channel in their lives that is like the central channel in the part..... You're edging towards the part so that the part becomes them.[2]

If you've not been fortunate enough to have had extended rehearsals before shooting, and frankly very few directors are so fortunate these days, you will have to do it on the day of shooting. Rehearsal is viewed by bean-counting production executives either as some arty perversion designed to cost them money or an opportunity for the actor to undermine the script. The truth is quite the opposite; rehearsal saves them money because most of the script problems, actor questions, and staging concerns get explored in even brief periods of rehearsal. Sidney Lumet proved this film after film, year after year. He would consistently shoot his films in four to five weeks when every other director was taking ten weeks for the same kind of film. In rehearsal a thirty-minute discussion is no big deal. A thirty-minute discussion on the set on a tight shooting schedule is a disaster. And when is the shooting schedule not tight? James Cameron after a jillion days of shooting on *Titanic* and *Avatar* still says he needed more time. If there's a protracted disagreement about a scene, not only is shooting time lost but as importantly the tension of the situation causes tempers to shrink like wool sweaters in a Jacuzzi. Producers get frantic, angry, even; directors smell hot cigar breath on their necks and actors wonder, "What's the big deal, I just asked a question?"

---

[2] Jeff Young, *Kazan* (New Market Press: New York, 1999), 130.

There is an art to proper rehearsal. Take a look at Judith Weston's excellent book *Directing Actors*, which has a terrific section on rehearsal. As Jessica Lange said in her Academy Award acceptance speech for *Blue Sky*, "I want to thank our director Tony Richardson for giving us permission to play in rehearsal." Or Harvey Keitel: "When I met Scorsese the work between us was never 'you walk over here and then turn around.' It was about finding what we were searching for in my own being." These are not the kinds of things you hear from actors when they get jammed through the process.

On the Day

So you've not had the benefit of rehearsal beyond what you might have gotten done in the auditions and callbacks; beyond what you worked out with the actor over dinner. You're now standing on the set promptly at call time, 7:30 a.m.

That's your first mistake.

You will be seized by the AD and frog-marched to the DP who wants to know what's the first shot. You don't know, do you? Because you haven't rehearsed with the actors. Then the prop man comes over to ask if you want a ballpoint pen or a lead pencil in the scene and the line producer comes up with a heart-stopper that they've lost the next location.

When will you talk to the actors? Oops. Too late! The juggernaut is rolling. You may have an idea of camera placement but you really need to pull the cast out of the makeup trailer to work it out, find the marks, show the crew, and send the cast back to get dressed.

Oh, stop right there! Are you thinking you don't need the actors on set to place the camera? Don't do it! I'm telling you. Even if the star sends word that he'll stand wherever you tell him, *don't* believe it. He *will* screw you. He's not evil, he's not out to cause a problem, it's just in his nature; like the scorpion and the frog. When you're all lit and he gets called to the set, he's guaranteed to look at the mark you set for him and say, "No, I wouldn't stand *there.*" Argue with him you will... and lose you will. Now you'll have to wait for a little re-light, a big loss of momentum, and a couple of layers of enamel are ground off your teeth.

If you think I'm kidding, give it a go.

Instead get to the set early. Forty-five minutes before call ought to do it. Go to the makeup trailer and corner sleepy actors in their chairs. What you'll talk about doesn't have to start out like anything more than a "good morning, did you sleep OK" kind of hello. Then look in their eyes. What do you see? Relaxed people? Confident people? Do you see frozen grimaces? Thousand-yard stares? Their eyes will tell you all you need to know. The grimace and the "deer in the headlights" look are sure signs they're worried about today's work. No matter how confident they looked on other days, today's scene is probably the scene that scares them. Now is the time you'll earn some of that obscene paycheck you get. This is when you get to play therapist, coach, and friend.

Okay, so we're still in the makeup trailer and you want to chat with everyone for a minute or two before you get trapped back out on the set. Very important, never neglect the day player who is there for only one or two scenes. She is more nervous than anybody. She may only have one line but she is Jell-O inside. Obviously she is coming to work not knowing quite what to expect, hoping for the best, but nervous nonetheless. She probably doesn't know the other actors. If you got to audition with her, you at least are a friendly face. You are her lifeline. Ask her how she sees her scenes today. Of course she will try to do it any way you want, but ask her for her thoughts. She's agonized over it quite a bit and may, just may, have something worthwhile to contribute. She is a collaborator too. You cast her because she had a good handle on the part. Take advantage of what she brings to the party. Listen to her.

"How are you feeling about the scene today?" is always a safe question. "When you were thinking about the work last night how did you see playing it?" You hope her vision agrees with yours. If not?

Do not panic; do not go directly to jail. If her thought is different from yours there are three possibilities:

1. It's really interesting and you can use it with your idea or instead of your idea.

2. It's the same idea just spoken in different words.

3. It's a terrible idea for any number of reasons.

Whatever you do, don't panic. Remember, this is just a discussion, not a demand. Most of the time it's an idea that the actor thought of last night or this morning and just wants to air it out. The best thing you can do is listen with interest. Sincere interest. You want to stay open-minded and keep saying the mantra, "What if it's a good idea? Now without showing any sweat, you can reply, "That's really interesting, I never thought of it that way before. Tell me more." Whether the actor's idea is good or bad, say something like that, *but always focus the actor on the action.*

> **Elia Kazan:** What you talk about is what they want out of a scene —why they are going into it. You keep them concentrated on the action, what we call the "objective." If you do that, at least you'll have clarity. If you talk about what the character is feeling, you'll get nothing but simulated emotion.[3]

Let the actor explain himself before you stupidly jump in and say, "That's wrong. That'll never work." Why? Because if you jump on his idea without at least looking like you're considering it he *will* get defensive. When actors get defensive they get emotional. When they get emotional their egos get in the way. When their egos get in the way, there is no talking to them. Reason has flown south and the chill of winter descends. You have to allow the actor time to express himself and really hear him out before you say, "Wow, that's so interesting because I had thought it might play this other way. Tell me more." Now you hopefully have a dialogue going, a dialogue that will lead to understanding between the two of you, not a monologue from you, O, Ozymandias, all-powerful director.

---

[3] Young, *Kazan*, 72.

An understanding that should try to land on the best version of what you're both thinking.

John Rich: On *All in the Family* we'd read the script line by line and anybody who had a question could speak up. Sometimes I'd say "Does that make sense to you?" If they said "No, not really," I'd ask, "What would you say instead?" Some writers were very upset by that. But I got tremendous performances. When we were staging I never told them how or when to move on a line. "Find your own way, I'll help if you get tangled up." Paying attention to any actor's instincts really brings out the best in them. They are so much happier than one who's been told to stand here, move there and so on.

Remember, we're talking about actors who don't trust directors; actors who are used to being run over roughshod by directors. Directors who wake up singing "My way, or the highway" in C minor. Which is a stupid egotistical way to be. You always have to ask yourself, "What if they're right? What if there is something here I can use?" If there is nothing useful and an actor's idea is harmful, you need to search for clues about what's *really* bothering him. So "tell me more about how you see the scene" is not just pampering him and manipulating him through the process; it's the therapist's time-tested way of getting to the bottom of the problem.

Very often, though it's hard to believe, it can come down to something very minor in the scene like a stage direction or a wardrobe or prop choice. Even a particular line of dialogue can throw an actor off. That's why I love having the writer on the set. Actors respect writers and what they do. A writer can tell the actor the very same thing you just told him and the actor takes it positively, whereas he may think the director is shining him on.

Isn't it better to have this conversation *before* you get to the set? Of course it is. It's not a public forum, which is always stress-provoking. Don't give actors audiences to play to, which can be both stressful and humiliating or performance-provoking. Either actors or you start trying to prove who's got the biggest stick. Aha! Caught you, didn't I? You thought I was going to say who's got the biggest trick. This is a family book. Really.

Patty Jenkins: The most important thing that I try to seek out is a few moments, whether in person or on the phone, to sit and talk through the script with the actors. "Here's why I see this happening. Here's where I see the turn. I felt like so and so would be angry here. What do you think?" "Well, I was thinking that they are angry and that they'd hide it." "Oh, very interesting." So that you at least are completely on the same page about what performance you're trying to achieve. "OK, we agree." So now you're not fighting that out on set. You're not standing on set saying, "I think I'd walk over here." "Well, I want you to walk over there." And if you're arguing about a deeper-level issue that's going to be a problem, you can sit and talk, and try to get on the same page before shooting begins. "OK, let's look into that and we'll decide."

By listening, you not only get the actors' thoughts but you have an enormous relaxing effect. They get to see your face, not just on the set amongst a horde of other faces. They get to see it up close and personal. You're there to ask about them, not to give orders. Suggestions maybe, but not orders. It's a lot like the doctor coming to check in with you in the hospital just before you have your appendix out.

A while ago I took my wife to the hospital for a procedure that, though not a humongous deal, would scare anybody. She was no exception. As she lay on the gurney in the pre-op room her heart ran a two-minute mile and her breath came in gasps. Soothing words from me had little effect.

After a few minutes the curtain parted and the anesthesiologist came in, gowned for the procedure. He introduced himself and paid attention to her as though she were the only person in the world. Nothing much was said beyond "how do you feel" and "do you have any questions" and "we'll take good care of you." He said he'd see her in a few minutes and traipsed off to the operating room. The change in her breathing and heart rate was beyond dramatic. It dropped like a stone and a smile returned to her face. When they wheeled her into the operating room she was calm like you've never seen calm.

Afterword: The procedure was very successful and her recovery was definitely helped by the anesthesiologist's visit beforehand. Why would that work when my words were not heard? Of course the anesthesiologist's bedside manner helped, but what is more important was that his being the doctor carried gigantic credibility. So with the director. No matter the actor's trust level before you came to visit, it will be greater afterwards. You'll be able to tell it right away on the set as you rehearse.

Brad Silberling: What I always make a point of doing when I'm shooting is to get in as early as I can and spend a little time with the cast and just ask them questions to get to know their characters. And of course, you learn about what they're going to be like as actors. You can get a real quick sense of someone's process by asking a few questions about how they like to work.

For me, some of the most constructive times that I ever had to direct the actor was at the audition, where you have a somewhat calm place to sit and make adjustments with them and really see what they're like as an actor. When they show up on the set, I could say, "Hey, do you remember the work that we were doing in the audition? Keep going that way." So you use your casting time as directing time. I find that even happens with costume fittings. I'll make sure that I drop by at costume fittings so we can keep talking about the character and the scenes. Use any moment you can. Because otherwise you may not get any other rehearsal time.

Failure Is OK

A final note on this subject: major psychological studies of people show again and again that one of everyone's biggest fears, by far, is speaking in public. If you thought that this did not apply to professional actors you would be very wrong. More than anyone they understand that what they do today, especially on a recorded medium like film, video, even YouTube, is going to be around forever. For Ever. Long time *n'est-ce-pas*? That will make anyone nervous. And sometimes the more someone acts, the more she understands the long-term ramifications of what she is doing and the more nervous she becomes. It's a vicious downward spiral.

This means that the director has a big job with every single actor, every one, not only to encourage them, to make them feel comfortable, but to let them know that it's OK to fail. It's OK to screw up. Because only with that attitude can an actor feel free to experiment, to try new things, to go outside his comfort zone. Only in that way can the actor let go of all the safe, proven crutchlike solutions that he's relied on for years. To do that he needs the express permission and encouragement from the director to leap off the high diving board, to go for the bungee jump; because the director is there to catch him.

On an episode of the TV series *Psych* we had an actress whose character was written to go crazy, physically berserk, writhing, screaming in one scene. She was supposed to be so violent that Shawn and Gus couldn't hold her down. We could tell in early rehearsals that the actress clearly did not like having to go outside her normal quiet comfort zone. She was afraid of looking stupid or foolish. Even though that big scene of her going nuts was several days away I had to start working harder to gain her trust. I told her several times on several occasions that my job was to make her look as good as possible. If she looked stupid it would make all of us look stupid, it would make the episode stupid. I promised her I would not allow that to happen. If she went "over the top" we would not use that take. However, she needed to feel free to go over the top, knowing that I would protect her both on the set and in the edit bay. This took a lot of conversation, and a lot of letting her see that I took care to make her look as good as possible in other scenes.

I told her about Jack Nicholson's work shooting *The Witches of Eastwick* where he played the Devil. He would do five or six or more takes on every scene getting bigger and bigger, and more over the top until he exhausted his choices. Then he and the director, George Miller, would look at the work and decide what worked and what didn't. They both believed that exploring the role of this fantastical character this way was the only way to find the right level for the character. The terrific results speak for themselves.

On the day we shot the crucial scene in *Psych* I kept encouraging the actress to let her inhibitions go, that I would protect her from embarrassment. The writer, who had been worried sick about her being too bland in the scene, was standing beside me sweating bullets as we rolled the cameras. When the scene got to the part where she goes nuts, we all held our collective breath.

Suddenly, she let loose with a scream that woke the Teamsters... I mean the dead. Her body seemed to levitate off the bed and Shawn and Gus, who were twice her size, couldn't hold her down.

That's what we needed! We did it several more times from different angles and I praised her after every take and encouraged her to try anything different that she felt like. By the end she was hoarse, sore, exhausted, sweaty, and glowing. She said she never felt so free acting before. The writer, the producers, and USA Network were themselves over the top in praising her work. I have to thank a friend who years ago helped me in his blunt way:

Mark Rydell: I like to tell them that it's OK to fuck up. Fucking up is just fine. Don't worry about it. Just don't come unprepared. Don't come not knowing anything. Other than that, you can fuck up all you want.

SUMMARY

1. Actors often distrust directors they don't know. It's the director's job to gain their trust; all the actors, not just Number One on the call sheet.

2. Every actor is quite different from every other actor and has to be treated differently. There is no one-size-fits-all solution for working with actors. The director must adapt to what works best for each actor.

3. Get to know your cast and crew. Learn their names before you shoot and work with them. Showing that you care about them will encourage them to work harder to achieve the goals of the film.

4. Directors need to be present at auditions. Otherwise they only learn part of what the actor can do.

5. Use auditions as mini rehearsals. Work with auditioning actors to see what both they and the scene are capable of. Actors are much more receptive to ideas before they get the job.

6. Often actors who are not right for the film have terrific ideas about the scenes. Experiment in the casting session with anyone if the inspiration strikes.

7. Encourage actors you are interested in to talk about themselves personally. You can learn as much from this as from their carefully crafted, and certainly truthful resumés. You can learn what makes them tick and what directions will work for them.

8. When an actor is cast, make contact ASAP, on the phone if not in person. Tell the actor how glad you are to be working with him.

9. Ask the actor before shooting if he has questions about the dialogue or the character, the wardrobe, their hair, anything. Don't wait until the day of shooting. You may get some nasty surprises otherwise.

10. Rehearsal before shooting is an invaluable tool for ironing out problems and finding creative approaches to the film.

11. Never stage scenes without the actors present. You *will* be sorry.

12. Arrive at set earlier than crew call. Begin your day in the makeup trailer with the actors. Discuss the day's work with them and make sure that everyone feels comfortable. Keep an ear out for any potential problems that you can troubleshoot now and solve before they happen.

13. Keep an open mind when hearing actors' ideas for any scene. It's part of building trust as well as encouraging creativity. You don't have to agree to their ideas; you do have to listen openly.

14. Let actors find staging with minimal help from you. Take advantage of their creative imagination. You can assist if they get tangled up.

15. Let your actors know you are looking out for them. Create an environment where they feel safe to experiment, knowing you will make them look good, and you will reap the benefits of wonderful performances. Be like the surgeon coming to see you before an operation.

16. "It's OK to fail" is a calming mantra for an actor. Relaxation is a key precursor to creativity. Assure your actors you are there to catch them if they go over or under the top.

Chapter 2

Mistake #2: Know-It-Alls Rule

On the set of my first movie, *The Bingo Long Traveling All-Stars & Motor Kings*[1] (what a title!?), I was working with Richard Pryor, Billy Dee Williams, and the amazing James Earl Jones. For 1976 it was a medium-budget film about the Negro baseball leagues, that took place in the 1930s so it was also a period picture, which meant period set design, costumes, automobiles, trucks, and busses. That meant it was going to cost more to make than Universal Pictures thought it could earn at the box office. Executives were on  the phone every day with ideas galore about how to cut the unreasonably huge budget of $4 million! Even in 1976 this was cheap. After a while when you've cut everything you can think of that doesn't hurt the picture, you... surprise surprise, start to hurt the film. My partner Rob Cohen, the producer, and I spent

---

[1] http://www.amazon.com/s/ref=nb_sb_ss_i_2_5?url=search-alias%3Dmovies-tv&field-keywords=bingo+long+traveling+all+stars+and+motor+kings&sprefix

more time fighting off the bean counters than making the film, or so it seemed. I had gotten so defensive I greeted any suggestion almost automatically with a *"No way!"*

One morning in the hundred-degree heat of the Georgia sun in July with the humidity bubbling at 90%, Billy Dee Williams, who was playing the pitcher, steamed up to me with an idea about what he could say to the batter, James Earl Jones, at the plate. Nothing much was scripted but Billy Dee said he thought these two were very competitive in a friendly way. What if they were to "play the dozens" or hurl funny insults at one another? Jokes on the level of "Yo mama is so fat…" was what he had in mind. They could make fun of each other's age or athletic ability, or family traits.

My very first instinct hearing this was to think that we didn't have time to stand around and make up a bunch of silly insults. We barely had time to shoot the scene as written. The first-time paranoid feature director in me was thinking, "This is how it starts; they try to take the picture away from you a little bit at a time. Don't do it. Stand up to them."

> **Donald Petrie:** I've seen more than a few, where the first-time director on the set wants everyone to know that they know what they're doing, and they're in charge. So when someone tries to give them a little friendly advice they go, "I know what I'm doing, no, no!" They become these little Hitlers and if they do well, great, and if they don't, nobody's gonna help them. You don't have any friends there on the set.

While Bill Butler, the DP, was still lighting up his giant carbon arc lamps to overcome the glare of the sun James Earl Jones joined the conversation and said, "This is a great idea playing the dozens! We learn about the characters this way."

So there I was, director on the spot, all alone. Rob Cohen was not yet on the set, he was out trying to persuade some old Georgia cracker to let us shoot in his grocery store. I had a negative attitude, because I was scared and defending our movie from people wanting to "ruin it." "I don't know if we can do that," I said. "We don't have the writers here. What would we say anyway?"

I found out.

Next thing I knew the entire baseball team, all black, surrounded me, one skinny little white boy. They started throwing out suggested "dozens" right and left. "It ain't nice to be throwing hard at old men." "You couldn't hit the floor if you fell out the bed." "Don't be makin' excuses for yo arthuritis now." "Yo mama so fat when she haul ass she gotta make two trips." Within two minutes we had enough insults to repel the Normandy Invasion. Before Bill Butler had finished lighting the scene we had a scene that was not only much funnier than what we had before but also told us more about the characters than we ever knew. Great idea. I almost turned it down. What was I thinking? When Rob Cohen showed up on the set and heard the scene he laughed so hard he had to change his Depends... twice.

> **Ron Howard:** Because I was an actor, I was playing every role in my mind and trying to make puppets out of everybody. And because I was young, I was terrified that people would second-guess me. I was so prepared, and pretty dictatorial about how things had to go. It took me a while to figure out that people weren't going to try to undermine me, that it's in everybody's interest for the director to succeed.[2]

Little did I know there's a name for this: "First-Time Director Syndrome." More common than pimples on a teenager... only less attractive. The director is terrified that he won't be like all those directors he's watched over the years who seem so sure of themselves. You know the one — the cliché director seen in the movies who is always yelling and who never listens to reason. One would think the directors who made these films would be better protectors of their images. Or even worse, maybe they think that's the way directors should act? Yikes.

---

[2] Terrence Rafferty, "Ron Howard" *DGA Quarterly*, Fall 2009, 38.

But you can be certain it's definitely characterized by fixed ideas, by stubbornness, by obsessive attention to petty details and over-looking important ones.

Paris Barclay: The number one problem that young directors have is a misconception of what the job really is. I think something in our culture is this idea of the tyrannical director, and maybe it came from the jodhpurs and the big microphone. They've gotten this idea that the director is a kind of god, and the director can't be wrong, and the director doesn't need to collaborate because the director has "the vision" and therefore it is all about the director. It's so not all about the director.

But a lot of young directors, and I've seen it, twenty-one years old, twenty-two years old, they'll come on a show, they'll get a great opportunity and they'll kill themselves by thinking, "I am the director, and therefore where I put the camera is the only place the camera can be, and this is the way the actor needs to do this, and this is my vision, and you need to walk there." On *In Treatment* one season, we had a director who said during the take, "Stop!" Not "Cut," but "Stop. Everybody, right where you're at." He was calling out from video village, not where the action was happening. He ran up to the actors, who were slightly frightened, frozen in their places. Gabriel Byrne as the shrink was seated and his patient was standing. The director says, "Move there, a little to your right. Two more lines before this is when you should've sat down. OK, let's go again." And from that day on he lost the actors. They paid no attention to him. I don't know where people got this idea that these are their meat puppets. I think this goes back to conceiving of the director as the master manipulator of events who controls everything, and is the only person who really knows what can go on.

I asked Jodie Foster what does she know now that she didn't know when she started directing. And remember, she had been acting professionally since she was only five or six years old and had many opportunities to watch different directors at work.

Jodie Foster: My first movie was ... *Little Man Tate*. I was young, twenty-five, and I think that I had this very black-and-white idea about how everything must be. I had a very young idea about life. You have the black on one hand and the white on the other hand. I don't think I had enough appreciation of complexity. That just comes with age. But that extended to my relationship with the actors too. I think it was very hard for me to let go of a preconceived idea of what I thought the performances should be. That was fine with Adam Hann-Byrd because he was a little boy, but it was harder on the other actors. I wanted it told a certain way and I couldn't allow them to breathe in their characters' bodies. But by the time I got to the second movie, *Home for the Holidays,* I thought, "I'm not doing that again." Because I could see that *Little Man Tate* had a very linear, plodding character to it. The same way the little boy did. He's very methodical, A leads to B leads to C. But I didn't want that in my second film, so I made a big effort to ensure that there was managed chaos and that all the actors could be more complex.

I've done many movies with first-time directors. I have a whole list of pet peeves about the things that they do. I did Alan Parker's first movie, *Bugsy Malone*, I did Adrian Lyne's first movie, *Foxes*, I did a thousand other movies with first-time directors. Sometimes they trench in on things that are unimportant because there's something solid to get their teeth into. I worked for a director, and in the script the character had a chipped tooth. There really wasn't any reason why she had a chipped tooth. She just had a chipped tooth. So he insisted on me having false teeth.

We were filming in Canada, in the winter, so it would freeze whenever I went outside and I couldn't talk. To him, that one little detail was something he could hold on to, he could grab on to with all his talons, and say, "This scene doesn't make sense to me unless she has a chip!" He was overwhelmed by the enormous questions in the movie that he couldn't answer, but that one he could answer in some very hands-on, controlled way.

So that's my biggest pet peeve, that they don't know which battle to hold on to that really is important and which ones aren't.

The fixed idea is the death of the creative person. It's one thing to have a strong concept and a strong belief in what you want to do. At the same time just because something is being created doesn't mean it's perfect, or even right. It would really be nice if our first idea were always the best one. The truth is a lot harder and any creative person has to be ready to modify, change, alter, chuck, deep-six, or destroy an idea if it's not working.

Nobody cares if it's your first idea or your jillionth idea. What they care about is very simple: does it work, does it speak to them. Authors rewrite books endlessly, Rembrandt painted over earlier versions of the same portrait. Picasso redrew *Guernica* many times and Spielberg reshot parts of *Jaws* so many times the studio took away all his cameras. As he was editing the film he kept having good ideas. Shut out of resources, he had to improvise. For one of the most terrifying moments in the picture he borrowed an underwater camera from Panavision, scammed some short ends of film, and built an underwater set in the swimming pool of the editor Verna Fields' house. And no executive was ever the wiser, until the money started rolling in faster than they could shovel it up.

On the other hand, stubborn directors who refused to alter their approach to a film even when it was clearly not working have caused some of the greatest film disasters like *Heaven's Gate*. Flexibility not egotistical stubbornness is always the way to go. Flexibility in the interest of making the best film, telling the best story, not in who had the best ideas.

Paris Barclay: I guess I have two things to say to new directors. I know you don't have to really be humble, but you must present an appearance of humility otherwise you're not going to get anyone to work with you. Everyone's going to be against you. They're going to be talking about you behind your back and you're not going to get the best work from them. It doesn't mean you have to go up to everyone and say, "I don't know what I'm doing, and I'm really stupid." It means you have to be open and accepting to collaboration with other human beings. The true definition of humility is an accurate appraisal of your own abilities. You have to accurately know what you're good at, and what you need help on, and that's humility. Humility is not overstating the things you're weak at. Humility is knowing this is what I'm good at. Like I know I have a certain expertise in music, but at the same time I know I need work when it comes to a fight scene. I need help. I'm not really great at choreography. I have many ideas that always come off a little stagy, or like things I've seen in other movies. I'm not the guy who's going to do the fresh fight scene. So I know I need the stunt coordinator who's creative. I need to give him some free rein. I need to have him come and show me stuff. I need to give them their challenge, which is I want something fresher than I've seen in the last thing, and that helps. I know that. I mean, if you're the director and you're afraid to let people know that these are the areas you're weak in, whatever you come out with is not going to be as good as it could be, and certainly not as pleasant. The takeaway is you need other people. You do. You need actors, you need other collaborators. You need to inspire them. You need to treat them like family, which gets me to number two. Bob Fosse once said, "Directors are directors because they're always trying to recreate their broken family." So usually directors are people who have come from some sort of disturbed or broken family. He said they're trying to recreate and rebuild their family with each project, and they're trying to do it in a way that they think is healthier and better than the way that they grew up.

SUMMARY

1. Good ideas can come from anywhere. Listen to anyone, even if it's the craft service person or a Teamster. E.g., *The Bingo Long Traveling All-Stars* finding dialogue through improvisation.

2. First-time directors are scared of being second-guessed and try to act dictatorial to cover their fear. E.g., "First-Time Director Syndrome."

3. Be open to suggestions. In the end you are the decider. If you never let yourself hear the suggestion, you could be passing by gold.

4. Not all suggestions are good ones. However, sometimes hearing something that wouldn't work can shine a light on the scene and lead you to discover what will work.

5. Fixed ideas are the death of creativity.

6. Have a vision for your work, but don't become a slave to it.

7. If you can't be truly humble, at least pretend to be. Otherwise nobody will want to work with you. Understand your strengths and weaknesses and ask for help when you need it. You'll get help... and respect.

Chapter 3

Mistake #3: Filibusterers

Kurt Vonnegut? I get to direct a Kurt Vonnegut short story? That was great! By this point I'd only been directing for a couple of years. How could I screw this one up? I was sure I could find a way.

Kurt Vonnegut's *EPICAC* was part of a TV film, *Three Faces of Love* hosted by Rex Harrison. *Epicac* is about a giant computer that falls in love with a beautiful female programmer and destroys itself when it realizes it can't do anything about it. Funny and sad at the same time, it starred Bill Bixby and Julie Sommars.

One day on the set of the ginormous computer that in 1973 took up half a soundstage at Universal, but had half the memory of my iPod Nano, Bill Bixby (playing the head programmer) asked me to explain a simple line of dialogue to him. It was a bit tricky so I floundered about before I came up with a good explanation. Or so I thought. I stood there and talked, and talked, and talked, with logical ideas, quotations from Plato, analogies from my own life. When I stopped to take a breath he looked at me, not unkindly, and said, "I have no idea what you just said." I think I turned eight shades of crimson for being such a Chatty Cathy. After that I started watching good directors much more carefully and listening to how they spoke with their cast. One thing was really clear. The good ones, not just the great ones but the good ones too, know to keep it short and to the point.

Why? To avoid being embarrassed by Bill Bixby?

No.

> **Taylor Hackford:** You can easily over-talk to actors. When you try to intellectualize too much they can go, "Why are you talking so much? What do you really mean?

Keep it short; give them something they can *use* while acting the scene. They need to hear it expressed as an action verb. That is something they can *act*, something they can *do*. Persuade, seduce, attack, destroy — these are all action verbs, actable verbs. Professor Andy Lane, my colleague at Chapman University, teaches his directing students to give directions in ten seconds... or less.

> **Steven Soderbergh:** Don't tell actors what to think. Tell them what *to do*. Give them things to do. Less and less I'm telling them what to think, because I don't want them thinking. I want them doing. I want them behaving. So I think it's more helpful. Instead of saying, "You know, he's a guy who in school took these kinds of classes," it's better to say to the actor, "Don't walk like an athlete. You walk like an athlete. You walk like somebody who has an athletic background. That's not that guy. Find another way to carry yourself, because you look too physically comfortable."

In Bill Bixby's scene the computer wasn't behaving right. All of his dialogue, which was very technical, had to do with fixing what was wrong with the machine. If the objective was "I want to find a solution," what he needed was a verb that actively drove what he was doing in the scene. It could have been *fix it*, *debug it*, *curse it*, *attack it*, or *engineer it*. Any of those verbs would have been better than the vomitorium of irrelevant words I spewed on him. Maybe they were nice ideas, maybe they were terrible. One thing is for sure: not only were they obtuse and unclear, but they were also all intellectual and not emotional. And intellectual is not playable or actable... even if you're Mr. Spock, Data, Hal, or Joshua. You have to find a verb that will give life to what a character is playing.

James Woods: Whenever I have a problem with an actor, I say to them, "Tell me the story again. What's happening in this scene? Tell me the story of just this scene." The actor says, "Well, I feel that she's been abused by her stepfather..." Oh, please! Don't give me all that politically correct crap. I just had lunch. Just tell me what's happening in the scene right now. "Well, I'm coming in to get the money from the guy. He's not going to give it to me. So I'm going to try to have sex with him to get it." Aha! So you're seducing him to get the money, right? So seduce him already! What's the problem?

As we directors gab on and on, we don't even notice the polite actor's eyes glazing over, probably thinking of Booze, Blondes, and BJs. The impolite actor has pulled out his iPhone under the table, and is checking his email, texting his agent, and playing Angry Birds in Hell. When you're done, the actor waits for the camera to roll and does exactly what he was doing before. If you're lucky he'll blunder into some facsimile of what you wanted, but no props to you, oh mighty blabbermouth.

Elia Kazan: Many directors talk a lot and show off, and then the actors think, "How the hell am I ever going to get that?" You can't unload the whole problem of their part on them. You never feed them more than they can eat and digest. And never talk about the significance of the movie. When you start talking too much, it's usually because you're floundering around and don't know yourself.[1]

Stephen Collins: I think the thing that drives most actors crazy is that a lot of directors leave you alone when you need the most attention and give you the most attention when you wish they'd go away.

I was lucky enough to sit in on a rehearsal of *The Seagull* that my talented professor at the Yale Drama School, Nikos Psacharopolous,

---

[1] Young, *Kazan*, 134.

was directing. I wanted to hear what he would say to the actors, what pearls of wisdom, what gems, would emerge from the master's mouth. At the end of a scene he stopped the cast and asked them to do it over again. He pointed to the ingénue and said, "This time, when you enter, carry the mail in your other hand."

That was it?

Carry the mail in the other hand?

WTF!

I asked him later what he meant by that direction. He said that the mail had nothing to do with it, the actors just needed to do it again and they would find the right path all by themselves. The mail was just an excuse. So it goes. The trust he had for his cast to be able to decipher the problem on their own was not just Pollyannaish, it was based on the surety that if they figured it out on their own they would grasp it forever. It would be theirs, they would own it. They would respect him for giving them that space. And if they needed more help, his words would be heeded more gladly than from some chatterbox who explains everything... but says nothing you can work with.

Tom Mankiewicz: In *Hart to Hart* Stefanie Powers did this scene with Lionel Stander and it was just awful. And I said, "Cut, let's do it again." I knew she had to leave. And she turned around and she said, "Let's do it again?" I said, "Yes, do it again." She said, "What was wrong with that?" I said, "I just want to do it again." She said, "You mean you have no direction to give me whatsoever?" I said, "That's right. I just want to do it again." Because I knew she knew that she was terrible. She's a pro. So she was really grumbling wanting to get out of there. And "Roll Camera... Speed." She did the scene. It was way better. I said, "Cut." She said, "What was wrong with that one?" I said, "Nothing. They were both perfect. Which one do you want me to print?" She said, "The last one." I said, "Great." Next morning, she came in and she said,

"I'm so sorry." I said, "Well, I just couldn't let you get out of there with a bad performance like that." And she really worked on the second take. And the whole point is that professionals that are good... she knew she was terrible on that first take. If I'd let her go, she would have written it off. You have to remind somebody, "Excuse me, you weren't very good. No, I have no direction to give you. I'm not going to tell you in front of the crew you weren't very good and you can do better." I'm not even going to say it to her. I know she knows she was not good. She gave four times the performance in the second take."

Donald Petrie: Listen, I had heard that Gene Hackman punched out directors. I'd heard on *The Royal Tenenbaums* he wouldn't do anything that the director asked. I had zero problem with him on *Welcome to Mooseport*. I just realized very quickly he doesn't suffer fools. Don't try to direct him. He does his homework. He knows what he's doing. More often than not, directors try to direct too much.

The moral is really simple... and really hard to follow: Directors talk too much. We love to explain, expound, and extol to our captive cast. We spend our days explaining what we want to our designers and crews, DPs and ADs. We're working our way to a vision and we have to explain it, over and again. The difference should be that we only explain what pertains to the job at hand. We don't need or want to go into the macrocosmic view of the script. Say as little as you can and when you do, make it about:

A. What the character is trying to do in the scene; and

B. How the character feels about what he's trying to do.

Sydney Pollack: An actor will say something and I will say, "What does that mean to you?" They say, "What do you mean?" "You just said I'm never going to speak to you again. What does that mean to you? Are you sorry you said it? Are you thrilled? Have you been wanting to say it for two years? I can't tell what it means to you. I hear the words but I don't understand what it means. The only thing that I understand is behavior. Nobody understands words, otherwise there wouldn't be all these misunderstandings. Too many directors just explain intellectually what a scene is about.

Don't stuff their ears with palaver about what happened in a past life, how this is an allegory for the evolution of the universe, how their mother had ingrown toenails which made her grouchy. Remind them what they're playing and get out of the way.

Sports coaches have this down to a science. We can learn from their manual. They are very specific with their directions. The tennis pro working on your serve doesn't go into the physics of the ball and racket or the history of the game. She keeps it simple. You want to hit the ball into the opposite court? Her direction: toss the ball more to your left. Simple. Direct. Uncomplicated. It's hard enough to do a good serve even this way. In the same way it's hard enough for Stanley Kowalski to get Stella to come home to him without the director having to spew a treatise on why Men Are from Mars.

Always remember the KISS principle: Keep it Simple, Stupid.

James Woods: It's like in golf. Never tell somebody what *not* to do in the swing. "Don't look up." Well, you can't do a negative. Tell them what *to do*. "Get over to the left side, or whatever, with the club." That'll take care of the other problem. So always find something positive. If an actor's stuck, don't dwell on the problem. Give them something else to do.

Here's a little example. I was doing a scene once, and a coffee table was in front of me. Somebody said, "Oh, you're having a little trouble getting up around that coffee table. We'll just move it." I said, "No. The coffee table is a real obstacle in a scene. If it's a real obstacle, something interesting will happen in my explosive moment with him." We rolled on the scene and when we got to that blowup part, the coffee table was in my way. I kicked the stupid thing over and went and throttled the guy. All of a sudden, that became a captivating, explosive moment, because there's nothing worse on film than tedium, and nothing better on film than excitement.

SUMMARY

1. Directors talk too much. Don't overexplain. The actor may drown in your "helpful" words.

2. Give an actor behaviors and actions for his character, not intellectual ideas.

3. Ask the actor:

   A. What his character wants in the scene; and

   B. How does the character feel about what he wants?

4. Encourage the actors to figure things out by themselves. When they make discoveries themselves, they will possess them totally; more so than if you had given them the very same idea yourself.

5. Never tell someone what *not* to do. Give the actor an action *to do.*

6. Above all — KISS — keep it simple, stupid!

Chapter 4

Mistake #4: Too Many Notes

Potentially the most helpful and possibly the most destructive aspect of working with actors is giving notes. Notes on staging, notes on character, notes on story, and, most critically, notes on their performance. The latter, notes on performance, is where actors decide you're either a genius or you "have no clothes." This is where the director can be really helpful or a worthless wing nut. As far as actors are concerned performance notes are the make-or-break point for any director. He can do dumb staging, pick mediocre camera angles, be no help with character or story, but when it comes to performance, actors are the most vulnerable. This is where they're looking for real validation. When actors ask a director, "How was it?" they're not asking about the scene, they're asking about themselves. It is the acting equivalent of "Do I look fat in this dress?"

If you say, "Of course not, you look great," actors think you are feeding them a line. If you were to say to your wife, "Yeah, that dress might be a little tight on you," forget about going out to dinner that night. Certainly don't look to get lucky anytime soon.

This is not some great revelation to anyone reading this book. What is interesting however is how directors give notes to their cast. Combine poor social skills and a lack of ability to interpret the material as discussed in the Director's Checklist section (see page 181), and the result is directors who either don't know how to give a note or just wimp out and don't talk to their actors at all. Beyond their no-brain, no-gain directions of "let's go again," "pick up the pace," or "smile when you say that," they opt for the safe harbor of Muteport.

Oliver Stone: I have the feeling that most young directors are afraid of actors. They come from film school with a heavy technical background, but they don't know how to deal with an actor. Some of them barely even talk to their actors. I am amazed to hear that some directors who make excellent films just put the actors in front of the camera and shoot. They don't talk, they don't rehearse. I don't know how they do it because, in my experience, actors will give you a good performance only if you force them to look into themselves and get out of their comfort zone. So as a director, you have to find the raw material, then take that person to a place he or she has never been before. That's how you bring out the best in actors.

Most film schools realized in the last few years that many of their students come from technical backgrounds and need a lot of help and practice dealing with human beings, in this case, actors. This is not something that can be taught in a couple of semesters. It can take years to get good at it. Some fortunate directors have a natural affinity with people and how to connect with them. Others need a lot of practice to get out of their shell and engage with their actors on a level the actor can relate to. This is one of the most exciting parts of directing. Since all actors are totally different, two scenes are never the same. Every scene is a new creative challenge for the director to find a way to work with his cast and help them give their best performance.

Try these easy steps for starters:

Step #1: Cut and Validate

Next to Elia Kazan and Mike Nichols, Sidney Lumet was one of the greatest communicators with actors. His forty films include *12 Angry Men, The Pawnbroker, Dog Day Afternoon, Network, Serpico,* and *The Verdict.* He understood the psychology of the actor as well as anyone ever has.

> **Sidney Lumet:** I understand what actors are going through. The self-exposure, which is at the heart of all their work, is done using their own body. It's their sexuality, their strength or weakness, their fear. And that's extremely painful. And when they're not achieving it in their performance, they pull back. They get shy. Paul Newman, who I worked with on *The Verdict* (1982), is one of the shyest men I've ever met. That's why rehearsal is so important.[1]

In his book *Making Movies* Lumet makes a surprising revelation of his directing technique that is so easy to follow it seems too easy to be true.

> I talk to every actor after every take.

Put yourself in the actor's place to understand how this works. Say you're doing a simple scene, not complicated or overly emotional. Walk to the front door, see who's there, find out what they want, if they're welcome, let them in. There is some tricky dialogue involved and you have to stay in your light. That's not hard, right? So you think. Remember you're the actor now.

So the camera rolls, action is called, the scene is done, "Cut." You're standing there waiting for a reaction from your director. What happens now?

As far as you, the actor, is concerned, not enough.

First off, the director is inside some stupid tent or room aptly named video village. The home of the village idiots. Apologies to

---

[1] http://www.imdb.com/name/nm0001486/bio

all real village idiots for lumping these trolls in with you guys. If an actress ever saw what went on in video village, laughing, snide remarks, phone calls, and a total divorcement from what the actors are doing on the set, she would go postal on the whole lot. It's all I can do to keep a civilized atmosphere in my own video village. As head idiot I try to keep everyone focused on the movie we're making, not local gossip, sarcastic comments, and whining. Video assist is a great tool, but a major distraction as people treat it like they're home watching TV. Many directors prefer not to be there but to sit beneath the camera close to the actors during the takes. Actors know the director is nearby and don't feel like they're performing in a vacuum. I carry a small wireless video monitor with me to check the operator's work as well as a headset to hear what's being recorded.

The biggest bug about the village is that timid directors and ones that don't like talking to actors hide out there and leave their actors in limbo wondering what the hell's going on.

Secondly, the director who is technically oriented can easily get caught up in the problems of the operator, the DP, the sound mixer, wardrobe, or any number of things. Meanwhile the actors are standing there hoping the take was OK. They stand and wait, and wait. More often than not they hear nothing from the director beyond "let's go again."

Al Pacino was asked by Rick Lyman in the *New York Times* if it was difficult to work with directors who are more interested in the technical aspects of a film:

> **Al Pacino:** You're acting and the director's off someplace else watching on a video monitor.... As soon as the take is over everybody says to the sound and the camera guys, well, did you get it? But the actor is finished. He's just sort of left standing there. You might have had something that you thought was very exciting happen. But to them, that's beside the point these days.[2]

---

[2] Rick Lyman, "Al Pacino Interview," *New York Times*, April 23, 2003.

The director who buys into Lumet's idea of talking to every actor after every take can still pay attention to all those technical things, just not right away. This director goes onto the set right away after a take and has a quick word, or even a touch or a look with everyone in the cast. He either reassures the actors they are on the right path, touches them lightly on the shoulder, or gives a nod that says the same thing. Then the director can spend a few seconds with anyone who can use an adjustment or some coaching. This is not a time-consuming process. Easily less than a minute, unless there's a big problem which means one would have to stop anyway to focus on the problem. I usually find that as I'm walking into the set to talk to the cast, I can call out any technical things that need to be done. The crew won't mind hearing that, as long as it's done civilly, as opposed to "Who's the idiot who frizzed the focus?" or worse.

The point is to offer feedback to the actors ASAP. It gives them a chance to digest it and focus on any change that's needed. If the shot's being taken again, it lets actors know why, so they don't think it's because of them, which they *will* think... I guarantee it. If it really is because of them, the director is there to give positive suggestions on how to make it better. Whatever you do, never leave actors hanging out on the set for any length of time without letting them know how they are doing. You are their support, their lifeline, and their validator.

If you think this will take too much time, just try it yourself. In the time that most good crews take to reset camera, reset props, reset the background artists, fiddle with the errant hair and droopy makeup, and adjust a flag, the director has more than enough time to give props or poops to the cast.

Michael Zinberg: Whether it's rehearsal or shooting, the first thing you do is deal with the actors. I know directors who will do a rehearsal. They'll say, "Cut, OK," and they'll go talk to the DP or the AD or something like that. The actors are standing there going, "Was that good? Was that not so good? Are we doing it again? Are we not doing it again? Should we go get made up after rehearsal? What's going on?" That is something that will turn an actor off in a heartbeat.

When you say, "Cut, print," or "Cut, good rehearsal," go right to the actors. Make sure they're taken care of before you deal with the rest of the stuff. I always ask an actor, whether it's a guy with one line or the lead carrying the whole scene, when I'm through with rehearsal and I'm through with shooting, whether it's a close-up or the master or whatever, I always ask them if they're happy. "I thought that was great. You OK with that? Should we move on? I'm ready to move on. Are you ready to move on? You want another one? You want to do one differently? You want to try something differently? You want to do one just for shits and giggles?" Nine times out of ten they'll say, "No, no let's move on."

How Not to Watch a Take

Somewhere in boxes of still film negatives there may be pictures of me sitting on a camera dolly during a take, going through a Saint Vitus' dance, shaking, quivering, twisting my body as though I'm playing an old pinball machine. Jerry Ziesmer, my AD for many films, used to do a great imitation of me watching a take. I could never get him to do it for me but his wife, Suzanne, told me it was hysterically funny. Watching the dailies was like looking at a 5.6 earthquake, the camera shook so much. One day in New York on *The Hard Way* a fearless dolly grip, Sergio Pendejo, told me to stop screwing up his dolly moves and find somewhere else to sit. I love New York crews, who else would do that?

I know why I was behaving that way. I wanted the take to be perfect and my body was just trying to help out. I was expending so much energy that not only was I worn out by lunchtime but I would also have a blazing headache.

Tired of being in pain and taking too many aspirin, Aleve, Advil, and Tylenol, I did two things. First, I went to a hypnotist in New York who treated actors for stage fright, and medical students preparing for their oral exams. Every Saturday morning for ten weeks she put me under and gave me posthypnotic suggestions to take away this terrible habit I had perfected. At first I thought this was silly, but I was desperate. After the second session, however, I noticed that the pain and tension headaches were less frequent. Four or five weeks later they were gone altogether.

The second thing, the epiphany, was that I realized I was watching takes in completely the wrong frame of mind. I thought, when I'm in a movie theatre watching someone else's movie, do I go through Saint Vitus behavior? No way. I'm either enjoying or not enjoying the movie but I'm not jumping up and down, shaking all over and giving myself headaches. What I need to do when I'm directing is put myself in a different place. When the camera rolls and the slate is clacked I will transport myself into a movie theatre or in front of my TV at home and watch what's going on objectively. I might enjoy it, I might hate it, but I'm going to stand back from it and be removed. That way I can be a much better judge of what's going on in front of the camera.

> **Allan Arkush:** I keep trying to tell myself, "You've got to pretend you're just home, this is not your show, you're just watching it on TV. You're not encouraging the actors, like with a pinball machine. You've just got to be totally relaxed like you're home and going, "This is shit." Sometimes I'll just sit there and take a big deep breath and close my eyes and just try to clear my head before this take so that I'm really feeling it.

Step #2: Privacy Please

OK, you called "Cut," jumped out of your chair, said you are going again for whatever technical reason and you spoke to everyone in the scene quickly. So far so good. And now you need to work something out with one or more of the actors.

How do you do that?

In private! *Never* give an actor notes within hearing range of other people, not actors, not crew, never. Take her aside and speak quietly so nobody else can hear it. Remember the embarrassment potential for her is high.

David S. Ward: Sometimes you have to tell an actor something that's difficult for them to hear. You have to tell them that what they are doing is not working. That they need to take another approach to it. That's not necessarily something you want to say in public. Because it could be slightly humiliating to the actor. You don't want the actor to feel that they are bad, or to announce it in front of everyone.

It can't be emphasized enough how critical this is. Remember how sensitive actors are about their work. Criticism of their work can easily be interpreted as criticism of them. Even tough actors like James Woods and Harvey Keitel respond better to a private conversation.

By being private, an actor can plan less stressfully how to handle the note you are giving. Because other people won't hear what you're saying the actor won't look as much like your puppet. However the actor responds in the next take can be seen as her own choice. There is definitely an element of "saving face" at work in all these kind of interactions.

Sydney Pollack: Actors usually feel because they're in a horribly vulnerable position of exposing themselves that they feel a strong kinship with each other. Often they're intellectually understood but emotionally violated by directors and by crews. The reason I don't ever like to direct actors when there's more than one present is they gang up.

They will form a resistance sometimes against you. You have to back off. When that happens you don't ever try to win that argument. An actress once said to me, "Well, I can't cross him. If he's sitting there like that, I would never move across him." Then the actor said, "That's right. What the hell would she move across me for?" I shut up then. Now, when I get the actress in the dressing room, now I can talk her into crossing him, but not with the two of them. It isn't adversarial. It's very understandable. There is a kind of — they're like animals that gravitate to each other. So it's just easier, I find, to work with actors one at a time.

Jeanne Tripplehorn: Sydney Pollack is a master at working with actors. I really like to rehearse but others on *The Firm* didn't. It was definitely an actor-by-actor thing. He would rehearse with me and work with me. That was how I came to trust him implicitly.

You don't have to be "precious" as Jodie Foster says but you do have to treat the actor with the respect of not calling her out in front of the other actors or crew.

> **Martin Sheen:** Acting is such a private thing. It's so deeply personal. You're revealing something. It may not be my wife or child that's just died, but somebody or something has died in me that I'm going to have to get in touch with. That's what we do. We have this store or this well that we go to and it's personal. If it's not personal it's impersonal and if it's impersonal it shows. And you'll only go there with someone that has confidence and that will protect you.

There is an exception to this rule. What if the actor did something right or terrific? Then not only let her know it, let everyone know it. Don't be shy. It's the equivalent of applause and nobody turns that down. Take advice from the best seller, *The One Minute Manager*: "Catch them doing something right."[3] Just don't overuse it. On Broadway nowadays if actors don't get a standing ovation they think they've failed. That's stupid. It's like grade inflation, everybody gets a gold sticker, and everybody gets an A. The smoke-blowing director who cries "terrific, fabulous" after every fart from an actor is a total fraud. We know it, the actors certainly know it. Use your praise wisely. Spend it with care, but do spend it.

The way to spend it carefully involves one other phrase from *The One Minute Manager*: "Be Specific." Tell the actors what they did right. "I really believed you when you turned at the door," "I

---

[3] Kenneth Blanchard and Spencer Johnson, *The One Minute Manager* (New York: Berkley, 1982), 39.

loved how you persuaded him to buy that," "That was a very clever choice to play exhausted instead of gung-ho." Remarks like that are the difference between the smoke-blower and the wise director. General, nonspecific compliments are easy and mean nothing. "That was great!" and "Terrific!" are in one ear and out the other.

Penelope Ann Miller: I remember a director saying to me once, "Faster and funnier." I mean what a clichéd thing to say. It's like from the handbook of do's and don'ts. When you say, faster and funnier, what on earth does that mean? And then I'm thinking, Should I speed up my lines? And then you're overacting and you're speeding it up and it's just all superficial.

Specific compliments are remembered. All people, not just actors, feel good about them. This works whether it's the actor, the camera operator who pulled off a tricky move, or the special effects tech who solved how to make the street look spooky by laying down dry ice fog.

Paris Barclay: Tell them the good stuff first, always. Don't start any kind of notes with "what's wrong with this scene." Always spend some time, and not just one line, talking about what's good about what they've done. Be very specific and very clear. "You know what, when you stepped up to him I was blown away by X, Y, Z. This really moved me. I love how you listened to her, I knew you didn't believe a word of her speech." You don't have to lie. There's always good stuff.

New York Magazine published an insightful article that's relevant: "How Not to Talk to Your Kids."[4] Its main point is quite simple: general praise of anyone, kids or adults, is almost instantly discounted. In this age of over-praising, everybody gets a gold star for fear they will lose their self-esteem. This has turned out to have horrible unforeseen consequences. People expect an A just for showing up. When they don't get it they stop trying. The

---

4 Po Bronson, "How Not to Talk to Your Kids," *New York Magazine*, February 11, 2007.

people who do persevere in the face of challenges or failure are the ones who have been praised specifically for their *effort* in getting to where they are right now. Focused praise on specific things people do right encourages them to persevere when they don't get an A. Judith Brook, NYU Professor of Psychiatry, explains that "the issue for parents or managers is one of credibility. 'Praise is important, but not vacuous praise. It has to be based on a real thing, some skill or talent they have.'" The article further states that "Once people hear praise they interpret as meritless they discount sincere praise as well."

The ability to repeatedly respond to failure by exerting more effort — instead of giving up — is a trait well studied in psychology. People with this trait, persistence, rebound well and can sustain their motivation through long periods of delayed gratification. In this article, Dr. Robert Cloninger at Washington University in St. Louis states that "the key is intermittent reinforcement. The person who gets too frequent rewards will not have persistence, because they'll quit when the rewards disappear."

There are two schools of thought about being specific, however. The one we've just discussed encourages specificity. "I loved how you took her shoulders before you said 'blah-blah-blah.'"

The other school believes that being this specific can cause the actor to become so pleased that he will subtly start to overact the very moment you praised. He'll make it bigger, or camp out on the moment longer. This does happen:

> **Steven Soderbergh:** I've learned the hard way, as I'm sure you might have, that when the actor seems to be onto something, shut up and stay out of the way. Don't get them in their heads, don't get them thinking, and never call attention to something specific that they're doing that's great, because it will never be great again. Never say, "I loved how you picked up the such and such," because you'll never love it again.

I am going to be the last person to ever contradict Steven Soderbergh, though Francis Ford Coppola believes the direct opposite. So if these best of the best directors disagree like this perhaps there is some truth to both sides. They certainly can over-react to praise and at the same time they need encouragement that is not vague and generic.

My personal inclination would be to avoid going overboard with praise and hope that the actor may only overdo the moment for a take or two. If it's a strongly emotional moment he may not ever do it the same way again. Actors are not robots. I would rather praise them for what they did right and watch out they don't get carried away with it in future takes than leave them in the dark.

Technology Sidebar

There are many arguments about shooting on film versus digital. But there is one terrific advantage to digital: when the set is quiet and the camera is recording the director can keep going for a long time without having to cut. You're not limited to a ten-minute film magazine. Why is that a good thing?

After calling "Cut" the set is invariably invaded by hair, makeup, lights, props, etc. Getting everything reset and quiet again can take a few minutes, which quickly adds up to hours in the day. With digital, however, takes can be repeated multiple times without needing to cut or fear of running out of film, often with lens changes on the same take. There's no invasion of the set; everything stays quiet so the actors can concentrate on what they're doing. Performance corrections and adjustments are easily made in this salubrious and peaceful atmosphere. What's fun is to watch everyone doing lightning-fast resets while the camera is still recording. The extras no longer trudge back to their starting points, they scurry back. Prop guys are flying in resetting the mashed potatoes. And they're having a good time doing it, because they're caught up in the spirit of getting the shot right. It all gets done in seconds. Everyone stays totally focused on the shot.

Some worry that this wears the actor out. Quite the contrary, the quiet focused set and the ability to go again right away without any delay is extremely effective. The stress factor is heavily reduced creating an atmosphere similar to a rehearsal ambience. Concentration and momentum are maintained, a state of being devoutly desired on any set. Even in many action scenes, keeping the camera rolling and repeating some actions that weren't quite right the first time allows the director and the actor to get the action done properly.

Any good script supervisor will make effective notes to help the editor in sorting through the extra work. In these days of Avid, Final Cut Pro, and Adobe Premiere editing systems even this is not a burden.

Step #3: Keep Them in the Loop

Talking to actors between takes is an excellent idea, as is saying it in private and keeping your directions concise and active, but *what* do you say to them, specifically? That's the hard part. Duh. Every scene is different as is every actor and every director. What is being sought exactly couldn't be covered in any book or series of books because each scene, each story, each character is so individual. What can be taught however, is how to deliver your notes in the most effective manner.

Michael Zinberg: When it comes to notes, directors who have the most success pose a note as a pitch, or as a question, as opposed to, "You should do this."

If a director says, "What would happen if?" or "How about this?" or "What if you did this? How would it feel if? What if you were to try?" and the actor picks it up, great. But if they don't go for it, there's no judgment involved. You're not putting the actor in a position of saying, "I like that or I hate that." You're not making them feel like they're making a judgment of you and your note, or that you're making a judgment of them and their performance if they don't take it.

After a note you can tell right away if they're processing it on a positive or a negative level. "Oh, I see what you're saying. That's really good. We can do this. We can do that." Or, "I don't know. My guy wouldn't do that." So once you have a feeling of what kind of actor you're talking to, then you can tailor your note in a way that will feed into that. If you know that an actor is going to try to talk himself out of whatever you're going to pitch, you pitch it in a softer way. If you know the actor's open-minded, you can go right to it. You don't have to pose it in such a way that it feels like you have to defend it. I'm not that clever myself.

I also think that with performance, the comfort level of an actor is so important. If you're asking an actor to do something that they are uncomfortable with, chances are the performance is not going to be as good as if they are comfortable. If you say, "Well, you've got to pick up that glass on this line," they're going to be thinking about the glass and not the line.

This kind of direction is posed as a nonconfrontational suggestion. That doesn't mean it should be wimpy or phrased in a passive-aggressive or sarcastic way. (One of the snarkiest things you can say to an actor is "Is that the way you're going to do it?") What it does mean is that the actor is being brought into the process and consulted. Whether we like it or not, that's happening anyway, it's just more in the open. As much as we would like to be Jim Henson, master puppeteer, with our actors, forget it. They won't let you treat them that way.

If we do need extremely specific physical things in a shot or a scene from the actor for technical reasons, we need to explain to the actor why it's important to do it this way and ask for his help. It becomes a challenge and he'll try his best to achieve it. When we need actors to bring their own creativity to a role or a scene, they are a key part of the process and they need some room to do that. Actors will put on insane outfits, wear horrendous wigs, walk like Quasimodo or be starkers... if they believe in the role. If we haven't enlisted their help and explained what we are trying to achieve, they'll never be happy. They'll do it maybe, but won't be happy. If they're not happy, there will always be some resistance to giving their all to the role.

There are some directors who take a much more aggressive approach to the actor. In earlier days this would have been the Eric von Stroheims, John Fords, Henry Hathaways, Otto Premingers, men who were equal-opportunity brutes to everyone, cast or crew. These are the kind of directors who created the cliché of the martinet maestro. Thin-skinned actors were pulverized and alcoholized from acting in their films. Oliver Stone, a tough director in his own right, takes a more enlightened approach: he likes to push actors to get out of their comfort zone. He believes without that approach actors fall back on their old tricks.

Oliver Stone: In my experience, actors will give you a good performance only if you force them to look into themselves and get out of their comfort zone. So as a director, you have to find the raw material, then take that person to a place he or she has never been before. And that's how you bring out the best in actors.

James Woods: Oliver doesn't like to talk about anything in a scene. He's one of my favorite directors in the world, no matter how much people criticize him. Everything I'm telling you is true, because I've had exactly these problems with him, and I was wrong. I'd want to talk about the scene, and he'd say, "Jimmy, just do the fucking thing. You're a genius. Just do it and shut up." I'd say "OK," and laugh and so on. I'd do it, and you know what, it'd work. The less I talked about it, the better it was. Everything I've directed, every time I got somebody who's quirky and a little difficult, it'd be a pain in the ass, and guess what, they always give the most interesting performance. Not that I'm promoting that people should be a pain in the ass. It's always more interesting and compelling.

The answer to whether to take the soft line or the hard line is totally a matter of the actor's personality and character. There are no firm rules. This is when the time you spent with the actor before shooting really pays off. This is when the time you spent breaking the scenes down dramatically comes to your rescue. With a tougher actor, you sense right away that you can be more direct, you can push harder. These actors may resist initially but that's just part of their nature.

With a genuine pro like Jodie Foster, James Woods, or Michael J. Fox, you can be very blunt in telling them what you want. There's no need to be delicate or precious about your directions — just clean and to the point. If you can express it in an active verb, so much the better.

Now you're communicating the essence of what you want. Never go for vague metaphorical or philosophical concepts that are so hard to interpret. These kinds of amorphous directions often leave the actor either pissed off or shaking his head having no idea what you want.

Jodie Foster: My least favorite thing is when a director treats everything you do very preciously, and is incredibly quiet, trying to talk about the experience from underneath your skin. And my feeling is like, You just direct, you let me do what I do, it's kind of a private thing and I don't really want you in my skin, I just want you to tell me what you're looking for, and if you're not getting that, and don't come up with fancy mysterious precious ways to get me somewhere, because that's manipulation. You can speak to me in an intellectual way and I will translate that into my own emotions. Don't try and talk to me like you're a little walking heart. That doesn't work for me at all.

On the flip side if you have a great director like Dick Donner, he's so crazy. He just talks to you during all of the scenes while the camera is rolling, and I love it.

Richard Donner: God love Jodie Foster. I mean, I've been the luckiest guy alive with getting actors. With her or Mel Gibson you see something or you hear something or you get an idea… if you wait until the end of the take and do it again, it's lost something. But if you can just say, "the telephone," and you don't say another thing. "The wallet." You never say anything more. Bang, all of a sudden Mel has lost his wallet. Or Jodie eyes the telephone and makes something out of that. I love her.

Most directing books will tell you never give "result-oriented directions." And that's really good advice... for most actors. But with many real pros, they just cut through the bull and go for the gusto. They'll say, "Oh, I know what you want, I'll give it to you." Then they process it through that amazing talent they have and come up with something special that you never expected. Makes life a lot easier.

It is dangerous though. Do that with the wrong actor and you'll get a clichéd and generic version of what you're after. You can never go wrong with directions that are either phrased as active verbs — persuade, coax, seduce, celebrate, escape — or strong *as-ifs* — "*as if* you have to catch a plane," "*as if* you know the ceiling is about to fall on you," "*as if* you just figured out they're lying." Everybody can interpret those directions. It's not just for one type of actor or the other; it's a universal shorthand.

The Bull in the Arena

Just as many, many actors get defensive about notes on their performance, many, many directors get very nervous about giving notes. They look at a strong-willed actor and only see a bull ready to charge.

Jodie Foster: They either say nothing or they get all precious like they're dealing with a mental patient. It's a turnoff.

That kind of director needs to man up, strap on a pair, and give the note with confidence. Because the truth is, *no matter what you say*, many actors are likely to resist you at first. That's why it works better, much better, to phrase the note as a pitch, not a demand.

David S. Ward: I had to learn how to talk to an actor in a way that didn't communicate a sense that they had failed or somehow they weren't measuring up on the talent level, but that it was simply a matter of making an adjustment in the approach to the character and to the scene, because once an actor feels like you don't have confidence in them they tend to withdraw from you. I think it's always better to deal with an actor privately about most things.

Jill Hennessy is a talented actress totally devoted to making her work the very best it can be. Whether she is excited, or tired, charged up, or bored by waiting, she attacks every scene with energy and commitment. She has thought about the work thoroughly beforehand. Playing the lead on *Crossing Jordan* for six years meant that she had a lot of herself, her emotions, her creativity, her life tied up in the choices she made. They were almost always the right choices, but as happens with everyone, sometimes not quite right for that particular story. So the director who goes to her with a note had better be ready to encounter some resistance not out of ego but conviction. Giving her a note she might reply, "I'm already doing that" or "I'm playing against that" or "I don't like that character, why be nice to him?" At this juncture a director could suggest, "Of course you don't like him. What would it be like if you tried to hide that from him?" So in essence the director is validating her choices but asking for more or giving a new twist on the idea. When I've been unable to make headway and run out of ideas I've even said to Jill, "OK I hear you, do what you think is right."

So the director has brought it up, planted the seed and it will have started to grow in her subconscious. There's no need to argue with her or get her any more defensive, because after the director walks away, she'll start thinking about it. It's the old What If He's Right Syndrome. Nine times out of ten Jill will make that change in her own special way in the next take. She won't feel forced, or bullied, but a participant in shaping the film. This works with almost any actor. It's not a trick. It's not a manipulation; it's keeping the actor part of the process.

A similar twist on that would be if an actor was making a very wrong or very strange choice. You can approach her and comment something like, "That was really interesting how you did that, I didn't expect it to go that way." You'll have a double effect on her. First, she's pleased you noticed what she was doing and second her alarm sounds: there is something you're not telling her. "How do you mean?" she asks. You can reply, "I always thought you were going to seduce him" or "you were going to ensnare him." So in essence you're not attacking what she did, you're just saying it was an interesting choice. Which is the truth, right? You were interested enough to pay attention to it.

Now she will certainly ask you what you had in mind. There's no need to keep selling your idea because it will already be working in her brain.

> **Allan Arkush:** "Shelley" is very mistrustful of guest directors. She doesn't like scenes to be changed. She prepares them in a very specific way. Sometimes she may not get what the scene is about. She has certain rules of acting in her head. If it doesn't fit into those rules I have to guide her to it. When a part of a scene, say, is not working, I'll go in and comment on it. "That was interesting, the way that went." She'll reply, "Oh wow, what do you mean?" So all of a sudden her focus is on it. "Well, right in that section, I never expected it to go there. You know what? What if we were to go this other way with it." Shelley will think and then say, "Oh, OK."
>
> So it's something that was not working right, but I draw attention to it, and make it seem like I'm praising the actor. I'll get them to focus on it and then I'll get them to connect it to something else.

Step #4: Make It Fun

One of the hardest things to do when making films is to keep remembering that no matter how serious the subject matter we always need an element of fun. Any creative endeavor has to come out of a playful mind, not a mind stuck in mechanical ruts and rote behaviors. It's no surprise that exciting new ideas seldom come from big corporations and bureaucracies who survive and thrive through tightly controlled thinking. Microsoft as a small startup was a whirlwind of ideas. Microsoft as a big company has gotten its back wheels stuck in the mud and is working hard to get free. Several people worry that since Steve Jobs' passing, Apple could fall prey to the same situation. The Maps app debacle was a harbinger of that possibility.

Films of any sort, even instructional videos, need constant creativity. They cannot be treated like cans of Coca-Cola or Chevrolets rolling off the line. TV series need constant infusions of creativity to stay alive. There is even a phrase for what happens to long-running shows running out of ideas: "jumping the shark," which came into play on *Happy Days* when Fonzie, in his leather jacket, water-skis over a shark. See it on *www.jumpingtheshark.com*.

It's obvious how this applies to actors or "players" as they are often called, as they play a role. In the theatre they still appear in "plays." We are bringing imaginary events to life, which is no mechanical process. Actors and directors have to be in a playful, imaginary place to do good work. The minute they start to do it by rote the whole soufflé goes flat. Even the *Happy Days* episode was a mighty effort to avoid going flat.

Peter Hyams: I had a discussion with a very prominent actor who said, "I think great work comes from conflict." I said, "I think you're wrong. I know you've won Oscars. I think you're wrong." I said, "Because of my family, I grew up among the greatest concert artists that ever lived. That was my family's business. Arthur Rubinstein didn't work the piano. He played the piano. Michael Jordan is not a basketball worker, he's a basketball player. When they showed up at the United Center Floor or at Carnegie Hall they played. They did all the hard work, all the rehearsal, and all the rejection, and all the other things you have to do, and all the weightlifting, it's all done before." I said to the actor, "Do you know what they call you guys? They call you the players. They even have a thing that says the *Playbill*. It doesn't say the *Workbill*. I've never heard anyone say, 'I'm going to go and watch a Broadway work.' It's a play."

As actors and directors are picking actions and ways to play a certain moment or scene they need to be looking for things that are "fun" to play. Things that are interesting and offbeat, things that enrich the moment or the scene. No one should be offbeat just for wackiness's sake because creativity has to be organic to the film being made. Otherwise it clashes horribly and rips the viewer out of the film. Perhaps this is a reason that mashups like *Cowboys and Aliens* don't work as well as hoped.

> **Donald Petrie:** It's the game of make-believe. This is why children are so fascinating to watch, because they're in the moment and they're just trusting their instincts. If you see a child being a fireman, he's just spraying water on the building, calling on the radio or whatever he's playing out in the backyard. You go up to that child and ask what he's doing. "I'm a fireman." There's no, "Well, I'm playing the fireman." He is the fireman. As adults we start to say, "OK, now we're acting." And all of a sudden, "I'm not a fireman. I'm playing the role of a fireman." So I encourage a childlike acceptance that says "I am the character" not "I am playing the character."

Penny Marshall, whose wonderful comedies include *Big* and *A League of Their Own*, knows a lot as an actress as well as a director about the inner process of acting. She talks about directing Tom Hanks in *Big*.

> **Penny Marshall:** I knew what it was like for an actor to find the right note, and I enjoyed watching Tom's process. He would try everything in rehearsals. "Just let me get it out of my system," he'd say.... He was playing a kid and didn't drive any of the scenes as an adult would. He reacted to things. The secret to getting all that right was that we let ourselves play. I let Tom play. I let myself play, too. We always gave ourselves those precious five more minutes of rehearsal. It wouldn't have happened otherwise. Tom had to find the kid in him and let that out rather than simply act like a kid."[5]

---

[5] Penny Marshall, *My Mother Was Nuts* (New York: Houghton Mifflin Harcourt, 2012), 221-2.

Things that are fun to play appeal to the actor's sense of play. They get inspired and really into doing these actions. Instead of "talking to somebody" at a party, "flirting with them," "teasing them," "flattering them" can be much more fun or perhaps inspiring to the actor. Try playing against the obvious way of doing something. This always shakes up a scene and helps you find more meat in it. Even if the choice is totally wrong it will bring some insight that you and the actor can and will use.

> **Michael McMurray:** They like to play in Imaginationland. "Who am I now? Oh boy, that's fun." So they're big kids. And it's OK to treat them like big kids. You want to talk to them like you're Imaginationland. "Wouldn't it be fun if blah, blah, blah?" That really gets them going. "Oh, that sounds like fun." I get it because I'm a big kid, too.

> **Betty Thomas:** I was doing a *Moonlighting* episode. And it was a big scene between Bruce Willis and this woman. And they're talking about their lives. It turns out that Bruce's father is going to marry this woman and Bruce has slept with her. But she was so drunk that she doesn't remember. He spends the whole episode talking about how he'd won her in a pool game. The surprise of the scene is, she used to do this all of the time; she would get really drunk and play pool and let guys pick her up. We do the first take and she's just full of self-pitying, "Woe is me," and "Oh, I have to get drunk," and Bruce looks at me like this is terrible. I took her aside and said, "I think you're missing the point of the scene. The reason that you're fitting in so well with the whole Addison family is they're all assholes and you're an asshole. That's what holds you all together. And what makes you fun to be around is you think it's funny, what happened in that pool game. As if you were saying, 'You want to hear something funny? I used to get so drunk...'" The actress went, "Oh, I see." I said, "You're telling the story because it's amusing, what used to happen." The punch line is they get up and walk out and she says to Bruce Willis, "Wouldn't it be funny if you had walked in there and we had slept together?" Make sure

> the character doesn't feel bad for themselves. Even the worst characters, find something admirable in themselves. That was a big thing in Jeff Corey's class, about not prejudging the character.

When directors are preparing they should be looking for the kinds of verbs that tease the actor's imagination. If the actor picks an ordinary action, such as "Read out the charges to the defendant," the scene will be ordinary. If he *accuses* the defendant, both actors profit: the prosecutor and the defendant. Not only does the prosecutor have something interesting to play, but the defendant has something more powerful to react to.

> **Allan Arkush:** In a scene I did for Jeff Corey's acting class from *Gingerman* I learned a lot about trying crazy choices. The kid has flunked out of school and been thrown out of his apartment and he's telling somebody why he flunked. So I acted the monologue and Jeff stopped me in the middle. He said, "Oh, that's so full of self-pity. You know what? Can you balance a broom on your hand? OK. Pick up that broom and balance it on your hand. Now do the scene." So I'm doing the scene while I'm walking around trying to balance it and he says, "Now isn't that more interesting? That's the kind of person this character is. He's flunked out of school, he's thrown out of his apartment, and he's just more interested in balancing a broom than telling you how miserable he is."

In this example, Jeff Corey used a prop to divert the actor from the obvious choice of self-pity and head him in a totally different direction. Even if the broom was forgotten about in later rehearsals it would still have had a huge positive effect on how the actor played the scene.

> **Donald Petrie:** Often an inexperienced actor will come in totally over-rehearsed. They've stood in front of the mirror and worked out every bit, every nuance, and now they get to the set and they're wooden, they're totem poles. They look like they're acting. You may say, "Hey, try it this way," and it comes out the same way.
>
> **John Badham:** They will not change.

DP: So I call it "propping up the actor." What I do is say, "Why don't you be eating an apple in the scene here." Or I give them a notebook and tell them to take some notes. I suggest any kind of props that they could possibly use that's not out of character. This gives them so much to do they forget to act. They're so focused on eating the apple or taking the notes that they forgot what they rehearsed. When I'm ready to shoot I say, "Forget the apple. You don't need the apple, stupid idea." They're back to where they were, but all their gobbledygook for the most part is gone.

JB: But it's loosened them up.

DP: And sometimes I might just leave the apple in the scene. At least it doesn't feel like the rehearsed thing they came in with. That's a technique I found, that usually works when you've got somebody who isn't as experienced.

Step #5: One at a Time

Always rushing. Never enough time to shoot. We have a few notes for someone. Big deal. Give him the notes, tell him what you need. What's so hard about that?

Depends on when you do it.

If you give all the notes at once you'll have either a confused actor or one who is concentrating on too many things at once.

Sydney Pollack: If there are seven things wrong with the scene, just talk about one. Then once it's fixed, talk about another one, and so on. Solve problems one at a time. You can't ask an actor to think about five different things at a time. You have to be patient. I never spend too much time on rehearsals because I'm always afraid I might get it right in the rehearsals and that it'll be gone in the performance. So once I think we're getting there, I bring the crew in and send the actors to their trailers for makeup and wardrobe, and then I go see each of the actors privately and talk to them some more about the scene. That way, each actor has a different sense of what he or she will bring back to the set. I always try to roll the camera too soon. It makes the actors a little tense, it catches them off guard a little, and it tends to give better results.

To go back to the sports analogy, the good baseball coach or the good tennis coach will only tell you one major thing at a time. If you're having trouble with your swing he might have several corrections to make. "Stand closer to the plate. Choke up on the bat. Keep your eye on the ball. Swing from low to high. Step into the ball." The wise coach keeps it simple: "Just stand closer to the plate." It takes the player time to get used to that adjustment. Then deal with "choke up on the bat." If this stuff were easy then Derek Jeter would only hit home runs and all of Rafael Nadal's serves would go in.

Don't Let Things Slide

OK, you've followed all the steps above and it's still not happening. What do you do when you're not getting what you need from the actor? Can you tell why? Is he fighting the scene, is he not prepared, does he have the wrong stuff, is he high, did you cast the wrong actor? Every one of these problems, and there are probably dozens more, will have to be dealt with in its own way. Some problems, like being unprepared, are maddening and time-consuming but can be handled. Others require a lot more finesse. This is no job for sissies. Usually, the first line of attack is to bring the actor into the problem, again in private. Ask him how he sees the scene, what are his goals, how does he feel about the goal. These are the basic questions that we always want to ask. Also we're trying to keep an open dialogue going; we don't want to put actors on the defensive because we know how that works out.

> **Richard Dreyfuss:** I feel that I have on the set the right to say to my director, "I don't think this works. How about this?" To duke it out to some extent with the director about the script. I want to be able to feel with a director that I'm a creative partner in this endeavor. Anything that happens that makes me feel otherwise I am going to resent.

You can ask, "Is there something that's bothering you in the scene?" What always surprises me is how often an actor is thrown by a word in the stage directions or one line of dialogue that could easily be changed. Many experienced actors spot this themselves but others take the script very literally and either don't realize they can bring it up or are too timid to do so.

Patty Jenkins: My new favorite thing, when you note, note, note an actor and it's not quite working, is finding some core underlying change, a one-word change that changes everything.

JB: Your favorite thing being the one word?

PJ: Figuring out what that one thing is. There's something wrong in the whole performance or not quite getting there, and figuring out what that one misunderstanding is or one word that'll change that whole performance. I think it's true in life, too, and that fascinates me. Gratitude, for example — can change the attitude that you're feeling in life, you can be in a much better mood all the time. I've met people who have said, "Wow, I had a near-death experience and now I feel so grateful. I appreciate everything about my life." One change changes the lens through which you're seeing everything. So finding those corrections in directing that are so simple yet change the performance completely.

Brett Ratner: When an actor's not getting what I want, I have a trick that I do. Take a break, "I've gotta go to the bathroom, please take ten minutes." They're not giving it to me. Maybe they're thinking about something else. Even if I don't have to go to the bathroom I'll just walk away. Then the actor will sit in the corner, and will be worried about making me happy. He's stressed out. I know he'll calm down. It's like if you're walking really fast, your heart's pumping. And then the minute you sit down, your heart rate goes down, you relax. Maybe he goes and has a cigarette, and he comes back. Every time he comes back he's perfect. I break him out of that trap where he's caught in something that he can't break out of.

Or the other trick, is to say, "Got it, we're moving on" and the actor thinks, "Really?" And all I do is say, "We're going in closer." But... I keep the camera the same distance. We'll pretend we're changing the lens, so the guys go around the camera and fiddle around.

This gives the actors time to relax and boosts their confidence at the same time because it sounds like we're moving on.

Or, I'll say, "Let's go take a walk." He thinks I'm gonna say "What are you doing?" but I'll talk about everything except the scene, and say, "Oh my God, last night you wouldn't believe what happened. This beautiful girl came in and she was looking at me from across the room, you wouldn't believe it," and I just start to tell him a story. We go back and he's like a different guy. It got him out of his head, you know? It's just breaking that logjam, that block.

Betty Thomas: When we're shooting and I'm not getting what I need, I say, "Look, this is stupid. It's fucked up. It's not working at all. Let's try something else. Let's try a whole different approach." I mean, I don't know what else to do, so I just say exactly what is on my mind. I say, "It's not anyone's fault. We've got to try something else and see what happens." That could mean that we try doing the scene totally the opposite way in order to break through or it could mean that we scrub it and come back to it another day. That's way better than beating it to death. A good night's sleep can do wonders for a scene.

In *Saturday Night Fever*[6] there's a scene where John Travolta's character, Tony, helps Stephanie (Karen Lynn Gorney) move her furniture to her new boyfriend's apartment. In the apartment Tony meets the new boyfriend who is a bit of a snob, and when Tony and Stephanie walk outside and get in the car they start a big argument driving back to Brooklyn. A very emotional scene where she tries to justify her behavior to Tony. At least that's the way it was scripted.

Saturday Night Fever, *Japanese poster.*

---

[6] http://www.amazon.com/s/ref=nb_sb_ss_i_1_20?url=search-alias%3Dmovies-tv &field-keywords=saturday+night+fever+blu-ray

We had cameras rigged on the car to shoot both of them at once, and because video assist wasn't used then, I was crouched down in the back of the car listening to the scene. What I could tell was that Karen wasn't getting to the emotional place she wanted to reach. She was making herself cry and the whole scene felt forced. We worked on it all afternoon doing several takes and sent everyone home exhausted but thinking we got the scene.

The next morning at 6:30 I went to look at dailies at Deluxe and it was obvious that the scene did not work. Luckily we were back shooting at the apartment location that day and decided to reshoot the scene right on the sidewalk outside the apartment in the car parked at the curb. Everything that did not work driving in the car the day before worked like a charm now. Everyone knew this scene so well that we reshot it in an hour and a half and didn't get behind on our schedule. But we had an infinitely better scene.

Part of the problem from the day before was that riding in a moving car was too distracting to the actors. They did much better when they could just sit still and be in one place. I also believe that taking the night off and trying it afresh the next day gave their minds a chance to rest so that they could come at the scene recharged.

There are always emotional scenes like this that look very simple on paper but turn out to be devilishly difficult in the actual shooting. It constantly fools production people who think to themselves, "This is a simple little two-page dialogue scene, we can shoot this in two hours." Then it winds up taking four hours to shoot and they freak out. Oh, and heaven forbid the scene has any kind of kissing or sex. That will add even more shooting time. Actors get really spooked when it comes to intimacy in a scene, even kissing. This is where the director has to be extremely patient with the actors and know that the emotional or intimate part of scenes don't always shoot as easily as the production department thinks they should. The actors are not robots on a Toyota assembly line.

Cut me a little slack here for generalizing and stereotyping. But many will agree that many American trained actors approach scenes and characters differently than many British actors. The American actors have generally been trained to work from the inside out, where they play the objectives in the situation and the emotion should come out of that. British actors on the other hand often tend to work from the outside in. For example, the character's walk or posture will be the basis for a character. A costume can make a huge difference even down to the kind of shoes that the actor might be wearing. Laurence Olivier like many British actors often immersed himself in the character by using false noses, different accents, different walks. They can even find a character using props whether it's glasses or a cane or cigarette lighter. These work from the outside of the actor inward, helping him get into a state of mind where he is able to "just pretend" and give a very convincing performance.

American and British acting techniques are really just two different ways of achieving the same result. Each has its benefits. The American technique might seem more honest and real and the British technique will be more reliable especially in a theatre for eight performances a week. One cannot tell how a great British actor like Anthony Hopkins gets to what he does and does it really matter? At the end of the day it's not about how the actor gets it done, it's about how effective he is. Does he communicate to the audience? It doesn't matter if the actor thinks to himself, "I really felt that scene," if it doesn't come across to the audience.

Make It Their Problem

William Ball, the longtime artistic director of the American Conservatory Theatre in San Francisco, talks about the "crowbar technique"[7] where the director doesn't try to answer questions from the actors but puts it back on the actors and makes them work through the problem themselves.

---

[7] William Ball, *A Sense of Direction* (New York: Drama Book Publishers, 1984), 91.

> **William Ball:** Some directors desperate to cover for lack of preparation manage to get through the entire rehearsal period on these two sentences alone. In fact there are some directors who, unable to be bothered with refinements, have built an entire career on these two sentences:
>
> "What are you trying to *get* from him?"
>
> "What are you trying to *make* him give you?"

Michael McMurray, a longtime DP on *Psych*, made this comment after directing his first episodes:

> **Michael McMurray:** The questions that actors ask you, you can often throw back in their face. "What do you think? Well what do you think your character would do if this had happened? I don't want you to do what you'd do — I want you to do what your character would do." And then they'd start talking, and they'd figure it out all by themselves, most of the time. After you fill them in on where they came from and where they're going — "What would you do if this was happening? What would Lassiter do as a police officer in the Santa Barbara Police Department? A fairly straight-laced police officer — what would he do?" And Timothy Omundson playing Lassiter started to tell me what he'd do. Well, I told him, "Do that. Let's see how that works." The action was going through the door where there may be a body in the room. He wasn't sure how. "How should I get in there? Kick the door in?" I said, "I don't know, what would he do? How would he approach a crime scene where he has no idea what's in there? Someone ready to blow his head off? I don't know, what would he do?" And then Tim figured it all out by himself — he decided that he'd go in very quickly, gun drawn... come quickly and quietly. So he said, "OK, let's try quickly and quietly." It worked like a charm. It was absolutely the right thing to do.

SUMMARY

1. Giving notes can be a tightrope walk. It's the make-or-break point in a relationship with an actor. Stupid notes are a major turnoff. Intellectual notes are unplayable. Use the "crowbar technique" for starters.

2. Communicate with each actor after every take, even if it's just a touch or a look. They need feedback.

3. Make yourself relax before watching a take. Pretend you are home watching someone else's movie, not your career going down the drain.

4. Always give performance notes privately. Give praise publicly and be specific about what people did well.

5. When working in digital, take advantage of the calm, disciplined set. Let the camera run as long as needed to repeat takes or even get added angles.

6. Give notes as a pitch: "What would it be like if your character...?" Make the process a collaboration not an order.

7. Many pro actors, e.g., Jodie Foster, James Woods, prefer the director being straight to the point and not precious. Know what your actor prefers.

8. Some actors need a bit of time to process and warm up to notes. They may be negative at first, but give it a chance. Plant the seed and let it grow.

9. There's a reason actors are called "players." Use verbs that will spark their imagination and creativity.

10. Don't overload your actors with too many instructions. Emulate the football coach. Give them one note at a time and let that adjustment work before going on to the next.

11. When the scene is not getting there, all is not lost. Sometimes you need a break to let the stress dissipate. Or try the scene in totally the opposite way just to shake up the brain cells.

Chapter 5

Mistake #5:
Enamel Grinders

You arrive at the set and you get a call. The star or one of the supporting players, or even the guy who has one line, has a problem, a problem with something, wardrobe, props, smoke on the set; it could be anything from dialogue to breakfast burritos. You take a deep breath and head off to address it. So confess. What's the first word that goes through your mind?

Usually said under your breath and with a hissing sound. Am I right? I knew it.

To mangle Thomas Paine, "These are the days that try men's souls... but he that stands it now, deserves the love and thanks of man and woman... the harder the conflict the more glorious the triumph."

So you head off to the trailer or wherever this confrontation is going to be. Remember, breathe deep. Stop grinding your back teeth! They have to last you for a while longer. You may or may not know what the problem is but, just in case, you should be ready for an angry person. Her problem could be very real, it could be overblown, and it could be imaginary. But always remember *it's real to her and you can't treat it lightly*. Blow it off and it will blow up in your face. Guaranteed.

> **John Frankenheimer:** You never want to get into a confrontation if you can help it because no one wins a confrontation.

The ideas in this section are inspired by Thomas Gordon's *Effectiveness Training* series of books. In particular his book *Leader Effectiveness Training* is extremely helpful in dealing with any difficult actor or crew situations.[1]

Entering the trailer or the office, you need to be neutral, but sympathetic. Keep it on a polite civil level. If the actor is already agitated enough to send up flares, there's no need to irritate her further. Start with something that gives her the opportunity to get the problem out in the open. "Hey, good morning, what's up?" "What's happening?" Say it with concern because that way you're already acknowledging she has a problem. You're not being judgmental or demeaning her problem *even if you think it's going to be crap*. It might be, but... wait for it.

> **Richard Dreyfuss:** Oftentimes you'll get a director who gives you the impression that your saying anything to them is simply taking up a little bit of their time. They can't wait for you to shut the fuck up. So I like them to enjoy it. I like them to appreciate what I have to say. And also if it's possible I like people to dispense with ego when it comes to saying, "That's not good" or "That is good." I have worked with directors who walked away from good ideas merely because they didn't think of it."

Give them a chance to ventilate and be heard. Be like the doctor listening to a patient. Imagine what would happen if you were telling your physician about a pain or worry you had and he blurted out "Oh, that's crap! You're fine." That would be the end of your relationship with that doctor. All your trust would be gone. But believe it, there are plenty of directors and producers who will react that way. Then they wonder why the actor is being such a jerk. Like the old theory of spontaneous generation, one jerk often creates another jerk. Don't be drawn into that death spiral.

---

[1] Dr. Thomas Gordon, *Leader Effectiveness Training* (New York: Perigee Books, 2001).

Ridley Scott: I learned engagement with an actor, where you assume partnership. It's not Svengali, it's a partnership. The best results are with partnership. If the actor says, "But...," you learn to listen, see? It's a good idea. Then they love the fact that you accept them. With Russell Crowe there is constant discussion. Constant. From stage one, even when I think I've got a good screenplay, invariably, Russell thinks it's no good, that the screenplay is terrible. So then we've got to sit there and go right through it. Then I realize, he really means a third of it, or maybe twenty percent, is no good. And the other eighty percent is quite good. So we talk, talk, talk. It's a build.[2]

Let's say the actor is having a problem with his wardrobe, which is a loincloth for the scene that day. And let's also say that you see a solution to it right away. So should you jump in and tell the actor "No problem, you don't have to wear a loincloth, a Speedo will do"?

No, don't do that!

When they've run out of gas the first thing is to feed back to the actor what you understand the problem to be. You want to be really clear that you acknowledge he has a problem. So feed it back like "Yes, I see. Sounds like you're not comfortable with that wardrobe. Go on, tell me more." This may sound simpleminded, as you're just repeating what he said in different words, but the actor needs validation of his problem. He needs to know you're taking him seriously. Anyone who tells him he looks great in the loincloth and the dialogue is just fine is demeaning his problem, not helping it.

It works the same with kids. Because parents have more life experience than children they can usually see the solution right away and have a tendency to jump in with some bromide along the lines of "Don't worry, nobody is looking at your zits," or "Someday you'll look back on this and laugh." No the child won't look back and laugh. It hurts right now and statements like this just make

---

[2] Kenneth Turan, *DGA Quarterly*, Fall 2010, 33.

the child feel put down, patronized, and pissed. So acknowledge the actor's problem. You don't have to agree with it. When you're saying, "Sounds like you don't like the wardrobe," it doesn't mean you agree that the wardrobe is wrong, you're just tuned in and listening. This is a huge step ahead.

Judge Reinhold: If you were to ask me what's the most important thing that I require of a director, it would be that if we have a half hour of light left, the generator just broke, it's started to rain, the other actor is cranky, I'm cranky, and I forgot what the scene's about, I need somebody to tell me, "Look, this is what the scene's about." It's like the quarterback saying, "Here's the play." That's it in its simplest form for me. It's dealing with a subjective reality. Actors are subjective. The director is objective. Sometimes you get lost so subjectively in things — details — that you need to be reminded what the scene is about. Sometimes it's a question of just getting overly emotional and losing your perspective. When I can rely on somebody who can bring me back to where we are in the story and exactly what the scene is about, that's enormously comforting, the simplicity of that.

No surprise that actors just want to be heard, they need to express their feelings whether it's to let everyone know the scene needs work or they don't like the way they look.

Jodie Foster: The director has to listen carefully to actors because the actor has to feel comfortable. It's your job as director to make them feel comfortable. Sometimes you'll have to explain to them why a little bit of personal discomfort is good for this moment. Remind them that their character has three PhDs, and a huge IQ. The character can't say, "Um-ur-um-ur-um-um-um." That's not helping the character. It may make the actor feel comfortable because he says, "Ur-um-um-um," or it feels real and like the character is discovering what to say, but the character is more articulate than that and doesn't need to cast about for words.

Keep encouraging the actor to talk about his problem, and it is his problem. He is trying to make it your problem. The goal is to get him to solve it himself and be happy about it. You can force a solution but you're risking resentment, resistance, and rollback of your communication with him. And if the building is burning down or you're losing the light, that's what you may have to do.

In my film *Whose Life Is It Anyway*, the great John Cassavetes played the head of the hospital where they were caring for Richard Dreyfuss, who had been severely paralyzed in an auto accident. Dreyfuss' character is throwing a fit in his room about how he is being treated. Cassavetes, as his doctor, orders, "Give Mr. Harrison 10 mg of Valium IM stat." Cassavetes, the actor, said to me, "This is techno-babble gobbledygook. Why don't I just say, "Give the asshole a shot for God's sake?" To be fair, it's important to know that this was John Cassavetes' first day on the film and he had just come from another film that had finished the day before. So he was playing character catch-up.

I then had to explain to Cassavetes why doctors must be extremely precise in what they say when giving orders. If not, something may go badly wrong with the patient. It might have appealed to Cassavetes' tough street personality to be more casual but it would have made the doctor look like a quack. That would have destroyed his character and the drama of the film. Cassavetes gave me a sharp look, but then after a pause stepped on his mark and said the correct line. He understood the dramatic logic of the scene and his character now and was able to abandon his comfort zone of using more casual speech.

> **Donald Petrie:** Some actors need to live it, they need to encompass, they need to discuss, they need to question. They need a lot of self-talk — they have a target in the scene that they want to achieve, be it anger or love or whatever it is that they're looking to find in a scene, and they can seem very one-dimensional. Uta Hagen describes it as opposites. Nobody's just angry. They're angry because they love you. Two very opposite emotions, love

and anger, but how much more interesting anger is when it comes from a place of love.

Robert Sutton's telling book *The No Asshole Rule* is a goldmine of information for achieving a good perspective on working with difficult people, whether producers, crew, or cast. He reports for example that the Disney theme parks train new employees how to handle visitors who are upset or angry:

> "They learn to avoid blaming either themselves or their abusive guests. They were asked to imagine all the awful experiences the family suffered that whipped them into such a hostile state (e.g., to imagine their car broke down or they got soaked in the rain) and to not take their anger personally."[3]

He emphasizes that you should never expect assholes to suddenly become nice people who will treat you nicely and with respect. You can only look forward to being disappointed.

> "The trick is to keep your expectations for their behavior low but continue to believe that you will be fine after the ordeal is over. That way you won't be surprised by your colleague's relentless nastiness....

> "Prison guard Franklin Roberts said, when dealing with inmates, 'I never yell at them. They get mad and yell their heads off, they go wild. But you don't yell at them. You never want to lose face in front of these guys. If they start yelling, you start whispering. You just don't play their game.'"[4]

Tales from the Trenches

Every director has their war stories: times when they had to face up to one or more members of the cast, times when they were presented with tough problems. Is there a common thread that runs between them? Maybe and maybe not. It's the "All Actors Are Different" rule. Add that to "Every Scene, Location, and Film Is

---

[3] Robert I. Sutton, *The No Asshole Rule* (New York: Hachette, 2007), ebook locations 1528 and 1701.
[4] Ibid., Sutton.

Different" and the permutations are infinite. Wouldn't it be great if there were a director's version of a doctor's manual where you could look up every lame-ass, stupid, maddening, frustrating situation you find yourself in today? If somebody did write one it would be obsolete before it was published. The best thing is to learn from how others handled some situations and extrapolate from that to your own situation. So here are some tales from the crypt, some positive, some... not so much.

One of the most entertaining times I ever had on a set day after day was with Mel Gibson and Goldie Hawn on *Bird on a Wire*.[5] These are the most professional actors who seemed to always be up for anything, crazy scenes, crazy stunts, and weird characterizations. If Goldie had a concern, however, she was not shy about putting it out there.

One day we had several scenes at a carnival in Vancouver. In the first

Bird on a Wire *Norwegian poster.*

scene she and Mel would be riding the roller coaster and having a great time laughing and screaming.

At least that was what was in the script.

When I arrived at the set I went to her dressing room to say good morning. She was in the makeup chair, hair in rollers and even without makeup, unbelievably cute. Her eyes were not saying "cute," however. Something was up. Oh boy!

She said, "Close the door, we have to talk."

Anybody who has ever been in a relationship knows when you hear "we have to talk," something bad is coming.

Goldie said, "You know the roller coaster sequence?"

---

[5] http://www.amazon.com/s/ref=nb_sb_ss_i_1_7?url=search-alias%3Dmovies-tv&field-keywords=bird+on+a+wire+blu-ray&sprefix=Bird+on%2Cmovies-tv%2C227

"Sure, it's first up today."

"Well, I'm not doing it. I hate roller coasters."

WTF! That was half the day's work shot to hell, not to mention what it wouldn't show about the relationship between the characters she and Mel were playing. While I got over my shock I couldn't resist a smartypants question: "Do you mean you hate the *idea* of roller coasters or what?"

"No," she snapped, "They scare the living be-craptus out of me. I don't want to get on that thing!"

Now this was a very small roller coaster, not one of those Six Flags Poopyourpants nightmares. I knew this was a futile argument. Don't go there. Won't work. Not prudent. I did remember to actively listen to her and acknowledge her problem. I had just taken Thomas Gordon's *Parent Effectiveness Training* course before this film and was hoping I could apply it here, even though this was not a parent and child situation, it was two colleagues working out a problem. With any actor, especially one who has a leading role, you can't order her about like a slave or iPhone's Siri. Find solutions that work for both of you. Find no-lose solutions where everyone feels this is the best way to handle a problem right now. It's important to understand the actor's problem and for the actor to understand your problem, and to try to reach a solution that works for everyone.

> **Elia Kazan:** A director should never feel that he has to win an argument. Not everything you say is going to be right. Hopefully everything you say is going to be stimulating. If one thing doesn't work, go right back two minutes later with something else. You don't have to win. You don't have to be the boss man."[6]

I said to Goldie, "Sounds like that roller coaster really scares you. I'm not nuts about them either."

---

[6] Young, *Kazan*, 139.

"That's what I just said. Look at it, it's all old and made of wood, what if it breaks or falls down?" Goldie replied.

"You're really worried that it might collapse when you're on it," I commented.

"Oh yes!"

I said, "Wow, we really need those roller coaster shots in the movie. They'll add so much to your relationship with Mel's character and they're great fun to watch."

"Yes I understand, but I just can't get on that thing," Goldie replied.

"What do you think we should do?" I asked.

"Can't you do it with Dawn, my double, instead?"

"Sure we can. She's not as cute as you are (apologies Dawn, I was desperate), but we can get some wide shots. We just won't have any close-ups of you having a great time."

"What, you mean screaming my brains out? 'Cause that's what I'd do," she replied.

I then suggested, "How about this. What if after I do some wide shots with Dawn, I back up the roller coaster about fifty feet from where people get on, let it roll into the station, and shoot you just where the roller coaster is really tame? I really want to see your face, see you having fun."

She thought for a bit and then said, "And it won't go over any of those scary parts? Well, I guess I could do that."

"Will that work for you? You won't be scared?" I double-checked.

"For what you're paying me I shouldn't even ride twenty-five feet, but I'll do it." And then she laughed that Goldie laugh that would charm the Devil.

Let's look closer at what just happened, how I tried to apply the "no-lose" technique, then I'll tell you how it worked out.

1. I listened to her concern and didn't belittle her or put her down.
2. I acknowledged how she felt, and luckily could agree with her.
3. I kept feeding back her feelings, making sure I got it right, and that she knew I was listening.
4. I let her know clearly what my problem was.
5. Instead of my coming up with solutions I asked her for her ideas. If she had none I would have stayed quiet and given her time to think.
6. Goldie proposed a smart idea, which made good sense. I accepted the general version of it and pointed out that we wouldn't have a close-up of her. I wasn't appealing to her vanity; I was talking filmmaker language that she understands as well as anyone.
7. Goldie suggested a "mini roller coaster ride" would be OK with her.
8. I double-checked to make sure she was OK with that idea, then went off to get it set up.

So here's how it worked out for us. We shot the wide shots with Dawn the photo double, even a couple of close shots with Mel in the background and Dawn in his lap partially hiding her face, blond hair blowing all over the place. Then we backed up the roller  coaster fifty to sixty feet and put Goldie in Mel's lap. We rolled the camera and the coaster rolled down into the station, Goldie screaming delightedly the whole way. The camera assistants ran over to make sure the cameras had rolled, and I ran in to see how she did. As I ran in I heard her say to Mel, "Well that was nothing. Was that it?" He just laughed and said, "That's it. Fun, isn't it, no big" and he kept talking about the ride with her. I stood there slowly realizing what he was doing. He was talking her into it. I seized the moment, I sprang into action, and waved to the camera guys to roll the cameras. I waved to the ride operator and before Goldie could react, the coaster lurched off to do its thing.

When it came back around, her hair was wild, her eyes were as big as saucers and she was laughing like a loon. She was so proud of herself for having done it that she wanted to do it again.

The moral of the story is that I took her seriously and actively worked with her to find a solution that was good for her. Gently she changed from "no way!" to "one toe in the water," to "full header off the diving board." She never got angry and loved the experience. I took a big chance having the roller coaster take off without checking with her. That could have blown up in my face big time, but that's often the risk you take as a director, trying to read people's feelings and use what they're giving you. There was definitely a great deal of trust that had been built up between Goldie and me, which allowed this to work out in the best possible manner.

I could have played the bully and used the old Ford-Hathaway-Preminger intimidator approach. I could have tried calling in my partner Rob Cohen, the producer, who would soft-soap her. We could have tried threatening her... lots of luck. Let's say that she yielded and went on the roller coaster as a result of one of those dictatorial or manipulative other strategies. We had ten more weeks left to shoot on the movie; we would have been looking at fifty days of hell from Goldie. As mature and grown up as Goldie is, there would have always been seeds of distrust, dislike, and distaste. Her enthusiasm would have been affected and we would have hurt this comedy far beyond what we would have gained with the roller coaster sequence.

> **Jodie Foster:** You don't want to be a hero on the day and then get into the cutting room and not have what you want. So that's when you need patience. Patience is probably the best way to deal with people who disagree with you when shooting. I don't believe in tempers on a movie. I don't believe in people yelling on the set. I don't think you get anywhere by that, and it ends up being very destructive to the whole process.

In Brett Ratner's version of *Red Dragon*[7] he worked with both Anthony Hopkins and Edward Norton. Their working styles are totally different. Once Hopkins has committed to the script he takes it as his bible and prepares from that. Norton on the other hand takes the script as just a jumping-off point. He is always coming up with ideas and suggestions how to improve not only his part but those of others as well. When he arrived at Ratner's house before shooting began, with notes longer than the script, he and Brett had to agree that Ted Tally, the Oscar-winning writer of *Silence of the Lambs,* would be the decision-maker on which of Norton's notes to incorporate and which to ignore. But, and this is important, his notes were not dismissed or ignored. Attention was paid and his thinking was taken seriously. Several of his ideas found their way into the final film.

Brett Ratner relates the following events that transpired over the course of a couple of days of shooting.

Brett Ratner: We get to the scene where he goes to see Hannibal Lecter after Hannibal had tried to kill him. We're doing a shot of Norton and I can't tell if he's afraid of Lecter or what he feels. Let me preface this by saying Edward is a brilliant actor but his way is, I call it non-acting, which is... he doesn't give you much. He gives a very simple, very subtle performance always. I say to him, "Are you afraid of Hannibal Lecter?" He goes, "Of course, he tried to kill me, ruined my life." I say, "I'm not seeing any fear in your eyes." "Oh no," he replies, "I would never do that, I would never show him I'm afraid of him. I'm not Jodie Foster's character, an FBI student. I'm an FBI agent. I'm not gonna ever show him." I say, "But you need to let the audience know that you're fearful." "Well what do you suggest?" he says to me. "I don't know. Can we put some sweat on your brow?" "No, bad idea. That's indicating, that's not a good idea." "Can you move your legs? Can you tap your fingers... whatever, something?" Two and a half hours back

---

7   http://www.amazon.com/Red-Dragon/dp/B001LX50I2/ref=sr_1_1?s=movies-tv&ie=UTF8&qid=1348768037&sr

and forth, and me just pitching out ideas to show that he's afraid. Nothing. He goes, "Trust me, the audience is gonna see my fear." I keep saying, "I'm looking in your eyes and I'm not seeing it." So long story short, after hours and hours of arguing and holding up part of the day, my mind is scrambling to try and come up with something.

Finally I have an idea. At the end of the scene I'll have Norton take a break and say he's coming back later.

I go to the production designer and say, "Can you build us a little waiting room with a coffee machine?" He says, "Give me a few hours." Builds the waiting room. I go back to Edward and say, "Here's my idea. You go to the coffee machine, you grab some coffee, you take off your jacket —and your armpits are dripping." He says, "That, I'll do."

My point is, through all the arguing and all the challenges, it came to a good conclusion, probably better than what we started with. When I sat in the audience for the first time and I saw it — "Oh my God, he's scared!" People were sitting around me pointing to his armpit sweat. So sometimes a creative war can lead to something better. That's the moral to my story.

Donald Petrie is one of the most delightful directors working now. His sets are fun, his actors love him because he is an actor at heart and understands their problems from their point of view. He says he seldom has problems with anyone because he prepares his movies from each actor's point of view. He plays all the parts in advance so he can understand what the actors might want to play. He's clever enough to know that he can't impose his ideas on them. But he does anticipate their problems well in advance. Not all days go as planned. On *The Associate*[8], starring Whoopi Goldberg, he was dealing with a strong-willed actress who was not only playing a man, she was posing as a white man to save her failing business. It's great material for farce and Whoopi is sensational at that kind of comedy. But on one day she totally disagreed with the scene where she had to use the men's room.

---

[8] http://www.amazon.com/Associate-Whoopi-Goldberg/dp/6305428344

Donald Petrie: There was a scene in *The Associate* where Ms. Goldberg, in full white-man makeup, has gone to the Plaza Hotel, and is now trying to escape a female reporter who was on her case. In a moment when she's caught between two things, she runs into the men's room. Of course, in the men's room, the one stall is occupied, and one stall is out of order, and she/he has to stand at a urinal and we know it's a women dressed up as a man who has to pretend to be using it, and all that kind of funny "shake it" stuff that men do there.

Tim Daly steps up next to her not knowing that it's her, to try to get a meeting with her. Ms. Goldberg said in a very casual way when she was leaving the set the night before we were to shoot the scene, "Oh Donald, figure out what you're going to shoot tomorrow because I'm not doing that scene in the men's room." Mind you, that was pretty much the first I'd heard there was a problem with the scene. I relayed that fact to the producers, and indeed spent most of the night rewriting the scene four different ways. I asked myself, "What could she possibly object to? Is it this? I'll do it without that. Is it this part? I'll do it without that." I wrote alternate, alternate, alternate scenes. I showed up to the set the next day, running into the producers first. I said, "I've written other versions," and they went, "Nope, we're going to sue her if she doesn't do the scene as written." I threw up my arms and I said, "I'll be in my trailer. Let me know how that works." So I remember waiting about a half an hour, and then she came storming out of her trailer and said, "You'd better be using two cameras because I'm only doing this once." She then had two and a half to three hours of makeup to become the white guy.

So I shot the scene and she acted like a piece of wood. She went over to the urinal, stood there, and waited for her cue, said her line, with none of the funny physical stuff. Then she stormed out of the men's room. Tim Daly started to follow and she unexpectedly picked up a can of hair spray and sprayed his eyes. Squirt-squirt-squirt. She just picked it up and used it like Mace. I don't know why the character would do that, but that's what she did.

I managed to get one other shot, which encompassed the squirt-squirt-squirt business. What it did was bring her into the room and took her over to the urinal. Then on the way out it encompassed the squirt-squirt-squirt. In the editing room, we got an idea: as Whoopi's character came in the room, she glanced at the table where all the hair sprays are.

JB: I always kind of thought she looked like Marlon Brando.

DP: That's what she was meant to look like. I focused the camera on the hair sprays and stuff so that she was out of focus. Instead of going straight to the urinals, Whoopi now turns and goes to the counter, and picks up a big old bottle of Listerine and stuffs it in her pants. This was all added after the fact. I brought in an actress I could double for Whoopi and I got a shot.

Then it's back to the real Whoopi. Tim Daly starts to talk, I cut to her hands unscrewing the top of the bottle. I cut to Tim Daly. I cut to her pouring, I cut to his reaction — whoa, it looks like a horse, it's taking a pee — glug-glug-glug.

And then as she turns to leave she whips the hidden bottle so it splashes across his legs, and he says, "Hey, you kind of got me there." And then he goes out and gets sprayed in the face. So there's a case where we saved a scene by adding a whole other element.

So far we've been talking about adult actors. These are people who may have problems with the way the film is going, or personal problems, but can be talked to, reasoned with. They are able to understand the problems of the production company. But when the actor is a child, all bets are off. The younger the child, the more difficult it becomes. When casting the part of six-year-old Scout in *To Kill a Mockingbird,* Robert Mulligan and Alan Pakula were smart to realize that they would be better off casting an older child who was more mature, who had a longer attention span and who could understand what was going on.

They cast a nine-year-old girl, Mary Badham, who had never acted before but who had self-confidence and self-assurance in addition to a great personality. Mary was nominated for an Academy Award for her work in the film. What few people remember however is that their casting director, Alice Boatwright, traveled all over the country and interviewed nearly three thousand children before finding Mary and the boy who played her brother, Phillip Alford, in a community theatre in Birmingham, Alabama. Side note: She also happened to be my sister. I was a starving graduate student at the Yale School of Drama at the time. My mother called to tell me my baby sister was starring in a movie with Gregory Peck. Baby Sister 10, Older Brother 0.

Taylor Hackford: On *Ray,* I have two little boys, Young Ray and George, his brother, in very dramatic scenes. The boy that I cast for Young Ray, Eric O'Neal Jr., was fantastic. He was eight years old. That's young. But his parents were professionals. They were brilliant parents, and we were really lucky to find him. He was intelligent, and had a sense of wanting to please and wanting to excel. He'd seen his father in football practice doing things over and over and over again. He was such a gift. I didn't talk to him like an adult, but I was straight with him, and let him know how important things were and he listened. And he's really, really good in the film.

Now I needed somebody younger to play his little brother. The Bell family brought their boy, Terrone Bell, in and he was fantastic. He was filled with energy and personality and he was really smart. But he was a disaster because he was five, and somebody five hasn't come to the realization that you have to do it over and over and over until you get it right. And he would be terrific if I could roll the camera and allow the first take to happen. But when you're making a film, especially a technical thing like this where you've got to see him drown and the whole thing... I didn't shoot very many takes but I'd have to shoot more than one.

We'd do a little bit of an improv-ey rehearsal, he was great. When the camera rolled he was just terrible. He'd lost interest. "Well, now we're doing it for real." "Well, we did it before." "But the camera wasn't rolling." If we had to do Take 2 and how often do you not have to do Take 2, he would say, "Well, I just did that." "Yes, but you don't understand, there was a technical problem, the camera shifted, or we didn't get focus." And of course he wouldn't stand on the right mark, so we couldn't get focus. He said, "Well, I'm not doing it again, I did it once." How do you reason with a five-year-old? His mother came and couldn't get him to. His grandmother came and couldn't do it. His grandfather came and took off his belt and said, "Boy, if you don't do this again I'm taking you out in that cane field." I said, "You don't have to do that."

I got a performance from him but the problem was the young Ray was doing it every take, doing brilliant work. It wasn't fair. I spent all the time dealing with George, all the time. And without little George I've got no film. So you use anything you can. You've got a whole crew, a whole company standing there, and I'm sitting there playing in the dirt with a five-year-old boy trying to find some way to convince him to get up and do it. Finally it's attrition. He realized he wasn't going home until we got it, and then he kind of got it.

Taylor Hackford and any director who has wrestled with the problem of working with very young children and kept their cool are on my short list for sainthood. When a director finds herself in this situation she must remember she is in great company with thousands of other directors who have bald spots on their heads from tearing their hair out. Patience, patience, patience.

Of course there's always the director's fantasy — the one where we aren't so polite, where we don't pussyfoot around and say exactly what's on our minds. Kids, don't try this at home.

 **Peter Hyams:** In *Capricorn One*, when it came time to do O. J. Simpson's death scene, O. J. suddenly got something into his head about changing something, and I said, "You've got a choice. You do exactly what I say, and exactly how I tell you to do it or I'm going to go about a half mile away with a thousand millimeter lens and a double." He could hardly respond.

The No Asshole Rule recommends a similar tactic in extreme situations: call their bluff.

Risky, but it often works on schoolyard bullies. One woman had been verbally abused too many times by a retired army major.

> "She gave him a steely look and said if he ever spoke to her again that way, she'd take him out at the knees, and that she was not paid to nor would she stand for any form of abuse, insults or shit from him ever again. He got the message."[9]

At the end of the day there are never universal answers to any director's particular challenge with her cast. It so much comes down to trust between director and actor. If you haven't built up that trust in the time you've been together you're going to have a rough experience.

Of course, when all else fails, there's always begging.

> **Brett Ratner:** You have to be everything from a director to a psychiatrist to a mom to a dad, to a teacher, to a slave driver, to an asshole. And I'm the guy who just begs and pleads. For example, Chris Tucker refused to say "bitch." He became kind of religious on *Rush Hour 2*, and he said, "I will not say 'bitch.'" I go, "Bitch is in the Bible. It's a female dog. It's not a bad word." Chris tells me, "I don't believe that. You're gonna go to hell, Brett, I'm telling you." So I got his father on the phone. "Can you tell Chris that he can say 'bitch' in this movie?" Chris goes, "My daddy don't know Jesus. My daddy don't know..." And if you see on the DVD of the making of *Rush Hour* 2 I manipulated him when he was on camera. When the woman Ziyi Zhang, who was in *Crouching Tiger, Hidden Dragon*, is standing over him and he kills her, he says, "You're a bad girl. I liked you. I wanted to date you." I told him, "Chris! You're a bad girl?? Twelve-year-olds are gonna laugh in your face." So then Chris starts using all these dumb adjectives. "You're very naughty. You're a mean girl. You're a silly girl." I'm yelling out, "Call her a bitch." And when he did it, the audience cheered, because it was real and it was funny.

---

9 Sutton, *The No Asshole Rule*, ebook location 1743.

So there's everything from that to saying, "Well I'm the director and I want you to say it, you know?" Every actor says, "I don't want to say that." And I say, "Let's just try it." What I'm most proud of is that I'm great at manipulating my actors and getting them to say or do what I want.

In *Tower Heist* Eddie Murphy said, "Brett, I'm not dancing in this movie." I'm like, "What? Really? Why?" Eddie stood firm. "You ain't gonna see me dancing," and he was dead serious. If you look at the deleted scenes on the DVD there's a scene where he's dancing with Gabourey Sidibe, I mean, it was hysterical and he kept insisting, "No way, I'm not dancing, don't even ask me." I put the right music on during the shot and I got him moving a little. And then I told her, "Push your butt up against him." Next thing you know, he's dancing. Actors are always resistant, afraid they're gonna look stupid.

When I asked one of the smartest directors I know, "What do you do when actors are not doing what you want and get really cantankerous?" he replied:

Steven Soderbergh: Boy, it's hard. It's hard because sometimes the dynamic of the relationship makes it difficult for them to understand why you're making a certain request. Your job is to have the whole movie in your head. That's not their job. Their job is very, very specific and by design pretty myopic. And after you've exhausted all the rational explanations, at the end of the day it really comes down to whether they trust you or not. That's a variable that I think really isn't under anybody's control, because it's a combination of their experience with you to that point, their knowledge of you as an artist, the exact physical circumstances under which this discussion is taking place....

That's a mysterious issue, this issue of trust. It's the most important thing that you can have with an actor or your crew or the studio or whatever. I think one of the reasons I've been able to dip in and out of the studio world is they know that I can be trusted — that when I say something, that that's what I'm going to do.

SUMMARY

1. In a fight with an actor, even if you win, you lose. Bully directors only turn actors into zombies or cornered animals.

2. Always treat an actor's problem seriously even if it seems frivolous.

3. Don't jump in with your instant solution until the actor has had time to explicate and ventilate. Even if you're trying to save time and cut to the chase, the actor will insist on saying everything that he has prepared to say.

4. Feed back to the actor what he's told you so that he knows he's been heard. Phrase it nonjudgmentally. "Sounds like you don't like this (dialogue, wardrobe, whatever)." You'll get to the real problem much quicker.

5. Remind the actor of his goal or given circumstance, or what's at stake. It's easy to lose sight of these facts when people are tired or tense.

6. Encourage actors to come up with solutions themselves. You don't need to or want to do all the work. It's not effective.

7. Your relationship with the actor is important — you're both in this for the long haul of the film.

8. Often problems can be an opportunity for wonderful and creative solutions.

9. In the end, it comes down to trust. You must earn the trust of your actor.

PART II

Action and Suspense: The Five Strategies

Chapter 6

Strategy #1: Not Just a Pretty Chase

You want to know how *not* to do an action scene? Let me tell you. One bright Monday morning in beautiful downtown Burbank, on the Burbank Studios lot, I nervously gathered together the creative team to see the director's cut of my new film *Blue Thunder*[1]. Dan O'Bannon and Don Jacoby, the writers, and the producers, Ray Stark, Gordon Carroll, and Phil Feldman had assembled in Jack Warner's screening room to see what two years of work had yielded. Did we have a movie or six cans of crap?

For the year 1982 *Blue Thunder* was a very expensive movie: $25 million for a film about a super helicopter secretly designed by the government to suppress riots at the 1984 Olympics in

Blue Thunder *DVD art.*

---

[1] http://www.amazon.com/s/ref=nb_sb_ss_i_2_9?url=search-alias%3Daps&field-keywords=blue+thunder+dvd&sprefix

Los Angeles. As one of the government stooges tells Roy Scheider, the pilot of the helicopter, "We don't want any Munich massacres here, Frank," a reference to the terrorist attacks at the Munich Olympic Games in 1972, where eight Palestinian terrorists belonging to Black September broke into the Olympic Village taking nine Israeli athletes, coaches, and officials hostage.

In the film, the government, wanting to justify the expense of the helicopter, creates a series of mini-terror attacks on the white community. They made it appear as though gangs from the African-American and Hispanic communities perpetrated the attacks. In actuality, the terrorists were hired thugs inciting racial paranoia.

Roy Scheider's character along with his partner, played by Daniel Stern, get wind of what's going down and steal the helicopter from the Feds while trying to tell the media and the public about the conspiracy. The result is a wild chase throughout the city with the Blue Thunder helicopter flying at street level through downtown Los Angeles fifty feet above the pavement, pursued by police cars, helicopters, and Air Force F16s. Buildings, busses, and autos are blown to shreds. A bit of comic relief in the middle of extensive and frightening devastation was a heat-seeking missile that goes down the chimney of an Asian barbecue shack blowing thousands of cooked chickens into the air and onto the homeless population of downtown LA.

No Asians, homeless people, or live chickens were hurt, molested, or panhandled in this messy sequence.

BBQ chickens rain down on the LAPD.

Meanwhile, back at Jack Warner's screening room the director's cut of the film was screening for its elite audience to simultaneously criticize, condemn, and hopefully praise. Lots of luck on that last bit. As any filmmaker knows screening first cuts for the producers is less fun than a colonoscopy. At least with a colonoscopy there is anesthesia to dull the pain. Stories of directors throwing up before, during, or after one of these screenings are myriad. However one of the benefits of suffering this torture is that after being so close to the film for months in the edit bay the director and editor see the film afresh through the eyes of the audience. Things that seemed exciting now become tedious; things that were touching are boring; things that were funny fall flat. Sometimes these can be fixed, sometimes not.

We screened our way through the film, which mercifully didn't break, as rough cuts on film are wont to do. There were laughs, some applause, a bit of cheering but mostly a lot of jaded eyeballs mentally dissecting the film like pathologists at an autopsy. Finally, the theatre lights come up as Roy Scheider walks away from a blown up Blue Thunder helicopter and the government plot is foiled. SPOILER ALERT! Oops, too late.

Our audience ran to relieve their communal bladder and the editors Frank Morriss and Ed Abroms and I were left to wonder what they were really thinking. When they reassembled we started to hear their suggestions: trim this, shorten this, cut this scene, make this clearer... yadda yadda, yadda. All pretty painless stuff — but right on the money. If we were expecting great praise and laudatory comments we would have been sorely disappointed. Nobody *ever* gives praise at one of these screenings. No damning with faint praise, it's damning with damning. It's all about the negative, what has to be fixed. There's an old saying in Hollywood that after a film runs "the credits," you get to hear "the blames."

As we discussed the second half of the film which is all action, all the time — an hour of solid chases and explosions with real-time choreography the film world might never see again in a fictional film (for reasons best left to discussions of safety) — the writer

Dan O'Bannon raised a red-flagged caveat. Dan, one of the film's most supportive people during shooting and whose biggest complaint had been that the bagels at the craft service table were a bit stale now said that the "chase sequence through the LA River" goes on way too long. OMG!! WTF?!

We were especially proud of this action sequence where Scheider tries to outmaneuver the helicopters chasing him with machine guns ablaze. He flies Blue Thunder down into the LA River bed, which is more of a concrete flood control channel than a real river. It serpentines its way through the city under bridges, buildings, and train tracks. Because of the obvious difficulty and the dangers of flying helicopters five feet off the ground through narrow passageways, the action was terrifying to watch, not unlike William Friedkin's wrong-way freeway chase later in *To Live and Die in LA*. Our scene ended with a spectacular crash as the pursuing helicopter slams into a bridge abutment exploding apocalyptically.

SPOILER ALERT!

Damn, I did it again. Sorry.

The scene ran for four and a half minutes, plenty of time to make an exciting, dangerous chase. What were Dan O'Bannon and his partner Don Jacoby, who had now "me-too-ed" his opinion, thinking? Have they no sense of fun? Grrr!

The editors traipsed back with me to the cutting rooms, happy we had a pretty good film in the works. It should have become better, thanks to the feedback we had gotten. But we were troubled by the "river chase" comments because we didn't know where we had gone wrong, if we had gone wrong, or even what to do about it. But we thought WTH it wouldn't hurt to shorten it up a bit. So we went through and trimmed a minute out. That should do it, right? ...Wrong.

The next time we showed the film to Dan and Don, who we now called the DDTs (Dan and Don Team), they said "Wow! Much better. The film is sharpening up quite a bit..." *beat, beat, beat.*

> DAN AND DON
>But didn't you say you were going to
>fix the 'River Chase' scene?

> JB
> (protesting)
>We did. We took a minute out. What is
>that, like 25%?

> DAN
> (never a word mincer)
>Yeah, but it's still boring.

So again back to the cutting room, went we did, and another minute took we out. (I was so stressed I was starting to talk like Yoda). Screened it again for the DDTs and got the same reaction...

> DDTS
>Boring.

By now I was mad. These guys were cutting the heart out of one of the most exciting parts of the movie. I told producer Ray Stark that I wanted to preview this last version with a full audience, composed of real people... who don't belong to the Writer's Guild! We added great sound effects and the exciting music that Arthur Rubinstein composed for us, one of the earliest electronic scores in movie history.

At the first public preview in Tucson, Arizona, the film was playing well. The audience was definitely taking the ride and having fun doing it. And then it came: a two-and-a-half-minute version of the river chase I'd all been waiting for (I know, that's ungrammatical, but you're smart, you'll figure it out). As the film unspoiled and projected onto the seventy-foot screen in glorious John Alonzo color and Dolby Stereo it hit me like a ton of bricks. Like Marlon Brando in *Apocalypse Now*... "like I was shot... like I was shot with a diamond... the horror, the horror!" (Purple prose apologies.)

The reason the DDTs said it was boring was suddenly obvious, right in front of me all the time. ***Nothing was happening.*** Oh yes, many choppers flew into the riverbed and snaked under bridges and fired a lot of fake ammunition. Oh yes, there was even a crash and explosion at the end. But! That *was all* there was. There were a few clever maneuvers by Scheider's character to evade his pursuers. He zig-zagged back and forth and a few bullets hit Blue Thunder. But what the hell, it was heavily armored and the audience knew it couldn't be shot down, so who gave a flying flop? All the jeopardy was watered down; we knew Scheider would worm his way out of it somehow. Not good storytelling! When the audience stops asking, "What happens next?" the movie is in trouble.

What could we do? We couldn't reshoot; we had spent enough money already to feed a third-world country for a year. And we had a release date looming before us. We did the only thing we could do at that point... we cut the scene out of the movie... Just kidding!

What we had to do was cut the scene down even more so that the exciting parts of the scene did not become repetitive. One event had to lead to a different event, not repeat the same old, same old. That's boring. And the next event had to be bigger and cleverer than the previous one, etc. If Blue Thunder comes whizzing by the camera and then the police chopper whizzes by, the next shot better not be the two choppers whizzing by again. Somebody needs to do something differently. One of them needs to try a different maneuver, or another chopper has to enter the chase. In the old Hal Roach comedies two men would be carrying a giant pane of glass across the riverbed and the Keystone Kops would be sure to fly right through it.

We shortened the scene to one minute, forty-five seconds so that nothing was repetitive and there was no time for it to get boring.

The movie went into the theatres on time, Memorial Day, 1983, and did great business. It was among the top ten grossing films of the year and was nominated for Academy Awards for editing and sound design. What was so bad about that?

What was bad was that the mistake shouldn't have been made in the first place and we ought to have designed something that was much more clever. We were shooting in a scary, dangerous location and thought that would be exciting all by itself, just great, two degrees shy of fabulous.

Well it needed more than we gave it; all my fault. As the director I blame myself because who else is responsible for taking the writer's ideas and elevating them to be the most exciting they can be? You can't just take a sketchy idea, like "there's an exciting chopper chase in the riverbed" or "the Indians take the fort" and literally transpose it to the screen as is. Hell, if that would work the writer could just read the script aloud to the audience. Save a lot of money.

> **William Friedkin:** Great action filmmaking doesn't get anything like the respect it deserves, despite the piles of money studios have made over the years on screaming car chases, spectacular firefights, giant explosions, cops leaping from roof to roof, cowboys thundering after Indians (or vice versa), and so on. Back in the day, of course, nobody spoke about "action movies" per se. There were simply genres — Westerns, gangster pictures, war movies — in which swift, violent action was kind of mandatory, and there were directors, like John Ford, who knew how to create that kind of excitement on the screen.[2]

Almost as soon as the idea of the "action movie" took hold, the adjective "mindless" somehow attached to it — too frequently with

---

[2] Terrence Rafferty, "William Friedkin," *DGA Quarterly*, May 2012, 69.

justification. But the fact is that creating movement on the screen is a task that requires enormous intelligence and skill, because there are so many different kinds of movement to deploy. There's the motion of the actors (and their vehicles) within the frame, and, often, of the camera itself; the rhythm of the editing; the momentum of the narrative itself. And all these elements have to be marshaled in a way that both makes sense and delivers the jolts of adrenaline that action movie audiences tend to demand.

One of the problems action filmmakers face is that moviegoers crave novelty in their cheap thrills. Watching a hit action picture of even, say, fifteen or twenty years ago can be a fairly sobering experience because the stuff that amped us up then has been stepped on too many times since. Been there, blown up that.

Directors have to electro-shock moments so they zap off the screen and jolt the audience awake. How does that work?

That's what this chapter is about.

What Is Action?

If I ask my grandson Milo what is action I'll probably get an answer like what I heard from my grownup friend Scott last week. I recommended a lovely film I'd just seen, *The Best Exotic Marigold Hotel*. He asked, with tongue embedded in cheek, and smirk plastered on face, "Any explosions, or car chases in it?" I said there were some tuk-tuks racing around. "Like space aliens or superheroes?" he asked. "No, tuk-tuks are rickshaws with engines. They're all over Asia," I replied. Scott frowned and looked down to check the ice cubes in his diet Dr. Pepper. Somehow I got the idea that he wasn't going to see *The Best Exotic Marigold Hotel* in the next 500 years, if that soon.

Action happens in films, as in life, when ordinary responses are too tame to respond to a situation normally. Events have mushroomed to such a degree of intensity that behavior has to shift into a higher gear. All the senses go into overdrive and adrenaline ramps up. It's the "fight or flight response" in action. Time seems to slow down dramatically and we have a nano- by nano-second recall of what went on.

African Action

On photographic safari in Tanzania, my daughter Kelley and I watched a solitary Cape buffalo peacefully grazing in the Ngorongoro crater as a pride of lions crept up on him. This was definitely suspenseful in every sense. Kelley and I were asking the key question for suspense scenes: "What happens next?"

Our guide, Ally Mtumwa, cautioned us not to disturb the animals. Nature has to take its course and it's not for sentimental humans to interfere. So the suspense built inside us, and probably inside the lions as well. They crept as close as they could to the Cape buffalo until it was put up or shut up time. The Cape buffalo, who had seemed oblivious to the approaching danger, lazily raised his head at the last minute and barely took note of the lions surrounding him. Other animals like wildebeests would have been in full OMG flight by now.

If this were a film, from a storyteller's point of view the situation was perfectly set up. We knew what was likely to happen, we could see the jeopardy the Cape buffalo was in: he was about to become lunch. Because he was out–lioned he looked like the biggest loser of the week. Kelley and I were seeing this from the Cape buffalo's point of view and hoped he escaped. Interestingly, if we were telling this

from the hungry lion's point of view we would be rooting for them to kill the Cape buffalo for dinner and share leftovers with the circling carrion birds.

The lions were no fools. They were very cautious. They realized this was no baby zebra, no newborn antelope; this was a *big mother* they faced. Not being their first rodeo, they stood there on hyper-alert gauging their chances. And the Cape buffalo made no sign of running away. Something had to give.

And give it did.

The leader of the lions crouched, pawed the ground, said "F@*k it" and charged. (Pardon his Swahili, but lions have potty mouths.)

At that moment we went from suspense to action. Everything speeded up dramatically. The Cape buffalo saw he was being charged, made a decision in a heartbeat, dropped his head low, and charged right back at the lion.

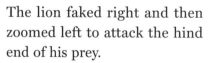

The lion faked right and then zoomed left to attack the hind end of his prey.

The Cape buffalo followed the fake and then reversed and went on the attack after the lion.

The two of them started to run in circles, chasing each other, which would have been funny were it not a life or lunch struggle.

The other lions just stood and watched this *mano a mano* fight, just like the bad guys in Hong Kong action flicks who hang around until it's their turn to beat up Jackie Chan. All the lions needed were cigarettes to smoke.

Which way would it go? Cape buffalo or lion? Right now it was an African standoff.

Until...

The Cape buffalo faked right, then surged up behind the lion and hooked a horn into the lion's side.

The lion howled in pain, then started to flee.

The Cape buffalo wheeled on the others who revealed their true character... and ran like hell.

Kelley and I, safe in the Land Rover, started to cheer for the Cape buffalo who took his bows and went back to eating his vegan lunch.

What can we learn from this true-life adventure that we can apply to our own storytelling?

First, we have a story that has its own **beginning, middle, and end**.

> Act 1. Setup: Lions sneak up on buffalo.
>
> Act 2. Development: Lions charge, buffalo charges back, they chase each other.
>
> Act 3. Resolution: Buffalo gores lion, the pride loses theirs.

Second, the **story can stand on its own**. We don't need a lot of back-story on the lions or the Cape buffalo to appreciate the struggle.

Third, each of the animals has a **clearly defined goal**. Kelley and I knew the goals of the scene without having to be told: The lions wanted to kill and eat the Cape buffalo. The Cape buffalo wanted to repel the attackers. If it weren't clear we might not have understood what was going down. We might not have appreciated the different moves the animals were making to get what they wanted. A poorly written version of this story would need a narrator to explain what's happening. The best film stories can be told visually and need no narration to stand on their own.

Mantra for filmmakers: Show it, don't say it.

Fourth, we see a **building of tension and suspense** as the lions get closer and the middle of the story develops. It bursts into full action when it can't progress any further without one of the characters making a major move. Either the lions are going to attack or the Cape buffalo is going to run away.

When the head lion makes his move and starts a charge the Cape buffalo has to respond: stand his ground and maybe get killed and eaten, run away, or charge right back at the lion. At this point things have speeded up dramatically and are happening very fast.

Fifth, the question becomes *how* **do they go after their goals**. What is their strategy? Get the Cape Buffalo. What are their tactics? Charge him. What does the lion do when one tactic doesn't work? Keep doing the same thing or try something new? In this case the Cape buffalo turns the tables and charges the head lion.

The lion doesn't know what to do for a few seconds and keeps going in a circle until the buffalo's horn gores him. He responds by running the hell away. The buffalo then turns on the other lions who wimp out and retreat ASAP. Resolution.

In films as in real life, there need to be different tactics to get to a goal. In directing and acting, these are the beats of a scene. They operate in any dramatic scene whether it's dialogue between two people, suspense scenes, choreography, or action. Any scene that doesn't have distinct and interesting beats will become repetitive and tedious very quickly. We know the animals in our wildlife adventure are not going to run in circles forever. Not only is it boring, it isn't working as a tactic and one of them needs to try something else if they are to reach their goal. Lunch or die. Which will it be?

Let's look at an example of an action sequence from *No Country For Old Men*,[3] winner of four 2007 Oscars, plus another one hundred and seven wins and fifty nominations for the Coen brothers, their cast and crew. NO SPOILERS! I promise.

After finding $2 million in the desert from a drug deal gone bad, a man finds himself running from a psychotic killer who is determined to get the money back.

At the beginning of the film the man, Lleweyln Moss (Josh Brolin) is in the desert in the middle of the night when the drug dealers come back looking for their money. He sees them coming and starts to run away on foot. Read this paraphrase of the screenplay[4] carefully to see how the chase works. Look for the goals and the beats.

> Near a big river gorge MOSS runs through the dark desert. He is being chased by men in a truck shining searchlights around.
>
> Moss sees the river and heads toward it.
>
> And just as quickly the truck closes on him. A shotgun is fired near him.
>
> Moss looks back and sees two men in the back of the truck aiming their shotguns at him.
>
> As he gets close to the steep river's edge, the guns fire again. One shot nails him in the shoulder and he falls head over heels down the steep bank.

---

[3] http://www.imdb.com/video/imdb/vi145883417/
[4] *No Country for Old Men* screenplay by Joel and Ethan Coen, based on the novel by Cormac McCarthy, 2006.

The truck skids to a stop and the men jump out and run to the edge of the bank.

Moss pulls off his boots and dives into the freezing current that sweeps him downstream.

A giant dog has leaped out of the truck and comes hurtling down to the water.

Moss looks back and sees the dog gaining rapidly on him. Shots are fired all around.

The dog leaps into the water and swims hard toward Moss who is slowed by the wound to his shoulder.

Moss looks back at the dog and tries to swim faster.

The dog is getting closer and closer.

Moss heads for a sandy bank and stumbles up on the shore. He yanks his revolver from his belt and tries to clear the water from the weapon.

The dog gains footing on the sandbar.

Reloading the pistol with difficulty he inserts a round as the dog bares his fangs and makes a flying leap toward Moss.

Moss fires.

The dog is hit in the chest and falls hard on the ground, jerking.

Moss scrambles to his feet and runs into the scrub brush.

This sequence is so classic that it could be in a John Ford Western or a Raoul Walsh gangster flick. Yet the modern sense of brutality and violence keeps it from feeling dated. The storytelling is spot on perfect.

Go back and re-read the sequence and see where the setup happens, where it breaks into full-blown action, how the action builds, and how it resolves. All the same questions that we will ask in Part Three of this book, **The Director's Checklist**, can be asked here. It's not hard, it's not string theory, but it is critical to ask the questions. What's the goal, where are the beats, where is the tipping point, what's the climax? Finally, is it exciting enough or is it predictable?

Directing Actors in Action

Thank God, there's an easy part to directing action: the actors. Unintuitively to us, they are the least of a director's worry. Actors specialize in scenes with a lot of dialogue. When they trained it was mostly with dialogue scenes from plays and films. They learned to analyze motivations, character, back-story, etc. If they studied at a first-rate institution like the Yale Drama School, they will have learned physical movement, fencing, even dance to be able to skillfully use both their bodies and their voices as instruments. But action is still the director's domain. He's the one who decides how a scene is to be shot, often like a jigsaw puzzle, made of individual bits that have to fit together just so. Like trained Dobermans, actors need to sit, stay, or attack when it comes to action. That doesn't mean that Matt Damon and Clint Eastwood don't contribute creatively to an action scene, it's just that their behavior is more circumscribed by the requirements of the scene. It is as much choreography as it is acting.

We often call actors "players" and action scenes take them right back to a totally playful and childlike state. It's imbedded in their makeup and begging to be released. Just like turning a bunch of ten-year-old boys loose to play *Cowboys and Aliens*. When we give directions to actors in an action scene we don't have to worry about esoteric back-stories, we don't need to come up with huge character motivations, we just have to tell them what their physical action is. It's always expressed as an active verb: "*Escape* the man chasing you by *Running* across the street," "*Reject* the pushy salesman's pitch by *Slamming* the door in his face," "*Punish* the man who just fired you by *Trashing* his office." These are simple, direct, easy directions. DO THIS, in order to DO THAT! SIMPLE. DIRECT.

Never make directions complicated. It's a waste of energy, waste of breath… and the actor stopped listening after the first sentence anyway. Remember the ten second rule for directing.

Of course the nature of the character will affect how the actor does the action; a timid man and the Hulk will perform the same active verb totally differently. Imagine how each would enact "*Trash* the office to *Punish* the man who just fired you." This can be a lot of fun in both drama and comedy. Watch some of the action in *The Hangover*[5] to see how this works.

Actors are quick learners. That's no surprise to anyone who's spent time around them. Since their job is to create the body, voice, and mind of a character they are excellent students absorbing like sponges what they need to know.

For example: Elizabeth Peña in *Rush Hour 2* plays a bomb disposal expert. It would've been easy/lazy for her to show up on the set and let someone show her a few moves. But being a good professional she made the effort to meet with bomb disposal experts to learn as much as she could about how bombs and detonators and wiring work. She wanted to look like she knew what she was doing and not just faking it.

For *Point of No Return*, Harvey Keitel, playing a professional assassin, actually managed to meet with someone who killed people for a living. Or so he told Harvey. Nevertheless Keitel returned from that meeting having a very strong idea of the kind of personality that would assassinate human beings.

Roy Scheider learned the basics of flying a helicopter from stunt pilot Jim Gavin on *Blue Thunder*. Gavin told me that he could teach any actor to fly very easily, much more so than a non-actor. This was a godsend one day in shooting when our cameraman nearly fell two thousand feet from the helicopter. Seeing a

---

[5] http://www.imdb.com/video/imdb/vi2105934361/

gorgeous sunset one afternoon in downtown Los Angeles we rushed to get the helicopter up in the air to photograph Scheider against the sunset. The cameraman, Frank Holgate, would have to stand on the skids outside the helicopter handholding the camera, attached by a very simple safety harness that he devised himself and used frequently.

As we scurried to get up in the air before we lost the sunset, I saw that Holgate was having difficulty setting up his harness. Seeing an accident in our future I told him to slow down, if we missed it we missed it. There would be plenty of sunsets that we could photograph later. Always confident, Frank assured me he would be perfectly safe.

Up in the air at two thousand feet he shot some really dramatic film of Scheider against the setting sun. I was riding in the back of the helicopter, and looked over the pilot's shoulder at Holgate to see if he liked what he was shooting. What I saw was a look I had never seen on any human being before. Frank had turned chalk white. There was absolute terror in his eyes. The straps of his harness were slipping and he was beginning to fall away from the helicopter. Both his hands were holding the camera, and he wasn't going to drop it over a populated area. Plus a lifetime of habit made him loath to lose exposed film.

Jim Gavin, the pilot, was sitting close to Holgate and quickly snaked his left arm around him to keep him from falling. Then he ordered Roy Scheider to take control of the helicopter. Like a  pro, Roy grabbed the cyclic and landed us at the heliport with only a little help from Gavin. Somewhere in the excitement, the Arriflex camera had been thrown back to me, and I continued shooting so we would have a record of Scheider landing the helicopter.

SUMMARY

1. *Blue Thunder's* lesson was that action sequences need new events and tactics to stay alive and interesting. The events and tactics need to increase in intensity.

2. Action happens when ordinary responses to any situation no longer work. Behavior goes into overdrive. E.g., the Cape buffalo and the lions in Tanzania.

3. Action sequences are individual stories within a larger story. They have a beginning, middle and end. Act 1: Setup, Act 2: Development, Act 3: Resolution.

4. An action sequence can usually stand on its own without depending too much on given circumstances.

5. The audience must understand the goals or objectives of a sequence either intuitively or from information given by the filmmaker.

6. Part of the fun of the action comes when we see the ways that characters go after their goal. What do they do differently when one tactic doesn't work?

7. Keep directions extremely simple. Use active verbs. It's called "action" for a good reason.

8. Actors are great learners. When they have to portray something they will work hard to look authentic.

Chapter 7

Strategy #2: Who, Where, and When

Point of View

Every form of storytelling has one key question:

From whose point of view is the story being told?

This question is on the top of your Checklist. Ignore it at your peril. Ignore it at the peril of breaking your story, of ruining your film. Not just the director needs to ask this. In filmmaking, which is such a collaborative art, everyone working on the project needs to agree on the film's point of view and work to support it. The writer, the director, the producer, the production designer, the cinematographer, the editor, the composer, the wardrobe designer etc., all must get on the same page. That's why the job of a director exists: to unify everyone working on a film. It only takes one of the creative team to ruin the whole film by having either no point of view, or worse, the wrong point of view.

> **Christopher Nolan:** I have an absolute concern with point of view. Whether in the pure camera blocking or even the writing, it's all about point of view. I can't cut a scene if I haven't already figured out whose point of view I'm looking at. I'm

always thinking of the camera as a participant. We always move the camera physically closer and put a different focal length on. Stylistically, something that runs through my films is a shot that walks into a room behind a character, because to me, that takes me inside the way that the character enters.[1]

Why such a strict rule?

Without a point of view, there is no art, no sympathy, perhaps only facts, and/or fantasies strung together somehow. It's bad storytelling. It could be scientific writing, or objective historical writing, or objective journalism but it's not storytelling. What storytellers do is subjective, not objective. They put a particular spin on their story that will make the audience sympathize with certain characters, facts, or phenomena over others. They create a tone to the tale that could be serious, might be humorous, or sad, ironic, or a jumbled mixture of many tones. Shakespeare mocked the playwriting traditions of his time when Polonius observed a play could be "pastoral-comical, historical-pastoral, tragical-historical, tragical-comical-historical-pastoral."[2] He was probably singling out plays that tried to please everybody, to have something for everyone.

Of course there is objective writing, just not in drama. Truly objective writing is usually not more than a listing of facts. Look in the newspaper's obituary section at reports of recent deaths. There'll be a list of facts about an ordinary person's life: birth, death, career, family, etc. But interestingly, the more famous the people are, the more the writing starts to take a point of view: how successful were they, what did people think of them, what is their legacy, etc. As a result, we get a feeling for the real person. Even this simple writing is hard to keep objective. Just the very choice of what facts to include in an obituary starts to take a point of view.

Historical writing might seem to be objective. Perhaps the historian even believes it is objective writing. If that were the case there would be little need for revisionist histories. But that's not going

---

[1] Jeffrey Resner, *DGA Quarterly*, Spring 2012, 29.
[2] William Shakespeare, *Hamlet*, Act 2, Scene 2.

to happen. We know that journalism can be horribly biased, even with the effort to separate the news from editorial opinions. In the new electronic media age it gets even harder as entertainment and news mingle into little more than gossip.

Documentary films usually try hard to be objective but of course it's extremely difficult, some say impossible, not to have a point of view in either the filming or the editing. Every choice that is made as a documentary is being created moves it toward a point of view. Ironically, the more truthful they appear, the more some people will complain that certain facts are missing and that the film is biased. It's not really a losing battle, just really difficult.

Whose point of view is the scene just referenced from *No Country for Old Men*? It has to be Moss', because we are seeing events the way he sees them. We find ourselves sympathizing with his character, hoping he gets away from the men who are chasing him.

Here's the cool part: the scene doesn't have to be this way. If we wanted we could tell it from the other character's point of view. Let's twist it around for example and say that we are seeing it the way the men who are trying to claw back their money see it. From their point of view they see a man in the desert at night where their money is supposed to be. He starts to run away and they pursue him to get back what belongs to them. From their point of view we hope they catch his sorry ass.

This swapping of points of view is not so far from what actually happens in *No Country for Old Men*. The character of Chigurh, played by Javier Bardem, is instantly seen as an evil, ruthless, Get-Medieval character, out to capture and destroy Moss. Along with Moss we learn to fear him and hope Moss escapes his sociopathic wrath. However, in the middle of the story when Chigurh gets injured in a gunfight we spend time with him. Unable to go to a hospital he cleverly creates a major distraction by blowing up a car outside a pharmacy, then stealing their first-aid materials to treat his wounds. In his motel room we watch him extract the bullets and sew up his own skin. Slowly we realize that we are sympathizing with him, admiring his resourcefulness and feeling the pain of the needle. Seeing things from his point of view gives dimension and some sympathy to Chigurh.

If skilled storytellers like the Coen Brothers and Cormac McCarthy can deliberately switch points of view to make their stories better, imagine how easy it would be for a director to change POVs by mistake. Sloppy choice of camera angles, or poor editing, just being in the wrong place at the wrong time, can severely weaken the power of a film.

Directors of comedies years ago devised a clever trick of introducing a third person's point of view to keep the comedy fresh. Blake Edwards was a master of this in his *Pink Panther* movies. As some of the car chases and action scenes would get crazier and sillier he would cut to a homeless guy or an old lady who just happened upon the scene. As this character looked at the insanity going on we the audience would suddenly see everything from a fresh point of view and be reminded how funny it was. This trick not only gets a big laugh, it refreshes the life of the scene.

One of the most insidious and yet delicate shifts of POV can come from an acting performance by a particularly strong actor intent on showing off to the detriment of other characters. It's called quite simply, upstaging, coming from theatre-speak where the rear of a proscenium stage is called upstage and the front nearest the audience is downstage. For trivia geeks this originated when stages were literally sloped on steep angles so that the rear was a foot or two higher than the front. It helped the audience see things upstage that might be hidden from view. So an actor who upstages another would go higher up the ramp, forcing the other actor to turn his back to the audience.

Upstaging now commonly describes an actor whose performance pushes others out of the way. This happens all the time in theatre where a director isn't always present to keep actors in the proper balance. In film it's rarer since the director has much more control over the fine-tuning of a performance. Even so, actors playing the bad guys or villains have juicier parts that may unexpectedly over-shadow the hero's part and skew the film in ways never intended by the filmmakers. The villains in the best Bond films are not only powerful adversaries as characters, but if the actor playing Bond doesn't bring his A game to the set we'll hear the audience coming out of the movie theatre humming the bad guy's theme.

ID and Locate

In these days of hysterical editing, crossing the 180-degree line, low-key photography, or just flat-out sloppiness, the director has to constantly watch out that the audience is following what is happening and where we are in an action sequence. We have to be sure that in the midst of the visual charivari and chaos that we're not losing the audience in the dust.

Look at Tony Scott's *Top Gun* to see one nasty challenge he faced making the film. On the ground, in the barracks, the bars, and the parties there's no problem knowing who everyone is. That's Tom Cruise, that's Anthony Edwards, that's Val Kilmer. Couldn't be any clearer where we are and who's who. However, when they put on their helmets, their flight suits, their face masks, all of which look alike, and mount their fighter jets, it turns into *Where's Waldo*. Scott is cutting rapidly from one pilot to another as they fly through their war games. As the action increases and the cutting speeds up it gets harder and harder to keep everyone straight and who's doing what to whom. Scott was smart to write the character's names on their helmets... if you have time to read them. Illiterate viewers will just be confused.

Why do we care about this? Isn't it enough to take the dogfight rides, to feel the excitement of flying at supersonic speeds? No, it's not enough. We need to stay invested in the characters, too. We're not being hurled around on a terrifying ride at Magic Mountain. First of all, the parks do it better than the movies can. They can throw us up, down, and all around with extreme vometic, (sorry, kinetic) action. They generate enough adrenaline in our bodies to power a small village. We identify with ourselves and the very real scary thought that we might die if thisdamnride breaks. When we take a commercial flight, they do everything possible to calm us down, to make us feel safe. On Magic Mountain's scariest ride "HOLY SH#%T LOUISE!" they do the exact opposite... freak us out! Deliberately. Else why pay fifty bucks to ride it?

In the movies the experience is very different. In any good film we get involved with the characters, we care about what happens to them. Even if they are bad guys, serial killers, and major weirdos, we can care about them. Otherwise why would *Silence of the Lambs*, *No Country for Old Men* or *Dracula* be such memorable films? The magic of the movies is that we can care about people who ordinarily we would flee from. Whether it's bug aliens from *District 9*, Hannibal Lecter, or Aunt Smellypants, we can care about them.

Just so long as they don't come to our house afterwards.

If we don't care about the characters in a movie it's going to be a very unsatisfying experience. My friend Scott thought he would hate the characters from *The Best Exotic Marigold Hotel* and didn't want to spend two hours with them. Maybe if we dragged him into the theater he might change his mind. But even if he goes to see his favorite Bond or Batman movie and doesn't wind up caring about the characters, he will flame it on Rotten Tomatoes.

In the various *Iron Man* films as well as *The Avengers*, Robert Downey Jr.'s character is often suited up in a titanium outfit that completely obscures his face. The directors Jon Favreau and Joss Whedon smartly shoot close-ups of him *inside* his mask so we can see what he's feeling. Otherwise, we would be completely divorced from him as a person. In *The Blues Brothers*, director John Landis took a huge risk by letting his two stars, Dan Ackroyd and John Belushi, wear sunglasses in every scene. He was counting on their amazing body language when performing to override the limitations of the glasses that kept us from seeing their eyes.

On the other hand, a television movie about a real disaster — the fatal climb up Mount Everest by beginning climbers — was totally frostbitten when viewers couldn't distinguish between or empathize with characters completely masked by layers of climbing gear. The characters were struggling, unable to breathe, snow-blinded, freezing, dropping dead and Lord knows what all but the audience had no idea who was who. We were distanced from the characters in their most agonizing and frightening time. Just to aggravate things, on the small, low-definition analog TVs of the time, their extreme distress was masked even more, to the point where it was almost impossible to care *what* happened to them.

Orientation

Knowing where we are in any action scene is very important. In order to understand, empathize with, and appreciate what's happening we must know where all the characters are in relationship to one another. There is a temptation among some directors and editors to get in so close to the characters that we lose any sense of where we are. If the bad guy is hundreds of yards away from the good guy that's one thing; if he is a few feet away that changes things. Alternatively, if someone is standing on a ledge of a building and we are so close to her that we don't see the street below, all sense of danger is lost.

Shooting the climactic bridge scene in *Saturday Night Fever* needed many close-ups of the characters as Tony tries to talk Bobby C off the railing of the bridge. Because of the tight shooting schedule we couldn't shoot the character's POV shots of the water hundreds of feet below that we needed. Once the scene was edited however, it was clear that the scene was emotionally flat without the sense of danger that the POV shots would provide. Fortunately we went back another night just to shoot handheld POVs of the water below, and they made a huge difference in the way the scene played.

A good example of confusion can be seen in the Bond film, *Quantum of Solace*. The opening sequence is a heart-stopping chase between Bond driving his Aston Martin and many bad guys chasing in their cars. At least that's the intention. The problem is that there are so many quick cuts and tight close-ups that it's very hard to keep up with what's going on and who is doing what to whom. It can take several viewings to be able to sort it all out. And who's going to do that? It means we are watching a lot of terrific chaotic action without much meaning. It certainly doesn't engage our emotions on anything but a very superficial level. The film footage exists to make all this clear and still be exciting. However, what happened is that the sequence is cut too quickly and shot too closely for a new viewer to stay oriented. My guess is that the more the filmmakers watched the scene in post, the more comfortable they got with it and kept cutting it tighter and tighter to keep their own sense of excitement.

We always need to keep putting ourselves back in the place of a first-time viewer so that we don't leave them behind because of our own overfamiliarity with the film.

> **Brett Ratner:** When I watch a movie and I'm in the middle of an action sequence, there's nothing worse than losing orientation. I have this weird equilibrium that needs to be balanced. I'm on a plane, I get freaked out because I gotta see the ground. I would not be a good pilot because I don't have that mind. And when it comes to spatial geography, and all of a sudden everyone starts throwing punches and we don't know where we are... they could spin around and then we're wondering, "Wait, am I upside-down?" If the whole scene is so confusing we don't know who is throwing the punch, or where we are, we've lost the audience. But a good action sequence allows you to keep your feet on the ground and understand it.

Jeopardy

Jeopardy is the oxygen that fuels the flame of any action. Jeopardy is the thing that draws us in inexorably, or not at all. If there's no jeopardy in an action scene that the audience can relate to, it is a tale, in the words of Macbeth, "full of sound and fury, signifying nothing."[3]

In the opening of *Raiders of the Lost Ark*[4], Indiana Jones is seizing a sacred statue from its pedestal inside a jungle tomb deep

---

[3] William Shakespeare, *Macbeth*, Act 5, Scene 5.
[4] http://www.youtube.com/watchfeature=player_detailpage&v=5a9NVDgKc4o

underground. Lifting it from the plinth triggers ancient booby traps, set to destroy tomb raiders. The tomb starts to collapse around Indy and his native helper. They begin to run out of the crumbling tomb, when Indy is double-crossed by the helper and falls into a deep pit. Rock slabs descend threatening to seal him inside forever. He must escape the pit in time to dive under the closing slabs, and ultimately outrun a giant boulder that chases him faster than he can run.

Now this is jeopardy!

George Lucas and Steven Spielberg created a sequence where the odds against Indy are stacked so high that we can't see a way for him to escape. We can't help but root for him. As the giant boulder is on the verge of crushing him any second he hurls himself out onto the jungle hillside. We are devilishly allowed to think he has avoided death for a heartbeat, only to see spears stuck into his face by angry native warriors.

Incidentally, to go back to the earlier point about orientation, notice the clever way in which Spielberg, his editor, Michael Kahn, and an uncredited George Lucas trick us two or three times into thinking the boulder rolling behind Indy is much closer than it really is. When we drop back to a wider shot we see he has a bit more time. Some critics complained about this at the time calling it "cheating." But they missed the point that those shots were really from Indy's POV and that's how close he thought (and we thought) he was to being crushed. There is a very funny variation on this in *Jurassic Park*. The T-Rex is chasing the Range Rover and the people inside stare at him approaching in the rearview mirror. Etched on the mirror are the words "Objects Are Closer Than They Appear."

It's clear why the opening of *Raiders of the Lost Ark* is a classic scene in cinema because we care about Indy and want him to succeed. We are involved at every second with his dilemma, see that he is clever and resourceful and yet is outmatched at every turn. Most importantly we see that he could be killed at any minute. He only escapes by the thinnest margin then is dumped right back in the soup of danger.

Jeopardy, jeopardy, jeopardy. The best!

Compare this with a sequence in another film, *The Matrix Reloaded* by the Wachowskis. Unfortunately, this sequence, "The Fight with a Thousand Smiths," impressive as it is, does not succeed as well. Why?

In the middle of the film Neo encounters his nemesis, Smith[5]. The two start to fight and in response Smith begins to replicate himself not once, not twice, not thrice, but *NINE HUNDRED AND NINETY-NINE* times. Neo is trying to fight every Smith simultaneously. And unlike our lions in the Ngorongoro Crater, these animals are not hanging about waiting their turn to enter the fray. If they could just get to him he would be crushed in a heartbeat. The fight goes on... and on... and on. Just as we think Neo has destroyed all the Smiths, a replacement battalion of them materializes and the fight renews. At an indeterminate point Neo suddenly leaps into the air and flies away from all of them, escaping their grasp.

What's wrong with this picture? Two things.

It becomes clear to even the most naïve viewer that though Neo has a hell of a job fighting these guys off, he seems to do it with relative ease. The plague of Smiths is more annoying than truly dangerous. It's more like standing in a swarm of bees or wasps. Yes, there is some danger but it doesn't seem like the kind of thing that will kill you or even be very debilitating. The jeopardy is minimized when we see that he's able to repel his attackers with relative ease.

Secondly, because there are a thousand Smiths, it takes a long time to even get the sequence built up to the point that we see a thousand guys either attacking, strewn about or just joining the fight. There are only so many ways that Neo can defend himself before we start to see repetitions of the same moves. Boring.

When a scene gets boring, audiences start tuning out... and that's a big no-way-won't-play. Unfortunately, many action directors are

---

[5] http://www.youtube.com/watch?v=lLXaRtc1f4I

seduced by their own shots. The filmmakers fall so in love with all the footage they slaved hard to shoot that they can't bring themselves to trim it down to a playable length. I'm as guilty of this as anyone. That's why films need to be previewed by average audiences. They are not shy about speaking out, "Too LONG, too REPETITIVE. BORRING!"

Don't repeat an action unless it's a clever variation of the previous beat. To paraphrase Harry Cohn, the cantankerous old boss of Columbia Pictures, when audiences' butts start to twitch, the scene's too long.

Finally, the ending of The Fight with a Thousand Smiths gets a ten on the Lame-Ass Scale because at a certain point Neo looks skyward and easily zips up and away from all of them. Well, hell! What was that all about?! Did he just get bored with fighting? Do you mean to tell me that he could have flown away from them all along? Was he just fighting for the fun of it, just to mess with Smith? Or did he unexpectedly acquire the ability to fly? "USE THE FORCE, NEO!" Oops, wrong movie. Many people felt cheated by the ending to this scene, which of course undercut their response to the whole film. This doesn't even qualify as a deus ex machina. Apologies, Wachowskis, sorry to nitpick; you are amazing filmmakers.

Make the ending of an action clever, ingenious, unexpected.

Countdown

Jeopardy is affected by another element: time. How much time is there before the catastrophe happens? If we know that time is running out, the audience's level of anxiety increases substantially. "Indy better get out of that pit before the tomb is sealed off... in the next five seconds." Every time the United States Space Shuttle launched from Cape Canaveral we heard the flight engineers count down "Ten, nine, eight, blah, blah, blah." Even after the jillionth time we heard it there was still a growing tension as the count advanced to zero. We wondered if this time would it launch successfully or would it explode, crash, or just plain abort? All real possibilities, so we took the launch seriously. Great suspense is that which makes the impending climax to action even better.

Of course a countdown like this is fairly obvious and relatively clumsy in our storytelling toolbox. Even the misnomered "reality shows" on television overuse the device to a fault. There are more inventive and subtle ways to keep the pressure on in any action or suspense sequence.

The classic device is a timekeeper, the clock made famous in *High Noon*, 1952's Academy Award-winning film by Fred Zinnemann that starred Gary Cooper and Grace Kelly.

The film won four Oscars: for acting, music, and importantly in this example, for editing by Elmo Williams and Harry Gerstad. They were the film editors who realized that this potentially exciting story of a marshal defending his town against a gang of outlaws bent on killing him was falling flat. Early preview audiences confirmed their worry. The marshal, played by Gary Cooper, finds out gradually that everyone in the town is leaving him to face the outlaws alone. He goes from store to home to store looking for support and learning that the whole town has come down with an attack of cowarditis.

Fred Zinnemann's highly realistic style of directing did not lend itself to artificially amping the suspense by having Gary Cooper frantically running around, or editing with quick cuts.

The filmmakers realized that one key to the story was the marshal has just learned the outlaws will arrive on the noon train. The original title of the film was "The Tin Star," hardly a bell ringer.

The marshal only has four or five hours to pull some kind of defense together, no time at all really. No phones, no faxes, no eager deputies to run around helping, just one man on foot. (What happened to the horses, was that their day off?)

But how to convey emotionally that time is running out? Using dialogue to do this is a C- solution. Movie audiences are not good listeners, as many a filmmaker has discovered to their dismay. Telling audiences something verbally without a visual aid is tantamount to not telling them at all. Visual information on the other hand almost always seizes audience attention in preference to what's on the audio track. Audio information frequently gets drowned by the eye candies of beautiful actors, gorgeous scenery, and dynamic action.

To repeat, **"See it, Don't Say It" is the mantra for all filmmakers since Georges Méliès invented the bloody thing.**

Zinnemann and his team needed a visual solution. That solution was staring them in the face: a wall-mounted pendulum clock, right over the desk in the sheriff's office. Cut to that clock at key moments and we can see how long before the train carrying bad guys arrives. If the marshal isn't ready but the train is almost here, the jeopardy and the suspense increase dramatically. Not only is the meaning of time built into our DNA, we are a time-centric culture who live our lives around specific times and diurnal rhythms.

The result of this simple change to *High Noon* was transformative. The film, which had played only decently at its early previews, now scored through the roof. The audience got it! And only with a few added shots of a clock ticking.

Since then, time-keeping devices of every sort have been used to keep us involved in the action or the suspense: sand falling through hourglasses, pages flying off calendars, digital computer clocks counting down. Even more imaginative ideas include a bathtub about to overflow in *Fatal Attraction,* a computer breaking into nuclear codes bit by bit in *WarGames,* and the real time thriller, *Nick of Time,* where Johnny Depp tries to save his daughter before she will be shot in the next ninety minutes.

We are always looking for more interesting ways to tell our stories. It becomes more difficult over time as so many techniques and tricks become familiar to audiences who have seen everything... several times. They can be so far ahead of the filmmaker that they can lose interest in the story and the characters in a flash. And when that happens, they don't come back. So on top of everything else, the filmmakers who succeed have found new ways to excite, puzzle, and tease their audience. Some will make their films more violent and bombastic, some more sexual or crazy. Quentin Tarantino continues to push the envelope as he plays with horrifying subjects like slavery and racial cleansing in *Django Unchained* and *Inglorious Basterds*. But these radical techniques would have no hope in hell of working if he did not also make us care about his characters.

SUMMARY

1. Directors must know from whose point of view a story is being told. Never shoot action generically without creating the right point of view. E.g., the men chasing Moss in *No Country for Old Men*.

2. It's possible to have more than one point of view in a scene or a film. E.g., *Rashomon, American Graffiti*.

3. Multiple points of view in a scene or a film are tricky but interesting. E.g., *Pulp Fiction, Psycho*.

4. Make sure the audience knows who is who and where they are. Otherwise they become disconnected from the characters and get bored. E.g., *Top Gun, Iron Man, Blues Brothers, Death on Everest*.

5. Jeopardy is the oxygen that fuels the flame of action. No danger, no suspense. E.g., *Raiders of the Lost Ark, Matrix Reloaded*.

6. Put a lid on the time to keep the suspense growing. How much time is left before this will be over? Countdowns, calendars, clocks. E.g., *High Noon, WarGames*.

7. See it, don't say it. Never explain something verbally that can be shown visually. "Motion pictures," not "motion talkies."

Chapter 8

Strategy #3: Quick Techniques and Safety

Directors and actors can use a few techniques when doing action scenes. Techniques that keep the energy of a scene alive and help the dynamics of the editing flow. They are seldom taught in acting or directing classes and get passed down only by observation and experience. Here are seven such hints and techniques.

1. Pointless Masters

Unless there is a stunning reason to do an action scene in one shot without cutting away, the time, energy, money, manpower, and other resources expended are a total waste of time. Of course there are some terrific examples of successful one-shot action masters: *The Protector*[1], a Hong Kong film, has an amazing one. Brian de Palma's *Snake Eyes*[2] combines action and dialogue in a tour de force ten-minute scene without obvious edits. But

---

[1] http://www.amazon.com/s/ref=nb_sb_ss_c_0_13?url=search-alias%3Dmovies-tv&field-keywords=the+protector&sprefix
[2] http://www.amazon.com/s/ref=nb_sb_ss_i_1_10?url=search-alias%3Dmovies-tv&field-keywords=snake+eyes+blu-ray&sprefix

99.99% of action scenes get chopped up into banjo chips and confetti. There is some old-school thinking that a master is needed to make the geography clear to the editor so she can make it clear to the audience. And clarity *is* very important in storytelling.

As we discussed earlier, in *Rush Hour* and all his other films Brett Ratner is very careful to let us know where we are at all times. Some shots are wide, some close, some are static, some move, but he never tries to create some overall master. If the editor can't figure out what's going on, the scene is either badly shot or you need a new editor. In either case, an overall master wouldn't help.

2. Few Actions

Three reasons: One, the editor will put his foot through your Rembrandt quicker than a butcher chopping chickens (block that metaphor!). Second, it's easier for the actor to get physical actions right in shorter bits. But it really is about as efficient to do the actions in manageable sections that don't try to accomplish too much in one take. Third, digital media allows us to keep the camera rolling without fear of wasting film, so an action can be repeated several times before cutting the camera: a missed punch in a fistfight, or a poorly timed reaction to something off-stage can be repeated several times before moving on.

> **JB:** On the commentary for *Rush Hour*[3], you described the scene with Jackie Chan fighting off a gang of guys in a poolroom. Now here we're talking about an absolute master, a genius of action. How much of a fight sequence will you shoot... before you've got to change angles?
>
> **Brett Ratner:** I'll probably shoot two, the most three events, meaning I could say skip ahead, skip ahead, skip ahead, and I'm manipulating him because he doesn't want to do that, because he might come up with another idea that might not connect back to the other... right? So I'll say, "Show me what you're gonna do in

---

[3] http://www.amazon.com/s/ref=nb_sb_noss_1?url=search-alias%3Dmovies-tv&field-keywords=rush+hour

this direction now," as if we're gonna shoot it. "Oh no, now come back that way." So I'll try to shoot that and I can only do that two or three times and then go back and fill in the blanks.

Jackie could do the whole sequence without a cut but it's always changing based on the limitations. If it was him fighting his Asian stunt guys they could do it, but he's fighting another guy who's an American stuntman not used to working in the Hong Kong style, right? So they fight in different ways. And it's like dancing. You dance with a girl that you just met, you might stumble or step on her toes. But if you dance with your wife, you are going to move in sync because you look in her eyes and you know which way she's gonna go.

That's how Jackie is with his stunt guys. He looks at them and they know exactly the way that they're going to move, and the unknown part of that is why he doesn't want to skip ahead. Jackie said, "I don't know if this guy is gonna be able to swing the stick at me without hitting me. I don't want to be hit, Brett. I mean, I'll be hit for the sake of the film but I'd prefer not to. So this guy can't swing it full speed and me have the confidence that he's not going to hit me in the head with a pool cue. Even though it's rubber and hurts, I don't want to do it, you know what I mean?"

JB: So it's a matter of getting the two, three, or four bits of action right, and then knowing that you'll cut. It's more manageable to do three or four bits, cover them and then move on to the next part.

BR: Well it's even more manageable to do the entire scene in one particular direction. If a stunt coordinator does it, he rehearses his guys and shows me the whole thing on video or however he does it, and we shoot everything in one direction, turn around and we shoot everything in the opposite direction. Jackie's inventing it as he goes and it would be more useful for me and for the cinematographer, unless we could light the whole room, which we never had the time to do, to come in and pre-rig the whole room in advance so you could turn your cameras around in a heartbeat. I would just say, "Jackie, keep going in this direction, please, please, please." But he goes, "But Brett if you can't do this with the pool cue we'll have to change it. But then he's got the stick in his hand, so what does the stick do, just appear? We ought to lose the stick if he can't hit me with the stick." So that's why he doesn't want to go too far ahead in one direction. But for practicality, it's just a different way of doing it. It's Hong Kong. They shoot in every direction. They don't care about the lighting. And every time we would spend more than five minutes lighting something he'd be like, "Oh Brett, let's go." I'd be like, "Jackie, it's gotta look good. It's not a #%$@ Hong Kong movie."

Exception

There are always opportunities where the director wants to do many actions without a cut. *The Protector* is a terrific example. The director spent days choreographing the action to happen all in one shot. The best Hong Kong professional stuntmen were determined to make this the most amazing action tour de force they could. But as actions are piled on and added in, the possibility for error and injury increase.

Observe the Three-Take Rule

During the first three takes everyone on the crew and cast are at the peak of their attention span. By take four, inevitably, one thing, two things, will go wrong. By take five something else will get messed up. The focus gets missed, the camera runs out of media, the key prop wasn't reset and so on. Hopefully nobody will get hurt but all too frequently it happens. The least harmful result is that time is lost and people are worn down. The worst that happens is someone is seriously injured — a twisted ankle, a broken nose, or worse. This causes problems everywhere, both to the injured and the production. All expensive, and potentially tragic. If you have to go more than three takes on any action shot keep everyone's heads out of their... clouds and refocus them on their jobs.

I always announce to the crew in a loud voice that this is the time when accidents are likely to happen. They mentally checklist what they need to do in the shot and double-check their equipment. Ironically this is easier the more dangerous the stunt. The easy stunts tend to be blown off. That's when something goes really wrong.

3. Overlap Actions

Since action sequences are composed of very short bits that are like jigsaw puzzle pieces cut to order we only need the actor to do two or three actions in a shot because the editor is likely to cut to something else. So to keep the energy flowing we have the actor overlap his action from the previous shot. That means he backs up by a couple of seconds from what he was doing before and repeats it at the beginning of the new shot. Example: On "Action," James Bond is shooting at Goldfinger. The wrong way would be for Bond to have his gun aimed at Goldfinger right from the top of the shot. He needs to be moving. The right way is to start as though he has just fired a shot and the gun was recoiling, then he would have to re-aim in order to fire again. In the wrong way we would have cut to him in a static position. In the right way a bit of energy from his previous action would carry over and the editor has many good choices where to cut into the shot. Mel Gibson is really skilled at this technique as are lots of actors who do action films.

4. Scissor Time

Even in short sections you may have to cut away to something else. Example: Bridget Fonda in *Point of No Return*[4] plays an assas-

Point of No Return *Japanese poster.*

sin who at one moment is trapped in a gunfight in a restaurant kitchen. She's ducked down behind a counter and pops up quickly to fire at the bad guys and then disappears just as quickly. Bridget is really quick and really accurate, so fast that after she fired, she ducked back down before the editor could get in his proverbial (and now metaphorical) scissors. In Bridget's very realistic mind she was doing the absolute right thing, but in

---

4 http://www.amazon.com/s/ref=nb_sb_ss_i_2_18?url=search-alias%3Dmovies-tv &field-keywords=point+of+no+return+dvd&sprefix

the editing world we needed to stretch time out so we could see what she fired at, *and* how she reacted to her target before disappearing. My direction to her was she should make sure she saw what her shot hit before she ducked down again.

NB: I did not say "take longer after you fire before disappearing"; I gave her a much more specific action: "Check how your shot landed so you know what to do next time you fire."

That's a more specific direction and not mechanical. Her imagination was engaged and her new reaction was real and organic, plus a big help to the editor.

5. Not That Fast

Oft-times actions done at real speeds are too fast for the eye to capture. In her case, she moved so fast that it was hard to capture what she was really doing. The first thing was to slow her down slightly so we had time to understand visually what she was doing. The direction was not "Slow down Bridget, you're going too fast." Rather, the direction was much more specific and actor friendly: "Make sure you have a good aim on your target before you fire."

As in all directing of actors, this specificity gives them so much more to do than if they are just told to slow down or speed up. In the second Bourne film, *The Bourne Supremacy*, Matt Damon has a fight in Victoria Station that goes so fast we are left saying, "What just happened? How did he do that?"

In the old Western gunfights, the gunfighters drew their guns so quickly that directors learned to slow them down a bit. Otherwise, the revolver would be in the holster and less than two or three frames later it was aimed at a target. It literally looked like a mistake.

6. Change-Up

Camera tricks are properly in the jurisdiction of DPs. They are the ones who are expert in their camera's capabilities. It's their job to stay on the cutting edge of what can be done with the camera and the media, whether film or digital. It's not only complicated but is always changing as new and inventive ways are created to make great storytelling images. However, that doesn't mean directors shouldn't learn as much as possible to be able to create visual ideas themselves in collaboration with their DPs. Good directors know their tools and how to use them. Directors need to know the different effects of slow motion, speeded up motion, skip framing, blurred motion, etc. They need to know the difference between 24 frames per second versus 36, versus 96. Every frame rate has a particular use and creates different effects from other frame rates. Directors need to know what happens when the motion in the frames is blurred or when they are hyper-sharp; what a 90° shutter does to the image versus an 180° shutter. Creative directors should know how to take advantage of these differences to better tell their stories. The slow motion horror of killings in *The Wild Bunch* is very different from the speeded up killings in *The Bourne Identity.* Whatever anyone thinks about the success or failure of Peter Jackson's 3D high-frame delivery of *The Hobbit,* both he and his cinematographer, Andrew Lesnie, deserve credit for pushing the creative envelope with their bold experimentation of 48 frames per second projection. Though the film's imagery has been disturbing to many viewers, it's not that long ago that so-called "dramatic films" were derided because they were in color. Comedies were in color. Black and white meant serious.

Camera tricks are totally useless and intrusive if they don't add to the story or the characters. Many new, in fact many old, directors think they can put their stamp on a film using fancy camera work. But this is never effective if it's not organic to the story or the characters. And it certainly will not cover up a bad story. "Lipstick on a pig" is a sty way to put it. It just mucks it up and evinces director desperation.

Test any new camera effect in advance of shooting. Never wait till the shooting day to experiment. There can and probably will be surprises. Things don't always behave the way you might want or expect. To complain that you didn't have time to test something is as lame an excuse there is. It also bespeaks lack of preparation, and the mother of all mistakes, assumptions. If you have to reshoot, think what that costs. Think what happens if you can't reshoot because you lost your actor, or ran out of time or money. *TEST IN ADVANCE.* You've been warned.

7. No Immutable Rules

Despite that rules seemed to be set out here, all are made to be broken. The effectiveness of each technique in filmmaking depends on how the filmmaker intends to use it. Just because a technique is bad in one circumstance doesn't mean that it's always bad and can't be used creatively another way. In the HBO series *True Blood*[5] the vampires often *WHOOSH* from one side of a room to another in a flash. It all happens too quickly for the eye to really know anything other than they moved *REALLY FAST.* The creative point is to show the supernatural power of the vampire. This is a very clever use of the camera that would make Georges Méliès proud.

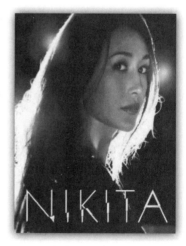

I recently adapted/homaged/stole a variation of this *True Blood* shot for an episode of *Nikita.*[6] A warning pager signal is sent from a house that's been broken into, to a man's pager many miles away. To get a feeling of the electronic message hurtling through space to his pager, the camera first moved through an empty warehouse, turning corners, until it reached his pager, which started blinking as the camera got close. We then speeded the shot up 1000% to get the neck-snapping effect we wanted.

---

[5] http://www.youtube.com/watch?v=XNFZezdnpsE
[6] http://www.amazon.com/3-0/dp/B009TNA07M/ref=sr_1_1?s=movies-tv&ie=UTF8
&qid=1351462526&sr=1-1&keywords=nikita+season+3

8. Booby Traps

Actors delight in the fun of action scenes, the harder, the better... well, up to a point. They love it so much that even adult actors who should know better frequently want to do their own stunts. And this is where a director has to draw the line and become "Dad."

Countless films have had accidents, even tragedies, as a result of actors doing their own stunts. In spite of great care and strong precautions, actors have been injured, maimed, even killed trying to execute what looked like the most harmless stunt.

In my own films there have only been a few accidents. They were huge lessons for me. The beautiful, talented Barbara Parkins came to guest-star in a *Night Gallery* playing a runaway bride. In the very first shot she is seated on horseback behind her "lover," Alejandro Rey, as they ride away, escaping from her wedding. The actors had to ride bareback and close to camera so we could see their faces. There was a stunt double on set, but this was an easy shot so who needed her? Right? Wrong. After "Action," Barbara and Alejandro had no sooner ridden past camera and he slowed the horse to a stop than she slid frighteningly, horribly to one side off the horse and impacted on the hard ground.

Mayday, Mayday! Nothing was broken, except her pride and my poor judgment but she still had to go to the hospital to be checked out. We couldn't shoot for the rest of the day and we had to replace her with Susan Strasberg. Not Barbara Parkins' fault. My fault. I should have ignored the desire to see her face in the shot. It wasn't worth taking the risk of riding bareback. Not surprisingly, I was not asked to direct any more *Night Gallery* episodes after that. A big lesson at tremendous personal cost to me and financial cost to Universal.

In *Saturday Night Fever* John Travolta's gang, the Faces, get into a huge fight with a Puerto Rican gang, Los Brujos. The film was shot in Brooklyn where there are very few stuntmen who are young and look Puerto Rican. It was a low-budget film and we couldn't afford to fly in eight Hollywood stuntmen. So we decided that our stunt coordinator would train all our actors, Puerto Rican and Italian, how to do some very simple fight moves. The actors were thrilled and were great students. They got it right away and were really convincing. So far, so good.

On the shoot day I gathered all the actors together including our newbie Puerto Ricaños. I told them, "What we're about to do will look like a fight... but it's *not* a fight, it's *not* acting. It's choreography. If you start 'acting,' that's when you may hurt somebody." The young actors looked at me the way you look at your mother when she nags you to drive carefully. "OK, John, we got it," they said, all twenty-four eyes rolling as one.

The first shot is our character Double J taking a swing at one of the Brujos. We rolled the camera. I said, "Be careful now guys. OK and... Action!" The Brujo took a swing and Double J pretended to take it on the chin. Good. Then he wound up and took a roundhouse swing... and connected. BAMM! CRACK! He broke the Brujo's nose! Blood flowed everywhere. "Cut, Cut! What the hell???!!" We stopped. Everything was chaos. Travolta left the set in shock and the stunt coordinator started to take the injured Puerto Rican to the ER. But he was a lot tougher than us wimpy Hollywood types and insisted that we shoot his side of the fight before he went to the hospital. So we swung the camera around, shot his side of it and in five minutes he was in a car on his way to the emergency room. His nose got reset, just the way it was. We offered to pay for a cute bobbed nose but he liked what he had when he came to work that morning. Travolta came cautiously back to the set and we kept on shooting. You could almost say, "No harm no foul," but there was no need to have this happen. There's no movie in the world that's worth injuring someone for.

Richard Dreyfuss in *Stakeout* was running from the cops and jumped into someone's backyard to hide. His stunt double, John Oliver, had jumped the fence in a wide shot and Richard just needed to hop into his close-up. I stood him on an apple box only twelve inches high. On action he hopped down onto the ground as though he had jumped over a big fence... and promptly twisted his ankle. Owwwww! Even though it wasn't broken he couldn't walk on it that day. We had to shoot shots of John Oliver until Richard could come back to work. When he did come back the next day he was still hobbling. Cost to the company: $25,000 insurance deductible. I don't think this one was my fault since the action required was no harder than stepping off a curb. Who knew Richard would land badly? He said later that he had weak ankles but had thought he could do this... it's hard to call it a... stunt. *But!* The point is that even the smallest action can turn sour quickly. Remember I said earlier that actors enjoy being playful. They regress to being little kids, who we know are prone to scraping their knees, bonking their chins, and... twisting their ankles. They get into the game so much that things just happen.

And that's why it's a very bad idea to have actors do their own stunts, no matter how enthusiastic they are. Some actors are great at it, like Mel Gibson and Wesley Snipes or Dwayne "The Rock" Johnson. But they are a tiny group in the midst of a huge clump of accidents waiting to happen.

In the bicycle racing film *American Flyers*[7], we put our actors through six weeks of training, riding bicycles for long distances through Griffith Park in Los Angeles. If they had thought before starting training that bicycle riding was easy, they were quickly disabused of this notion. When we began they could only ride for a couple of miles before they fell exhausted to the side of the road. They quickly grew highly motivated to become the most powerful bicycle riders they could be

American Flyers *Italian poster.*

---

[7]   trailer: http://www.youtube.com/watch?v=QxNWzbM7BjA
DVD: http://www.amazon.com/s/ref=nb_sb_ss_c_0_14?url=search-alias%3Dmovies-tv
&field-keywords=american+flyers&sprefix=american+flyer%2Caps%2C377

so they could keep up with the highly trained professionals who would ride with them in the film.

Kevin Costner, in particular, showed not only a great competitive spirit, but also great athletic ability. In one particularly difficult shot he and the other actors, along with fifty professional riders, rode down the Colorado National Monument on a series of severe S curves and switchbacks. At the bottom of the hill they entered a long tunnel, which then opened up onto another steep road. We set up at least six cameras to photograph this action. As the riders emerged from the tunnel, one of the actors, Luca Bercovici, hit a nasty bump in the road that catapulted his bike into the air and him into a rock wall, promptly dislocating his shoulder.

Kevin Costner was riding directly behind Bercovici and was hurtling toward the fallen bike. A second nasty accident looked inevitable. However, Costner somehow *levitated* his bicycle over the fallen bike and stopped safely. This was an amazing physical feat that could only have been done by an athlete in top shape. Even though the production department of the film had complained mightily about the six weeks spent training the actors, it all paid off at that very moment. If Costner had been severely injured there was the very real possibility that we would have had to stop filming. Luca Bercovici continued to work in the film even with a dislocated shoulder, though his physical movement was severely limited for several weeks.

What we take away from these examples is that actors are not only willing to learn to do complicated things and are capable of learning very complicated skills, but that if we are going to put them into dangerous physical situations, it is critical that we take as much time as necessary to train them. Having been trained, they will be able to perform some of the safer parts of a stunt, and the dangerous bits can be left either to stunt performers or the miracle of computer animation. The latter allows directors to do things with their characters that look much more frightening than they actually were in the shooting situation.

Brett Ratner: You know there's that jump at the end of *Rush Hour* where Jackie falls from the top of the Convention Center down ten stories. It takes forever to set it up and we didn't shoot it until six in the morning... the worst time to do a crazy stunt after you've been up all night.

So he goes up and does the fall. He's got a harness on and a wire, but come on! He's free-falling one hundred feet. The wire is only backup.

CUT! Everybody's cheering, what an amazing jump.

So we look at a playback and I tell him, "We gotta do it again." Jackie says, "What? That was perfect, you're crazy!"

"Jackie, you're not Jackie Chan falling from up there. You fell like you were floating on air. You gotta show fear. I want you flailing your legs and arms. That's what's gonna give the audience a gasp." He was ready to argue with me, telling me, "You don't know what you're talking about." I can see he's really angry, saying, "Respect me, I know what I'm doing with the stunts." And I say, "I'm not agreeing with you. I don't see the fear. You're falling like you're floating on air, like you knew you were gonna hit that banner. You have to let the audience know from one second before you're saved that maybe you're gonna die. If you know you're not gonna die from the jump, then the audience isn't gonna feel it."

So he goes back and does the fall you see in the movie.

If *Rush Hour* were being shot today there would be no good justification to have Jackie Chan himself fall from 150 feet in the LA Convention Center when so much of it could be done with computer animation. Yes, it's exciting to be able to shoot it for real. Yes, it's great to be able to say at the press junket that Jackie Chan actually did this but there is a nasty price to be paid for a major screwup: someone's life.

To repeat, there is no movie ever made that is worth injury or worse. Families still feel the pain and loss of lives on *The Twilight Zone*, on *The Crow*, and several other films where actors, stunt performers or crew died needlessly. Given the fact that so much can be achieved in computer animation it seems an unnecessary risk to try to do extreme stunts for real.

SUMMARY

1. Unless some directorial tour de force is envisioned, action masters are usually pointless. They are almost always cut into banjo chips.

2. When shooting pieces of an action sequence always overlap a bit of the action from the previous cut.

3. Don't try to do too many actions in one take. Work in smaller bites. It is safer, more efficient, and will be cut into bits anyway.

4. Allow split seconds of time between actions to allow for better editing. Too fast is too hard to edit. E.g., Bridget Fonda in *Point of No Return.*

5. Create the extra time with directions to the actor that will fill the space so it doesn't look like a stalled moment, i.e., "aim before you shoot."

6. Fast can be too fast. Audiences get lost and are knocked about. E.g., *The Bourne Supremacy, Quantum of Solace.*

7. There are no hard and fast rules about what works and what doesn't. Totally dependent on how the story is being told.

8. Learn to use the camera to help the action look more exciting, more dynamic. This includes lenses, speeds, film stocks, and postproduction tricks.

9. Camera tricks that are not organic to the story hurt more than help.

10. Test out unusual technical ideas in advance… thoroughly. Don't wait until the day of the shoot.

11. No film is worth hurting anyone to make. The director has a moral responsibility to protect his cast and crew from danger.

12. Actors are often too willing to do stunts that may look easy and turn out badly. E.g., *Saturday Night Fever, Stakeout, The Crow.*

13. If physical action really must be done by the principal actors, then intensive training is critical. E.g., *American Flyers.*

Chapter 9

Strategy #4: See It Before You Shoot It

Storyboarding

Storyboards are the Linus' blankets for filmmakers. Words can only take us so far and can be wildly misinterpreted by crew and director alike. An invaluable assist to filmmaking, storyboards express the idea of a particular shot in a very precise way, allowing for an easy understanding of the shots that will be needed to tell the story excitingly. They reduce the confusion that results when we try to translate from the verbal world to the visual world. "Give me a two shot over here on a long lens" will mean many things to many people. Even the simplest chicken scratches on a piece of paper will do better than hundreds of words. Ridley Scott may start filming a scene with elaborate storyboards drawn in advance, but as the filming progresses he will sketch out very quick indicators of new ideas that arise during the filming. He always backs up his verbal instructions with little drawings.

But storyboards are not the answer to every problem. There are plenty of situations where they can be a waste of time. It's easy to get caught up in the process of storyboarding and forget that they are only guides to what the filmmaker intends to do. Let's take a look at five common mistakes filmmakers make when using storyboards.

1. What's the Point?

Even though a storyboard is stressing the visual idea, the underlying story itself can be obscured. Every single storyboard needs to answer this question: What is the story that is being told in this shot? Every shot must add to the overall story and can never be random. Verbally describing the story of the shot will help prevent it from just becoming a static image that loses its meaning.

A: Rick jumps over cops headfirst into Marianne's car
B: Reverse- slight up angle as Rick sails into the car

Nikita Knatz, Bird on a Wire, *1989*

I was directing a film that needed several establishing shots of buildings we had been unable to shoot in the regular schedule. I sent out an experienced 2nd unit director with a camera crew to get the needed shots. When I saw the dailies, I realized that the list of shots had been treated like a "to-do list" of errands. Yes the shots were of the buildings I had asked for, but no, they were not what I wanted, or more importantly what the film needed.

They looked like tourist photos, bland in the extreme, barely advancing the story. An establishing shot of the Eiffel Tower or the Capitol Records building in Hollywood needs to be more than just a shot of the building. It ought to convey the mood of the film and contribute to the story. Does the Eiffel Tower look ordinary or exciting or frightening? What mood does it convey? Does the Capitol Records building convey the vibrant Hollywood of the '60s or the decrepit aftermath of the record industry collapse? A good storyboard would have helped in this regard, whereas just a verbal description, "shot of Capitol Records building" without further explanation can lead to a boring shot that adds nothing to the film. Imagine the iconic house in *Psycho* or the spaceship in *Star Wars*. These are stunning and memorable images that are carefully and creatively conceived to add to the story, not just move us from one location to another.

The hysterically funny TV series *Seinfeld* played many scenes in a diner. For nine years, and 200 episodes, every time they cut there it was preceded by the same establishing shot of a real place, Tom's  Restaurant, 2880 Broadway in New York. Of course it's unfair to beat up on any show that has a limited budget and relies on stock footage just to get through the week. With apologies to *Seinfeld*, it's clear that shot only said one thing: "Now we're in the diner." It didn't add to the mood, the environment, the tone, or any other dynamics of the individual story.

2. Dialogue Scenes

These are scenes that are obviously carried by the actors and that will be shaped by them in rehearsal. To spend time drawing out individual shots for a dialogue scene can be a complete waste of time. Unless the director has in mind very unusual angles and compositions for a particular scene there is no need to spend time and resources on drawing elaborate storyboards for a dialogue scene. For the majority of scenes, however, when the actors arrive on set and help work out the staging a more dynamic version of the scene can be devised that can use the input of the DP, the camera operators, and the director.

Alfred Hitchcock would have disagreed strongly here, since he storyboarded every shot in his movies. He often said that the most interesting part of making a film for him was the preparation, when the script and storyboards are created, like elaborate blueprints for a building. After that, shooting and postproduction were just following through on his planned instructions.

3. Overdrawing

It's easy to forget that the storyboard is just a guide and shorthand for telling cameramen and crew what the finished shot should look like.

> **Brett Ratner:** One of the greatest values of storyboarding is to familiarize the whole cast and crew with the overall plan of a sequence. It helps them visualize what the director is planning and how they can contribute to making it work.

However it's hard for the artist to resist the temptation to spend a lot of time making a beautiful drawing, filled in with shading and colors, when something much simpler will do the job just as well. The only value to a very elaborate storyboard is for presentation to producers, financiers, or actors when showing them what the film will look like. If the final product is to be some form of animation or CGI then of course it will be best to be as specific as possible as the drawings themselves may become part of the final product. But for nearly everything else, simpler is more efficient and cheaper.

4. Losing the Flow

Because storyboards are a series of single frames like a comic book it can be easy to lose the flow of the action only seeing single static visual images. Skilled and experienced storyboard artists know how to convey a sense of action to indicate how one shot flows into another. Look at the *Bird on a Wire* storyboards later in this chapter to see how it's possible to express the dynamics of a real action scene versus postcard compositions that feel static.

5. Slaves to the Boards

Always stay flexible. Just because there's a storyboard doesn't mean you have to shoot it. Good ideas don't stop because the storyboarding has stopped. The set changes, the scene works differently, the DP or the actor makes a great suggestion. There are so many inspirations that happen on a set. It would be foolish to ignore good ideas just to adhere stubbornly to ideas from a few weeks ago.

> **Taylor Hackford:** I storyboarded every frame of my first film, *The Idolmaker*. Now I only storyboard effects sequences or action sequences that are complicated and expensive. I got on the set, with my AD, and my DP, they'd all looked at the storyboards, and started blocking a scene. We were changing things a bit here and a bit there; different angles, combining shots. Out of nowhere the line producer appeared. "There's a big problem here, Taylor. We've got a lot of money at stake." "What do you mean?" "You're not following the boards." "Well I know I'm not following the boards." "Well you should be. We need these boards to get through the scene." I said, "Excuse me, where did those boards come from? They came from inside my head. I worked through five different ways to shoot this scene and the best way I've found, version five, was the one I put on the boards. But now I've discovered a different way to shoot the scene that's better. It's my prerogative as a director. Don't hold these boards up like they're the Gospel that I'm ignoring. It's my blueprint. Do you think I've gone crazy and I don't know what I'm doing? No! I just discovered a better way to do it."

Good storyboard artists are worth their weight in No. 2 pencils. They can and should be much more than translators of the director's wishes. They can do more than just draw what the script says; they should be also allowed to add their own creativity to any sequence. Just as a writer knows in first draft to allow his scene or description to go on a bit longer than absolutely necessary, a good storyboard artist will draw many ideas to see what works the best. Then the director can winnow the storyboards down to the quintessential shots. Allow your storyboard artist as much freedom as possible under the circumstances of time and money to be able to try out several ideas. In films of mine like *Blue Thunder*, *Short Circuit* and *Bird on a Wire*, many visually exciting ideas came from the pencils of the storyboard artists. I told them they had complete freedom to experiment, knowing if they were constricted to drawing only what was dictated by me, that is *all* I would get back.

Here's a very dynamic sequence from *Bird on a Wire* that was storyboarded by the talented artist Nikita Knatz. Nikita works in Los Angeles and the film was shot in Vancouver, British Columbia. To familiarize Nikita with the area, we took photographs of the specific locations from angles that could work well for the action. Nikita used the photographs to more accurately visualize how a sequence might work.

Watch the following:

1. There is a clear goal to the sequence. It has a beginning, middle and end.
2. There are constant obstacles that grow in intensity.
3. There are surprises once the sequence gets to the train tunnel. In this case they reinforce the comedy of the film.

Notice how he creates a sense of movement, a feeling of energy in the frames. This kind of storyboard is not only a great guide but a wonderful source of ideas for shots. The storyboard of Mel Gibson upside down in the car from the point of view of the accelerator is genius even given the inspirations of Kurosawa and *The Hustler*.

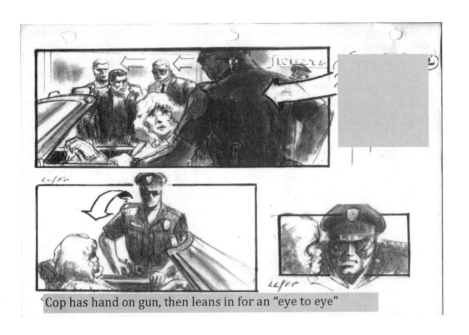

Cop has hand on gun, then leans in for an "eye to eye"

Rick dips down, displays remarkable ball handling....Then steps back as The 2 cops go down...Cop in other side of car

A: Rick takes a few steps & jumps over cops into Marianne's car

B: Reverse, slight up angle as Rick sails into the car

Con't-Rick lands inside

DS-Rick wedged under the dashboard (between her

Kurosawa/Hustler shot. Up angle past Rick on car

On floor toward Marianne. Rick: "Floor it, etc...."

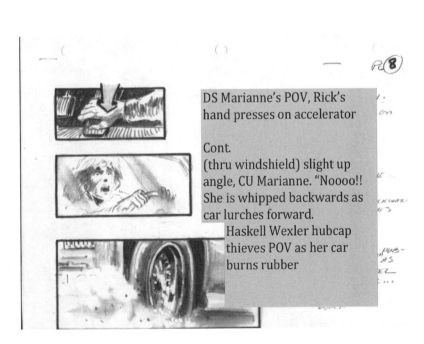

DS Marianne's POV, Rick's hand presses on accelerator

Cont.
(thru windshield) slight up angle, CU Marianne. "Noooo!! She is whipped backwards as car lurches forward.
Haskell Wexler hubcap thieves POV as her car burns rubber

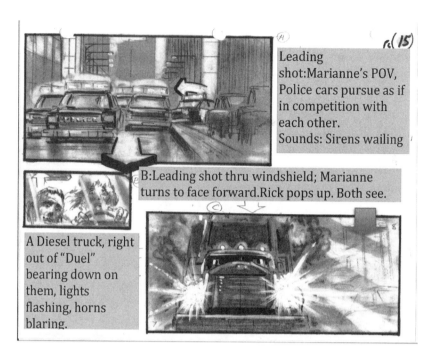

r.(15)

Leading shot:Marianne's POV, Police cars pursue as if in competition with each other.
Sounds: Sirens wailing

B:Leading shot thru windshield; Marianne turns to face forward.Rick pops up. Both see.

A Diesel truck, right out of "Duel" bearing down on them, lights flashing, horns blaring.

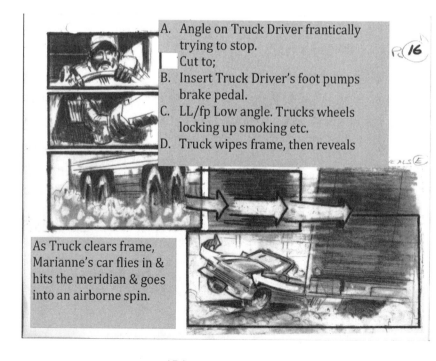

Pg. 16

A. Angle on Truck Driver frantically trying to stop.
   Cut to;
B. Insert Truck Driver's foot pumps brake pedal.
C. LL/fp Low angle. Trucks wheels locking up smoking etc.
D. Truck wipes frame, then reveals

EALS E

As Truck clears frame, Marianne's car flies in & hits the meridian & goes into an airborne spin.

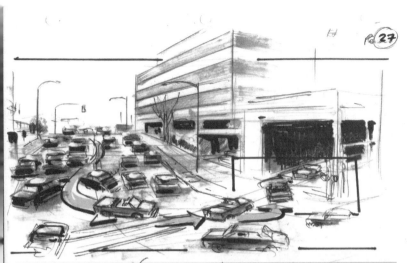

(intercut cu's Principals) LL/FP Long/wide shot as Marianne's car weaves downhill thru traffic (several hits/ accidents) then skids into Railroad Tunnell

a. Int. Tunnel, angle on Windshield.A light appears from OffStage and illuminates their faces. Move in on them with the light

b. Their POV A bright light coming toward them

cut to
Exterior Tunnel.
ECU RR crossing lights, bells start up. Barrier starts to descend, track with the barrier as it descends.

LL FP (fg barrier in soft focus) Cops stopped, get out call for ambulance anticipating

Reverse, Cops POV as her car comes backing out, fast.

Rick and Marianne come shooting out of the tunnel backwards. Reverse- High down angle as her car escapes.

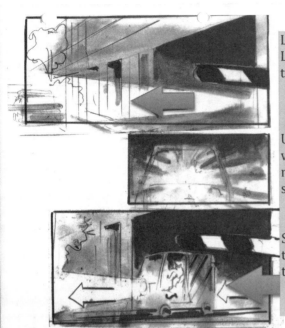

Low angle. Shaft of Light from out of tunnel.

Up angle. Bright light, very threatening-moves into & fills the screen
Wipe to

Small Rail checker trundles out of tunnel.

Tracking with the copcar as it tries to negotiate path through barrier to chase Marianne and Rick

2. Light comes out of the tunnel. NOTE: Light much brighter than the Rail Checker.
Cop clips barrier, breaks off the end.

Int. Cop car: they look to the barrier they hit and don't notice light coming from the other

Low angle. Train's light comes toward camera.

On Sound: diesel horn, etc.

Cont.

Int Cops car as they are blinded by the light, now very close and very loud.

Cont.

Cops POV train bearing down on them.

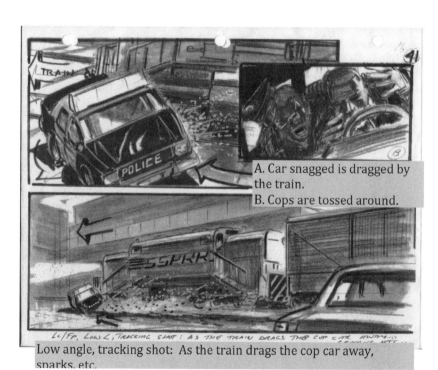

A. Car snagged is dragged by the train.
B. Cops are tossed around.

Low angle, tracking shot: As the train drags the cop car away, sparks, etc.

If one compared these storyboards with the final sequence in the film, many discrepancies and differences would be spotted[1]. This is the reality of filmmaking. The artist and director have many ideas but only so much time to shoot them. An unlimited budget would be terrific but that's rare. Also different ideas pop up during shooting. Rarely is the final film an exact translation of the storyboards.

In recent years software developers have created many good storyboard programs, both two-dimensional and three-dimensional. *Frame Forge*, *Shot Designer*, and *Toon Boom* are just a few. There are ones that work on the iPad, the iPhone, on Android, as well as laptops and desktops. Many are designed to work for directors who may not have the resources to hire a storyboard artist or who want to be able to express their ideas more directly. George Lucas has spent considerable time and resources developing a storyboarding program that would be completely intuitive for a director unskilled in drawing, and also allow images to be animated.

Though the results of some of these programs can be quite spectacular they have a hard time equaling the work of a good storyboard artist working with either pad and pencil, or on a computer. The storyboard artist brings an artistic sensibility to the job that few directors are trained to be able to do. Even directors who have great drawing literacy, such as Alfred Hitchcock or Ridley Scott, have always relied on storyboard artists to help realize their visions.

Can't Afford No Stinkin' Storyboards?

In the worlds of low-budget filmmaking and episodic television, there is often no time or money to produce storyboards. The director in league with the DP and the assistant director have to come up with a shot list that can be interpreted just on a verbal basis. If a creative team is well synchronized and used to working together, maybe no shot list at all is needed. There can be just an

---

[1] http://www.amazon.com/s/ref=nb_sb_ss_c_0_10?url=search-alias%3Dmovies-tv &field-keywords=bird+on+a+wire&sprefix=Bird+on+a+%2Caps%2C311

unspoken understanding, as the crew stands on the location, as to what shots need to be taken and how the sequence will lay out in editing. It can be like a great jazz combo that plays together without written music, creating something terrific in the process. However, if a filmmaker is going to work this way, he should know that there is a great danger in making things up on the spot; too many shots may be taken or forgotten, the angles chosen may be weak, etc., and the whole point of saving money by not having storyboards can be wiped out by poor storytelling.

In 1987 I was location scouting for *Stakeout*[2] with Richard Dreyfuss and Emilio Estevez. One of the first "buddy-cop thrillers," it took place in Seattle, Washington, (read Vancouver, BC) where Dreyfus' and Estevez's characters are in pursuit of an escaped convict. Jim Kouf, the writer of *Con-Air, Rush Hour,* and *National Treasure,* wrote a scene that had the detectives chasing the bad guy along the docks where hundreds of fishing boats are moored up. Kouf had written that Estevez's character would eventually get knocked into the water and Dreyfuss' character would have to abandon the chase in order to rescue him from drowning.

But at that point that's all we knew. Kouf had time to sketch out a rough idea of where a pursuit could happen but had not yet come up with the details. Both he and I kept going back to the location over a period of several weeks, to see if we could devise an idea that we would be excited about. Many times we left that location somewhat dispirited, but with the fragile wish that something would present itself as a good idea for a chase. We hoped. The pressure was on as the time for shooting was getting really close and we still hadn't figured anything out. We actually were at the point of doing a technical scout where all department heads go to the location to see what we intend to do and how we intend to shoot it. On the day of the tech scout we got to the docks, and still had no inspiration. Too stressful.

---

[2] http://www.amazon.com/s/ref=nb_sb_ss_i_4_7?url=search-alias%3Dmovies-tv &field-keywords=stakeout+blu+ray&sprefix

So we sent everyone for coffee while Jim Kouf, Connie Palmisano, my stunt coordinator, and I took one more frantic circle around the docks where the fishing ships delivered their catch to be cleaned, canned, and shipped. We spotted a giant steel hopper beside the dock we had never looked at. We climbed up above it to take a closer look. The harbor master explained that fishing ships dumped their catches into the hopper, which would funnel the fish below to a processing room where one hundred Asian women, none of whom spoke English, would WHACK behead, clean, and WHACK gut the fish with bad knives that slung fish blood in all directions.

As the three of us stood on a balcony watching cod flop into the hopper relentlessly, one single idea popped into everyone's minds simultaneously. We all looked at each other and started laughing. WHACK!

Almost as one, we outlined the missing link we had been searching for: Dreyfuss and Estevez, searching for the convict, would split up. Dreyfuss would go to the upper floors. When he came out onto the balcony overlooking the hopper, the convict would jump down on him from above. The two men would fall into the hopper as smelly oily cod poured onto their heads. The convict would knock Dreyfuss down, escaping while Dreyfuss was being sucked down into the black funnel along with thousands of fish. He would scream for Estevez to come and help, but to no avail. We then could cut inside the prep room as the Asian women see a very fishy, smelly Richard Dreyfuss on their conveyer belt; ducking their knives and begging their pardon he  would slide onto the floor and run to join his partner.

We never storyboarded this fight. We barely shot-listed it. Partially because we were shooting in a couple of days and there was so much pressure to save money that we didn't want to fly in a storyboard artist from Los Angeles. The third reason was that we felt confident we had such a clear idea of what had to be shot that we could get by with a good shot list and no storyboards. We saw all the pieces of the puzzle as a team and knew that we could shoot it well with just the images that were alive and buzzing in our heads. It had unexpected incidents, funny jeopardy, but jeopardy nonetheless, a good scene build and a final cap to the scene as both Estevez and Dreyfuss end up in the water.

I do not recommend this technique for anyone to do on a regular basis. But it can be done, and often is done in situations where there is no time or money to storyboard. It just means that the people who are carrying the idea around in their heads better have a *very clear and well thought out idea of the shots that are needed.* Otherwise, the result could be a horrible jumbled mess. There is probably nothing more embarrassing than being in the editing bay when the editor asks, "Where's the close-up of Richard Dreyfuss?" Or, "Where's the insert of the gun falling on the ground?" Even a half-baked series of storyboards would probably have reminded the director what was needed.

You have been warned.

Coverage

How many shots do you need? How much coverage is enough? These questions can haunt even the most experienced directors. There is no right answer since every scene is unique to every filmmaker. The Hong Kong style of filmmaking is different from the American style. In between there is every kind of mash-up imaginable. Brett Ratner talks about his approach to action in *Rush Hour* as compared to Jackie Chan's approach on films he directed. Ultimately it's an artistic choice that the filmmaker has to make. On one side the seemingly endless fight scene in *The Protector* is all told in one spectacular shot. Conversely, Lars von Trier might have used one hundred cameras to tell the same story as he did in the musical numbers for *Dancer in the Dark*. The shots are chosen on the basis of what the filmmaker wants to see. What detail is important to understanding the story and the geography? What makes the story more exciting? What creates suspense, or terror, or shock?

If there is a rule of thumb, it would be shoot as many angles as possible in the time available. The second rule: shoot as many shots as possible from a specific character's point of view. This will make the scene personal and connected to the characters. If the shots are generic, then the scene will become generic and depersonalized. If the heart of the scene, the part that the audience should be grabbing on to, is lost, they will remain detached from the characters.

Imagine watching exciting sports like football, basketball, or soccer as if you didn't understand the game. It looks like a bunch of people running around like crazies back and forth, back and forth. The strategy and tactics don't make sense. You're detached from the teams and players. The experience is boring. This is mostly because the games have to be shot in a generic fashion, even with many cameras. It's really hard to get connected emotionally to the individual players, except after the games when they are interviewed or appear in beer and underwear commercials.

If you understand the game and have a specific team to root for, watching it can be wildly exciting, often leading to riots and violence afterwards. The job of the filmmaker is to tell the story of the game visually in a way that will get anyone involved, whether they understand the game or not. Compare the way pro football is shot versus great football films like *Friday Night Lights* or *North Dallas Forty*. In pro football you are watching the game to root for your team, to follow the plays, to see the spectacle. In a great football film you are also getting involved with individual players, maybe the coach, maybe the water boy. Both things can be entertaining but each in its own way.

SUMMARY

1. Storyboarding is a vital part of planning any action scene. It ensures the right shots will be made, that everyone will know precisely what should happen.

2. Always articulate the story point of every shot. Just a drawing of a building isn't enough information.

3. Dialogue scenes only need to be storyboarded for unusual angles or staging.

4. Storyboards are just communication tools, not an end in themselves. Don't spend too much time making works of art.

5. The storyboard artist must express the dynamic movement of the cast and the camera in any scene. Otherwise the drawing will be bland.

6. Storyboard programs like *Frame Forge 3d*, *Toon Boom*, and *Shot Designer* can be extremely helpful designing scenes. They can be very time-consuming if we get carried away.

7. Don't be a slave to your storyboards. When new and better ideas come up incorporate them. When shots can be combined or eliminated do it. E.g., Taylor Hackford's *The Idolmaker*.

8. If you don't have the money for a storyboard artist, the drawing skill, or the time, then make a careful shot list in advance. Improvising on the day is fun but dangerous. Pressures of shooting cause things to be overlooked.

9. Get as much coverage on a scene as you can in the time allowed. You will be glad to have it. Your editor will buy you dinner.

10. In coverage, emphasize the point of view of the main characters as much as possible.

Chapter 10

Strategy #5: Mystery, Surprise, Suspense

One of the best thrillers in recent years is Adrian Lyne's *Fatal Attraction*[1], starring Michael Douglas, Glenn Close, and Anne Archer. It starts with an affair that Michael Douglas' character begins with Glenn Close's character. Realizing that he has made a terrible mistake he tries to end the affair. However Glenn Close's character refuses to let go. Determined to keep Michael Douglas for herself she becomes unhinged, and whatever the cost, sets out to destroy his marriage[2].

In the original version of the film, Glenn Close kidnaps Douglas' daughter and causes his wife, played by Anne Archer, to have a car wreck. Douglas confronts Close at her apartment. After a horrific fight where she tries to stab him with a giant kitchen knife, he escapes her apartment and goes home to his family. The next morning the police show up and arrest him for murder. Close has committed suicide with the kitchen knife that has his fingerprints on it. The family is in shock as he is taken away in handcuffs.

---

[1] http://www.amazon.com/s/ref=nb_sb_ss_i_0_6?url=search-alias%3Dmovies-tv &field-keywords=fatal+attraction&sprefix
[2] http://www.youtube.com/watch?v=k1QuLIPFZL0

The director of *Fatal Attraction*, Adrian Lyne, recalls that when the film went to previews, it played extremely well... until the ending. Instead of the audience being pleased, they seemed to have little reaction. The "movie seemed to go flat."[3]

William Goldman once famously remarked, "In Hollywood, nobody knows anything." But one thing Hollywood filmmakers do know is that if an audience is bummed out or let down by an ending and don't walk out singing the end credits they won't recommend it to their friends. And friends' recommendations are the most powerful advertising on the planet. They can make sleeper films like *Paranormal Activity* or *The Blair Witch Project* into monster hits. They can also destroy monster tent-poles like *The Hulk* or *John Carter* in a few tweets.

So a new ending was conceived and shot.

NO FOOLING AROUND SPOILER ALERT! PROCEED AT YOUR OWN RISK!

This time Douglas goes home after the fight and tends to his wife who is recovering from the car crash. He goes downstairs to make her some tea. She is running a bath when Close enters the bathroom and attacks her with the same kitchen knife we saw earlier. Douglas is unaware what's happening upstairs. Only when the bathtub overflows and Douglas sees water dripping through the ceiling does he react. He runs upstairs and pulls the crazy woman away from his wife, finally drowning Close in the tub.

Tension lets up and we all start to relax... when suddenly Glenn Close *explodes* out of the water wielding the knife. She plunges it toward his chest... only to be shot by Anne Archer.

At the next preview, this version sent the audience into orbit. The rating was one of the highest Paramount had ever seen.

What was the difference?

Suspense.

---

3 Robert Abele, "Girl Crazy," *DGA Quarterly*, Spring 2010, 24.

Suspense is the most powerful method of holding an audience's attention. We know that in any dramatic situation the essential ingredient is conflict. No conflict, no drama.

Rule #1. Mild Conflict, Mild Interest

When a film begins we follow along, waiting to see what develops. We'll grant almost any film a few minutes of attention. If the conflict grows in intensity we can become more curious about how this is all going to turn out. The beginning of suspense is when the audience starts asking, "What will happen next?"

> **François Truffaut:** The art of creating suspense must involve the audience so they become a participant in the film. The audience is required to play along with the film. "What happens next?"[4]

But… no involvement, no suspense. Also if we know how something turns out because we anticipated it or we have seen it already, the suspense is deflated. We know that Little Red Riding Hood is not going to be eaten by the Big Bad Wolf, but our five-year-old nephew doesn't know that. He's pulling at our sleeve demanding, "What's gonna happen now?" The pressure is on the filmmaker to stay ahead of the audience so they don't guess what's coming next; and if they *do* guess, their guess should be wrong, which is also entertaining and involving.

> **Alfred Hitchcock:** Suspense is a three-way dance between the director, the film, and the audience, who also have to play.[5]

Let's say by way of example that a man, Fred, leaves home to catch a plane to a very important meeting. He drives to the airport, parks his car, and checks in on time. Is this suspenseful? Of course not. It's a boring part of the story that would be cut from any film almost immediately. In the final film we'd cut it down so we only see Fred close the door of his house and then we'd cut to the gate

---

[4] François Truffaut, *Hitchcock/Truffaut* (New York: Simon & Schuster, 1960), 51.
[5] Ibid., 50

as he hands over his boarding pass. This is simple narration and the audience is only marginally involved. They saw what was going to happen ages ago and immediately get bored.

> **Alfred Hitchcock:** The public always likes to be one jump ahead of the story; they like to feel they know what's coming next. So you deliberately play upon this fact to control their thoughts.[6]

But suppose now that as Fred gets in the car, he looks at his watch and says, "Oh man, I'll never make the flight." Then the whole ride becomes a series of difficulties as things conspire to delay him: highway construction, traffic, ambulances, Shriners' parades. The more things that go wrong, the more anxious he becomes as he tries to drive around the problems and call ahead on his cell phone, which can't get a signal. Maybe he gets a flat tire or in an accident. If we have done our job as storytellers, we will have made sure to keep the stakes high, so that everyone knows how important the meeting is. Otherwise the audience will relax and think he can just catch a later plane. This is plot-driven narration that creates suspense. Fred's trip to the airport continues to surprise the audience and keep them from getting ahead of the story.

Plain Story: Jack is in trouble and goes to a lawyer to seek advice. The lawyer gives it to him and Jack leaves.

Plot-Driven Story: The lawyer is skeptical and reluctant to get involved. If we care about Jack and his plight we start to worry if he will get representation or not. By introducing a conflict, feelings of apprehension and anxiety are created in the audience that invest this ordinary situation with drama.

If you didn't get it before: What's said but not shown will probably be lost on the viewer. The events in these narratives must be shown and not just talked about in dialogue or narration. Remember the power of the visual over the spoken word. With poor Fred trying to make his flight, imagine how the scene would play if we didn't see his terrible trip, but when he settles into his

---

[6] François Truffaut, *Hitchcock/Truffaut*, 206.

coach seat he tells his new neighbor that he had a heck of a time getting there, running into traffic, had a flat, yada yada yada? It's just not the same is it? It would take a really great actor to be able to make that story live by words alone.

In *Jaws* Robert Shaw's fishing captain has to relate verbally the terrifying tale of the sinking of the US navy cruiser *Indianapolis* where the surviving crew was left floating in the ocean being devoured by sharks. There was no budget to shoot any kind of scene where we can actually see men floating in the sea and being attacked. So the whole scene was on Robert Shaw to make this come alive. Steven Spielberg was extremely wise to fly this great actor all the way from England to play a relatively small part. Without Shaw's talent the scene could have lain flatter than a dead skunk on the interstate. Moral: we don't always have Robert Shaw to carry the day. Show it!

They're Coming! Get Out!

In *Stakeout*, Richard Dreyfuss is a detective, Chris, staked out with his partner, Bill, near the apartment of a woman, Maria, where they think an escaped convict may show up... or not. After days of waiting and boredom, Chris breaks in through her bedroom window and starts searching for signs of the convict: letters, photos, messages, whatever. He leaves Bill on duty across the street as the lookout.

Suddenly Bill sees Maria driving up to her apartment. He tries to warn Chris on the walkie-talkie but gets no response. Chris has turned off his walkie so Bill gets more and more frantic with no result.

Now we have the beginnings of suspense. When they were just staking out the house we only had their hilarious banter to break the boredom of a stakeout. When Chris breaks in the apartment there didn't seem to be much danger. Nobody was home. When Maria arrives in her car, the danger elevated but Bill could warn Chris, who would get out of there quickly. But the second we find out that Chris doesn't know what's coming and there is no way to warn him, the whole situation elevates to the level of really good suspense.

Alfred Hitchcock: In the usual form of suspense, it is indispensable that the public be made perfectly aware of all the facts involved: otherwise, there is no suspense.[7]

The suspense has been created. Now what?

Keep it alive as long as possible is what.

It's not enough to just have the situation, it's time to keep it working, draw it out for all it's worth. The longer the audience can be gripped by the situation the more fun it is. How long it can be sustained is a matter of not letting the characters off the hook and keeping the situation alive and changing constantly. A standoff will get dull very quickly. If we don't do it right the question changes from "What happens next?" to "When is something going to happen?" That's when suspense is lost and along with it the audience.

Back to Chris in the apartment. Maria is heading upstairs and Bill is having a metaphorical heart attack across the street. The situation is shot with adrenaline when Chris hears Maria come in the front door and he "Oh Shits!" He tries to hide signs of his presence, and she's coming up the stairs. No way he can get out the window in time. What to do? As she hits the top step he hits the floor and rolls under the bed. Now she's walking around inches from his face and turns on some hot music. From his partial point of view, blocked by the bedspread, he sees her shoes come off and clothes hitting the floor. Bare legs head for the shower and he sees his chance to escape.

This is pretty good up to this point. Chris could crawl out the window and the scene would have finished nicely. But Richard Dreyfuss wanted to do more with it. So he added in action. As he

---

7 François Truffaut, *Hitchcock/Truffaut*, 50.

heads for the window he can't resist the fact she is in the shower. Got to peek! He sneaks to the bathroom door, a really bad idea... for him, not the audience. We know he'll get caught. He peeks around the door and...

Suddenly she turns off the water and Chris has to move... quickly. He heads for the window as the shower curtain is pulled back and she steps out to get a towel. Just as his feet disappear through the window, she steps back in the bedroom drying her hair. What a terrific extra addition to the suspense. It was not only scary but also funny and very sexy.

It proves that suspense doesn't just have to be serious and frightening, it can be many things, comic, sexy, romantic, tragic, historic. Maybe Polonius had a point: you *can* mix all these things up.

Setups, Builds, and Switches

One of the obvious things about storytelling is that the audience needs to know enough facts and prior circumstances, events that went before the story began, in order to follow what's happening now. *Little Red Riding Hood* is not going to be scary if the two-year-old who is hearing it doesn't understand how dangerous wolves are. *Star Wars* is going to be tough to follow if we don't know that "A long time ago, in a galaxy far, far away... it is a period of civil war."

If we are talking about building suspense in a scene or an entire film we need to set things up carefully in advance. *No Country for Old Men* does this skillfully in setting up the character of Chigurh, the sociopathic assassin. At the beginning we see him for the first time being arrested on a routine traffic stop. The sheriff's deputy takes him to the station in handcuffs where we see Chigurh violently garrote the deputy with the handcuffs and steal his patrol car. He then pulls over a motorist on the highway and kills him with an evil-looking pneumatic weapon used in slaughterhouses to kill cattle. Now the audience knows how dangerous this man is and they will be hyper-aware of this for the rest of the movie.

The first time that Chigurh kills someone, it is a shock, simple but not pure. Very effective. The second time, with the motorist, shows that his killing is almost random, out of control, not just to escape the police. For the rest of the movie whenever he appears, our anxiety level goes up and suspense is automatically created. In the scene at the gas station where Chigurh toys with the owner the suspense is thick, palpable. Though both characters are standing stock still, the owner's growing fear radiates from the screen. There is never a violent gesture or harsh word.

At one moment Chigurh tosses a crushed peanut wrapper onto the counter where it crackles as it re-expands. This tiny event is as unnerving as a bomb. But if the Coen Brothers had not done such a good job setting up Chigurh, this scene would not play nearly so well.

Alfred Hitchcock was a genius at telling stories that brilliantly set up characters and situations in ways designed to create suspense. He always took this one step further by withholding some crucial information from the audience and springing it on us later, confounding our expectations, surprising us with something we didn't expect.

In *Psycho* we are shocked — unnecessary SPOILER ALERT— when Janet Leigh's character is brutally stabbed to death in the motel shower. Anthony Perkins, playing the motel manager, discovers her bloody naked body and runs to his house yelling "Mother, NO!!"

He starts to clean up the blood and hide the evidence to protect his mother, who must be insane. The audience even starts to worry that he might not do a good enough job. This is a brilliant bait and switch by Hitchcock who has totally invested us in

Janet Leigh and her dilemma and in a few short moments turns us around so we become worried about a sweet, lonely motel manager who has a crazy mother. At the same time there is now an aura of danger around Anthony Perkins especially when he goes to see his mother.

> **Alfred Hitchcock:** When a burglar goes into a room, all the time he's going through the drawers the public is generally anxious for him. When Anthony Perkins is looking at the car sinking in the pond... the public is thinking "I hope it goes all the way down!" It's a natural instinct.[8]

And of course there is the final surprise switch revealing the mother has been dead all along and Perkins, deeply insane, has been posing as her all along. This skillful storytelling keeps us on the edge of our seats as Hitchcock sustains the suspense scene after scene.

In *Diabolique*[9], Henri-Georges Clouzot's masterpiece, he carefully sets up the story of a woman who is so abused by her violent husband that her girlfriend persuades her to kill him. His abuse and humiliation of her is so bad that the audience is rooting for her to get rid of the creep. With much difficulty, the two women manage to sedate him and drown him in a bathtub. They dump his body in a leaf-filled swimming pool for him to be discovered as an accidental drowning.

After three days when the body doesn't float to the surface the women start to panic and have the pool drained... only to discover the body has vanished. So far the suspense has been built totally on their efforts to commit murder and get away with it. Now this shocking surprise raises the ante by asking, "Where did the body go?"

The story continues to work so well because the stakes have been raised dramatically. It needed to build in intensity and suspense

---

[8] François Truffaut, *Hitchcock/Truffaut*, 207.
[9] http://www.amazon.com/s/ref=nb_sb_ss_i_1_10?url=search-alias%3Daps&field-key words=diabolique+blu+ray&sprefix

because what had been driving the story up till now had nearly run out of fuel. Just as any scene, whether action, suspense, or dialogues between characters, comic or dramatic, needs conflict, the conflict cannot remain static without becoming boring. It needs to grow, to build. As these examples demonstrate, the answer is often an unexpected surprise that changes everything.

Another Cat Skinner

How do you create suspense? Lee Child, the author of the *Jack Reacher* novels, asked this question in an article for the *New York Times*. His question is another way to skin the "What Happens Next?" approach. It's not as simple as asking a question like "How do you bake a cake?" because the answer to this is just a set of instructions. "Add flour, eggs, and milk blah, blah, blah." There's no puzzle here and it's certainly not compelling. Try a more fun question: "How do you make your family hungry?" Anyone?

What does Lee Child recommend?

Notice I haven't given you an answer yet. I could have, but Lee Child said to hold off and see if we could keep you reading. So I won't... yet. And you're still reading. That's part of the point.

He wants authors to create a mystery that the audience will want to solve.

"How do you make your family hungry?" Hold on... hold on... "And the answer is: You make them wait four hours for dinner." He believes that writers should "ask or imply a question at the beginning of the story and then... delay the answer."[10]

You know how almost every TV show, whether it's a reality show, a newscast, or an episode of *Criminal Minds*, always asks a question just before they go to commercial? "Will this couple 'Love it or List It,'" "Man thrown on subway tracks, details after this." "Will Poo-poo throw The Main Attraction out of the house? Find

---

[10] Lee Child, "A Simple Way to Create Suspense," *New York Times*, December 8, 2012, SR8.

out after these blatant efforts to raid your wallet." Clearly these are just shabbily-disguised techniques to keep you tuned to that channel. Like Siamese cats with ADD, our fingers hover over the remote control. The producers had to come up with a way to keep you from using your instant veto power. They create suspense by asking a question that (hopefully) you want to know the answer to.

Lee Child contends that "the success of the tactic [doesn't] depend on intrigue. Even viewers with no interest at all [stick] around to find out. Humans are hard-wired. They need to know. Even viewers who [know] the answer for sure [stick] around, in order to be gratified."[11]

Child says he asks questions early on in his novels that have to be answered before the story is done. Questions that the reader will want answered.

"Someone killed someone else: who? You'll find out at the end of the book," Child writes. "Something weird is happening: what? You'll find out at the end of the book. Something has to be stopped: how? You'll find out at the end of the book."[12]

That means the writer, or in our case, the filmmakers, want to hold out answers to these questions as long as possible. What keeps the story alive and burning is a slow unveiling of the final answer.

Mystery vs. Surprise vs. Suspense

Surprise and suspense are the offspring of mystery, which itself sprang from simple narration. Each new generation of storytelling genres has built on the previous one to be interesting for different audiences. To oversimplify, simple narration is like a straightforward news story. Journalists are taught to stick to the facts and leave opinions to the editorial staff. If at dinner, a doctor is telling her husband, Bob, the stuff that happened that day at the ER, laced with her opinions of the patients, the nurses, the Federal

---

[11] Ibid.
[12] Ibid.

government, and the food in the cafeteria, she is combining facts, opinions and perhaps fiction.

Mystery enters the room when the story becomes a puzzle. The doctor tells Bob about a patient with an unknown illness that they struggled to diagnose and treat. It can be very interesting to Bob to hear about something puzzling. He may try to figure out an answer, even though he's not a doctor. It's purely an intellectual game for him, in the same way Sherlock Holmes gets involved in the case of a man who had his throat torn out but was inside a locked room that no one could have entered. This is another puzzle that makes us start asking questions and looking for an answer. "What about the windows? Was there a key to the door? How about the fireplace chimney?" This is a puzzle that's fun to attack.

When does it become suspense? Whenever Bob starts to ask, "What happens next?" of course.

To return to the ER, our husband Bob thought about the patient's puzzling illness and is about to go back to his daily Sudoko when his wife mentions that the patient is the wife of his closest friend, Herman. Unless Bob is a heartless jerk, this news immediately gets his attention. Now he wants to hear more about it. He has more questions. He starts to think about calling Herman, sending flowers, going to visit the wife in the hospital. He wants to know more about the prognosis, tries to offer his own uneducated guesses and so on. He is emotionally involved with the characters, a big step forward. He wants to know "What happens next?"

This is the kind of effect we want to have on our audiences. We want to get them caught up in events. We want them to care about what's happening now and very importantly, what's going to happen in the future. Without that we don't have a suspenseful film, maybe only a bad synopsis of one.

Hitchcock is always acknowledged as the Master of Suspense but is seldom called the Master of Surprise. Yet when we look more closely than these clichéd MFAs, we see he deserves a PhD in both areas. He uses these techniques like a composer uses instruments in the orchestra. Suspense and surprise are like musical instruments and as such may be used whenever they are appropriate, not exclusively. Suspense without surprise can be monotonous, but the two together make good cinema. The converse is also true.

The classic illustration of surprise is a bus loaded with passengers coming toward us down the street. As it draws parallel it suddenly explodes, sending a fireball into the sky.

In an example of suspense, we would be inside the bus where we could see the passengers with perhaps a little girl in the middle. A man gets on and pays his fare. As he works his way toward a seat in the back we see wires under his jacket and he is clutching a button of some sort. We realize there is a bomb about to go off and we start to ask questions: "What happens now? When will the bomb go off? Will the people be killed?" Our anxiety goes up as we are suspended in time.

The difference is obvious. In the surprise incident we get a great shock as the bus explodes. It lasts for a few seconds as our adrenaline surges and then it is over. Very thrilling and very quick.

In the suspense example we are given time to get to know the people on the bus, even briefly. Little girls are always appealing so she's a quick, if well-worn, shorthand for the audience. Now we introduce the terrorist and his bomb. This probably won't take much longer on screen than the surprise example. Once they see the wires and the detonator, the audience is asking, "What happens next?" They are hooked. The scene can now play out for quite some time, sustaining the suspense all the while. We can show the terrorist trying to build up his nerve to detonate the bomb. We could have the little girl looking at him and smiling. How does that affect him? Does it unnerve him? What if she sees the wires but doesn't know what they are? The audience is by now screaming at the movie screen, "Get out, there's a bomb! Quick, tell somebody what you see! Show your mother!"

A talented filmmaker like Brian De Palma will jones on this, milking it for all it's worth. He can draw it out for several minutes, having the passengers realize what's going on and trying to subdue the terrorist who will detonate his bomb if he could only get his finger back on the button. Meanwhile the bus driver is trying to contact his dispatcher who keeps putting him on hold. And the woman in the back is starting to give birth, but gosh darn, she's not covered by "O-Busa-Care" so she wants to delay delivery till they get to the free clinic.

Hitchcock's point is when the filmmaker shares something with the audience in a suspense situation they become more invested emotionally than with a surprise where they witness events more passively. They get a great thrilling jolt that is brief compared to the highly intriguing and involving suspense which can last for a much longer time and make a much stronger impact on them.

There are some films and television series that have succeeded in building the entire film or series on one event that creates suspense right from the beginning. Jan de Bont and Graham Yost's *Speed* is entirely based on the simple premise that a terrorist threatens to blow up a bus on the Los Angeles freeways if it travels at less than fifty miles an hour.

Nick of Time[13] posits that if an innocent dad does not kill the governor of California in the next ninety minutes his daughter will die. The TV series *24* could draw a story out for twenty-four episodes, in real time, maintaining suspense throughout as Jack Bauer continually saved the world. He kept saving us for nine seasons, 216 episodes, a tour de force of storytelling.

---

[13] http://www.youtube.com/watch?v=o6trRzB8fiA

SUMMARY

1. Mild conflict = mild interest. Events must be heightened as sequence progresses. E.g., *Blue Thunder* LA River helicopter chase scene from Part I.

2. If the audience is not involved in the characters, there will be no suspense.

3. In suspense, the audience must keep asking, "What happens next?"

4. Visual trumps verbal. Verbal descriptions are seldom really heard by the audience unless the narrator is exceptionally talented.

5. The filmmaker must dole out just enough facts for the audience to appreciate the story. E.g., Chigurh and the Gas Station Proprietor in *No Country for Old Men*.

6. Suspense is enhanced when the audience knows more than the characters. E.g., *Stakeout*, Dreyfuss in Maria's apartment.

7. Keep switching the problems to keep interest alive and building.

8. Mystery stories present puzzles for the audience to solve but are not necessarily suspenseful.

9. Surprise comes out of nowhere and is exciting but is over quickly. Suspense can be drawn out for a long time. The bus exploding.

PART III

Preparing the Scene: The Director's Checklist

Before Rehearsal?

François Truffaut, playing himself in his masterpiece, *Day for Night*, likened directing a film to taking a long journey by wagon train through the Old West. At first you start with great excitement and anticipation. As the journey continues you meet with many obstacles that are overcome by your determination and skill. But over time these wear you down and by the middle of the trip you begin to wonder if it will ever be over. You start to throw away things to lighten the load. Valuables get tossed in the expediency of the moment. Even something that's really needed is not as important as just getting there. Finally that's all that seems to matter.

Of course this means that the preparation for the journey is everything. Supplies, skilled help, finances and finally a good, no, a great map. Without it our wagon train can veer off course, get sidetracked, lose focus. With the map we can adjust to unforeseen problems that come up along the way. But if the map is not good, not well documented and detailed, more problems can imperil the trip. When the infamous Donner Party wagon train set out for California in 1846 they had been persuaded that the way through the Sierra Nevada Mountains was a pass that led to the Great Salt Lake Desert. What they did not know was if they embarked after October they were likely to encounter heavy snows, which is exactly what happened. They were trapped for an entire winter in the eponymous Donner Pass. Few survived and cannibalism was rife.

As we begin to prepare any script we read it several times with care, making notes, getting visual ideas and casting notions, talking to the author, our designers and DPs, etc. This is well and good for whatever it yields. Our intuition and experience will do a lot of work for us in creating an overall vision of the film we want to make. However it is a bit haphazard for prime time. Some scenes may work wonderfully and others are problematic. It's not that we're not getting the right answers. It's that we're not asking the right questions.

We often reread the script we have labored over to better understand it. But after a while something inevitably happens: being too close too long blinds us. The inspirations and ideas that came easily to us on the first few readings have slowed to a crawl and the whole script starts to blur. This of course is why those first few readings are so critical. The same applies when we are running edited versions of our film in post: during the first few times through it's easy to see how to tell the story better. Then quickly a sort of movie macular degeneration sets in. All the scenes start to run together and lose meaning. I have often looked years later at movies or television shows I have made and been amazed with how well, or sometimes, how badly they worked. I saw things I had never noticed before. I've had ideas that I wished I had when I was shooting the film. Too late now. I have to take a very long break from a film before I can see objectively what I created.

Fortunately there are ways to escape this blindness. And fortunately these ways can be used during the making of the film, not afterward, when it may be too late. We are talking about the checklist one can run through at any point in the making of a film that will keep us on the path the film should be taking. The questions we can ask at the beginning of preparation can be re-visited time and again to help us stay on track. At any time during pre-production while casting, picking locations, choosing wardrobe; while shooting, picking camera angles, helping actors with performances; while posting, refining the edited versions or choosing music and sound effects, color timing and even titles — we can ask those questions to see if we're going the right way. The questions refocus our brain and keep us going toward our final destination: an audience to whom we want to communicate our vision. This list doesn't originate with me but has been developed and created by our best directors and writers over the years. We can thank Constantin Stanislavsky, Sydney Pollack, Frank Capra, Elia Kazan, William Ball, Nicholas Proferes, Judith Weston, and my professorial colleagues and students at the Dodge College of Media Arts at Chapman University, among others, for sharing their wisdom.

What's important to remember is that the list doesn't need to be asked or answered in any particular order. We don't necessarily see the answer to the "big picture" question first. We often start with a much smaller question such as: "What stops our hero from getting what he wants... in this moment?" and "What does he want?" We may think we are wandering in the dark, but as we keep digging and asking key questions, the big picture becomes clearer.

It's easier to scratch away at the corners, the nooks and crannies of a single scene or an entire screenplay first. Look at any scene, a good one or one that doesn't quite make sense and ask an easy question first such as "What does the villain expect to get at the end of this scene?" Nicholas Proferes, the author of *Film Directing Fundamentals*, calls this kind of questioning the director's "detective work" on the script. The analogy to police work is quite apt. When police come to a crime scene they know there is a story there with a theme, characters, plot, and probably dialogue. But what is it anyway? How does it all tie together? There are many interpretations of any crime scene but what's the true one? So the detective work starts in earnest, picking away at the facts and starting to create a picture of the whole that's based in reality, not just the imagination of the detective.

To illustrate the checklist we'll use as examples scenes from *Kramer vs. Kramer, Juno, No Country for Old Men* and the 2010 version of *True Grit*.

THE CHECKLIST

1. What happened before this scene?

2. What does it add?

3. What's different at the end?

4. Whose point of view?

5. Where are the beats?

6. Where is the Tipping Point in the scene?

7. What do they want?

8. What do they expect?

9. What's at stake for each character?

10. What's stopping them?

11. How do they try to get what they want?

12. How does each character look at the other?

Chapter 11

The Scene Related to the Film

1. What happened before this scene?

2. What does it add?

3. What's different at the end?

The first three questions deal with how the scene itself will connect and relate to the film as a whole. How did we get here? How does this change things? Where are we going next? Often the answer to these questions begins with the knowledge of the theme of the story you are telling.

Any film that has any quality at all will have an overarching theme that is the backbone of the film and from which every thing in the film develops. Without a strong theme the film becomes unfocussed and runs off the rails, if it had any rails to begin with. A film like *Tootsie* could easily have been dismissed as a gimmick comedy with Dustin Hoffman in drag. But the writers Murray Schisgal and Larry Gelbart (plus several other writers who helped) and director Sydney Pollack found the soul of the movie in the concept that a "man learns to become a better man by becoming a woman." On the other hand there are hilarious comedies such as *The Hangover* or *There's Something About Mary* that are great fun to watch the first time but whose themes are so thin they evaporate before we reach the theatre parking lot. They are like cool rides at Six Flags or the Angry Birds game on my iPad, great diversions and little more. That doesn't mean they don't have a theme even if it is airy light. Is the theme of *The Hangover* "Even innocent actions done in fun can have disastrous consequences"?

Here are some themes of the films we are about to examine:

Kramer vs. Kramer: A just-divorced man learns to care for his son on his own, and become a real father in the process.

True Grit: A young girl fights the adult world to avenge her father's killer and becomes a strong woman.

Juno: A pregnant teenager tries to find parents for her future baby and learns to become a woman and a mother.

Once we have found what we think is the theme of the screenplay we have found the password that unlocks the inner workings of the film. We have also found the key to developing the film further. We can use it to build the characters, the plot, and the dialogue. Because in the best of films, or plays or novels, even paintings, sculptures, and symphonies, the overall theme is embedded in every part of the whole work of art. In any creative work this theme is the foundation, the armature, of the whole. If this theme is weak then everything else is weak as well. The movie feels thrown together without unity or purpose beyond making a movie to make a movie.

It would be great if someone could tell us the theme right away. So much easier. We need the CliffsNotes of the film, right? Trouble is, Cliff doesn't make those notes until after you've made the film. In high school and college we depended on Cliff to bail us out of those annoying homework assignments. If we didn't have him we had the answers in the back of the book. There's no CliffsNotes in filmmaking and there are no answers in the back of the book. Create the answers yourself. You may not know if you are right or wrong until after it's too late to do much about it. It's frustrating, and at the same time exciting, to be on the cutting edge of a film project creating new frontiers with our imagination, our creativity, and intelligence.

Seldom do these themes originate as fully formed concepts. Rather, they usually evolve along with the screenplay. The writer's idea doesn't always spring forth like Athena, "full grown from the head of Zeus." The themes often come out of the writer thinking about something else entirely. He may have overheard a conversation between two lovers in a restaurant or seen a scrap of news on the Internet about a woman leaving her children. He may have looked at a magazine cover of a handsome man and wondered if his life was as glamorous as it appeared. It frequently gestates from a small scrap, a vision, a dream, or some other thing that later develops into a story held together by an overarching idea, which is the theme. Similarly directors often have to sneak up on the interpretation of the film they are making. When we do "get it" and grasp the theme, we do it with an insight and understanding that surpasses CliffsNotes because we have decoded it ourselves. Now our creative faculties have a full range of tools to use when we direct the film.

1. What happened before this scene?

The shorthand for this question is "given circumstances." Which is a pretty cold way of asking what events, facts, and feelings led up to this scene, screenplay, character, or situation. It's like the question asked of new couples: "How did you guys meet?" Once we know how two people met, we understand much more about them than when we only knew them as "those weirdos." What's their baggage? Where are they from? Were they married before? Are they straight or gay, liberal or conservative, black, white, yellow, brown or fuchsia? We can ask this question of almost any element in the screenplay: the production design and wardrobe, for example. It's obvious how the given circumstances affect the look of a film or what people wear. In *Django Unchained*, to take a recent film, the slaves are so poor and treated so badly that their clothes are ragged, unwashed; their living quarters are barely shacks. The white plantation owners are dressed luxuriously and live in splendor. Those decisions are all rooted in the characters' given circumstances. For now we'll concentrate on what directly affects the characters personally.

We have to discover what we can from previous scenes in the screenplay, from the stage directions that the writer gives us, sometimes even from what happens after this scene as more is revealed about the character. For example, the audience may not understand why a character behaves the way he does until the onion is peeled in a flashback later on. The actor playing the part and the director guiding him can't wait to find this out at the same time as the audience. The actor and director have to make sure that the character's behaviors are consistent with what the audience learns later.

In *True Grit*, what drives Rooster Cogburn's grouchy behavior? The Coen Brothers don't want us to understand him early on. He is meant to be a puzzlement at first. Although a pain in the butt, he is the only person available, though not willing, to help Mattie.

In *Kramer vs. Kramer*, what happened before the beginning that causes Joanna to escape from her marriage?

In *Juno*, what led up to Vanessa, the adoptive mom, meeting Juno in the first place?

How do we find these things out? We have to dig into the screenplay and look for clues to the prior history of the scene. If a character is described as being wheelchair-bound, we need to know how he got there. The audience may not need to know, but the director and the actor *have to know*.

Now guess what? All these questions can be a total waste of your time! You can kill many little gray cells asking questions and not be much further ahead than when you started. Why? Because none of this information makes much difference at all... unless... it affects how the character *behaves* in the scene in question. The information may be interesting by itself but totally useless unless it affects what the character does right now. Don't tell me that Rooster Cogburn lost his parents as a kid or was abused, or came from Kansas... or has an ingrown toenail unless it affects how he *behaves now* in the scene in question.

Say what? This homework can be useless? Simple, we are not historians, we are not psychologists or sociologists. We are storytellers. As storytellers we use the facts that we need to tell the story right now. If we were psychologists we wouldn't be doing our job unless we did a complete and thorough analysis of the history. But as storytellers we tell what we need to tell, when we need to tell it, to keep the story moving and comprehensible to our audience. We are not here to educate them; we are here to entertain them. History and education are in second place. We may hold back a huge amount of information until we're ready to reveal it. Tarantino's *Reservoir Dogs* is a great example. Choosing what to tell and when to tell it is a key storytelling technique.

The secret of given circumstances is that they must be connected organically to the screenplay, the scene, or the character. Example: Shakespeare's Richard III himself tells us in the opening of the play:

> I, that am rudely stamp'd, and want love's majesty
>
> Cheated of feature by dissembling Nature,
>
> Deformed, unfinish'd, sent before my time
>
> Into this breathing world, scarce half made up,
>
> And that so lamely and unfashionable
>
> That dogs bark at me as I halt by them...[1]

This gives the director and actor great leeway to create a character who is warped physically and mentally. He can have a hunchback, a crooked leg, bent posture, and strange speech. These physical attributes are an external manifestation of Richard's inner personality: twisted, negative. These circumstances fit organically with

---

[1] William Shakespeare, *Richard III*, Act I, Scene 1.

Richard's character. If we take these characteristics away from him the actor has a daunting challenge, how to express and show the character to the audience.

Richard Dreyfuss starred in *The Goodbye Girl* in which he plays an actor who is portraying Richard III in an Off-Broadway version. The "director" character will not allow him to use any physical "crutches," insisting that the character's behavior comes from Richard's soul and isn't dependent on external hunchbacks and twisted limbs. Intellectually the "director" has a good point but emotionally his argument falls flat. Dreyfuss' character's performance as Richard was a total flop because the actor had been deprived of key given circumstances that Shakespeare hands us gratis. Dreyfuss himself was a total success. He won the Academy Award for Best Actor that year.

As we read any screenplay or any scene we have to be on the lookout for those things that define the characters, whether they come out of their past or present circumstances. We can add to the circumstances if and only if it enhances the character the way that the writer would have approved. Yul Brynner totally defined the character of the King of Siam in *The King and I* when he forcefully placed his hands on his hips. This became the iconic gesture for the King. If it had not worked it would have been abandoned sooner or later.

The same thing goes for deleting given circumstances. We do so at our peril. In the case of Richard III, the "director" character in *The Goodbye Girl* deleted "unnecessary" circumstances, crippling his actor, making him unable to render the character effectively. Of course it's the director's right to change or invent given circumstances in a film or a play. But that doesn't mean it will work. It's part of the artistic challenge of interpretation. It's what peels our grapes.

Find, discover, create if you must, given circumstances and make sure that you can put them to use in the film. Watch out for past events that may be true but have no bearing on what is going on in the screenplay or the scene right now. It may be true that a character was abused as a kid, it may be true that she had tonsillitis as a teenager, it may be true that she won the Nobel Prize last week, but if you can't use it in the scene it's of little help and may even get in the way. Our job as directors is to help identify the circumstances that work for both director and actor and ignore the ones that don't. Sometimes we may give an actor a prop or business that may not be specifically called for in the script but that helps the actor with his performance and still can be seen as an organic part of the whole. Remember Donald Petrie's example of "propping up the actor" in Chapter 4.

A director's greatest sin is that of laziness; not taking the time to examine the whole screenplay and use our imagination and intelligence to dig out these helpful tools that are prior circumstances.

2. What does it add?

What do we want the audience to know at the end of the scene? Another way to put this is what would we miss if the scene were not in the film? In *Juno* there is a very short scene with a girl in front of an abortion clinic. Juno walks up and talks to her briefly and then walks away.

                    SU-CHIN
        No thanks, I'm off pills.

                    JUNO
        Wise move. I know this girl
        who had a huge crazy freak-out
        because she took too many behavioral
        meds at once...

                    SU-CHIN
        I heard that was you.

                    JUNO
        Well, it was nice seeing you.

She continues on toward the clinic entrance.

> SU-CHIN
>
> Juno!

Juno stops in her tracks but doesn't bother to turn around.

> SU-CHIN
> Your baby probably has a beating
> heart, you know. It can feel pain.
> And it has fingernails.

> JUNO
> Really? Fingernails?

She considers the concept, then pushes open the clinic door.[2]

Su-Chin is never seen again in the film and it could seem like an unneeded scene. But without it we wouldn't see or understand Juno's decision to keep her baby and find good adoptive parents herself.

In *True Grit* the first scene with Stonehill the Auctioneer establishes that Mattie is extremely sharp and able to outmaneuver people in a battle of wits. She wants to return some horses her father bought before he was killed. The Auctioneer does not want to give her a plugged nickel. So she has to convince him to pay her. This makes her actions in the future very believable, which is absolutely critical since she is only fourteen and not expected to be so clever and persistent.

3. What's different at the end?

This is another way to answer the question "What does this scene add to the film?" We hope with all our storyteller's heart that there is something that has happened during the scene that advances our story. Has someone's attitude changed, has a decision been made to do something... or not do something, has something happened that changes the story? If we can't find something that is different

---

[2] Diablo Cody, *Juno*, Fox Searchlight Pictures, 2008.

at the end of the scene... other than five minutes have passed that the audience will never get back, we have to ask seriously what is the scene doing in the film? If we can say that Juno is rethinking her decision to have an abortion, the scene has made progress in the story. If Mattie has tried to convince Rooster to help her out and Rooster has flat refused then the story has progressed, even though Mattie didn't get what she wanted. But if Mattie and Rooster just talk and seem to get nowhere the scene will fall flat... unless there is a clear disagreement or conflict between them.

Rapping at a door of rough plank.
After a beat, a voice—rasping and slurred:

                    VOICE
    The jakes is occupied.

Wider. We see that Mattie stands before an
outhouse.

                    MATTIE
    I know it is occupied Mr. Cogburn.
    As I said, I have business with you.

                    VOICE
    I have prior business.

                    MATTIE
    You have been at it for quite some
    time, Mr. Cogburn.

                    VOICE
             (roaring drunk)
    There is no clock on my business!
    To hell with you! How did you stalk
    me here?!

                    MATTIE
    The sheriff told me to look in the
    saloon. In the saloon they
    referred me here. We must talk.

```
                    VOICE
                 (Outraged)
        Women ain't allowed in the saloon!

                    MATTIE
        I was not there as a customer. I
        am fourteen years old.

No response. Mattie reaches up and raps again,
vigorously.

                    VOICE
                 (sullen)
        The jakes is occupied. And will be
        for some time.³
```

Mattie's goal is clear: to enlist Rooster to help her. Rooster's goal is to be left alone. Both characters are stubbornly sticking to their positions. At the end of this scene Mattie has failed to move Rooster off the pot. What is different is that Mattie knows this is no easy job and Rooster has prevailed.

One thing is critical in every scene: there has to be conflict for the story to stay alive. If there is not some form of conflict present in the scene, then our interest will fade faster than a hooker's smile. When this happens in the theatre the audience cough, stir about, go for popcorn, check their messages, talk, text their friends. Check for tension, conflict, and change in the scene before you get to this point. Fix it at the writing stage... not after it's been shot.

Lack of conflict is often the problem with expositional scenes where story points have to be explained to us. It can be a problem in scenes where characters are just getting to know one another, e.g., two people are making love or eating dinner. Any one of a thousand things where we see little or any change from the beginning of the scene to the end. Perhaps the writer wanted to convey information about a character or the plot, perhaps there was a clever situation or piece of dialogue that the writer was in love with and just couldn't give up.

---

³ Joel and Ethan Coen, *True Grit* based on the novel by Charles Portis, Paramount Pictures, 2010.

If there is no change from the beginning to the end of the scene there is definitely something wrong. Something has to be reconceived. In the case of *True Grit* or the *Juno* scene quoted earlier there is definitely change. In each, one character rethinks her position because of the effect the scene has had on her.

SUMMARY

1. Aggressively seek given circumstances to shape a character's behavior.

2. Given circumstances refer to anything that affects a character's behavior, history, physical state, environment, other people who may be on or off screen.

3. Given circumstances are created by the writer or added by the actor or director.

4. Given circumstances are only useful so far as they affect the characters' behavior in the film.

5. Something must have been added to the story, characters, or theme by the end of each scene, e.g., Juno at the abortion clinic. If nothing changes, the scene is weak.

6. Identify what is different at the end of the scene from the beginning to clarify the goals of the scene and the characters.

7. There must be conflict in a scene for it to stay alive.

8. With expositional scenes directors and actors often have to invent conflicts to keep the scene from being a mere listing of facts.

9. Identifying what the scene adds to the story as a whole can help determine the best approach to the scene.

Chapter 12

Architecture of the Scene

4. Whose point of view?

5. Where are the beats?

6. Where is the Tipping Point?

When you think of a scene as if it were a person, it's clear how important its structure is. If you were creating a person, you would encode him with DNA that answered all sorts of questions: How tall is he? What color hair does he have? Maybe he's bald? What sort of clothes is he wearing — or none at all? These questions are important, but without bones, without the structure, every person would be a pile of skin on the floor.

The questions in this chapter will help home in on the important structural questions that each scene presents, and allow your scene to stand up and be ready to have hair and clothes, and maybe a neat hat added.

4. Whose point of view?

Before firming up an interpretation of any scene, or for that matter any shot, answer this. We know dramatic stories are about incidents in the lives of characters created by the writer. And we also know that good stories have characters that we care about. They may be the hero of the story or the villain or even somebody who only appears in a few scenes. Smart directors know to ask right away *"Whose point of view is it in this scene?"*

When we talk about point of view, we mean more than just what a character literally sees from where he stands or POV.

Though a POV contributes to a character's point of view we really mean point of view in a larger sense, the sense of what a character may be feeling in any scene, especially the lead characters around which the story is centered. If we shoot a scene from someone's point of view we can better understand what he or she may be feeling at that moment.

Take as an example a movie about a sport, say baseball, though any sport will do. Now imagine that there are scenes where the game is being played. There are two obvious ways to film them. We can use several cameras to cover different parts of the ballfield just as they do on TV. Then the players enact the game the way it is written in the script. What would that look like?

It probably would look like the baseball games we see on TV.

That's good because it would feel real. Would we have any sense of what the players are feeling? Not likely. Would we know what the pitcher is feeling as he faces a powerful home-run hitter? Probably not. Would we know what the manager is feeling as his team falls behind? Doubt it. To bring the sport to life dramatically, we have to get inside the head of the characters we are following.

We do want the audience to care about the key characters in the film. Why? Because that is why the audience is watching it. If they just wanted to just see a baseball game they would go to the ballpark or stay home and watch it on TV. Games broadcast on TV are shot in a documentary style that is from the crowd's POV, not one particular person, except sometimes the pitcher. If we want them to get inside the heads of the players or the umpire or the batboy, we have to show a part of the game from those characters' points of view. Not as a documentary, not as a sports broadcast, but as something that gets us subjectively inside the story and the character, not from outside the story.

For example, there was an item on the Internet recently about a girl who heard an intruder in her house in the middle of the night. She hid in the closet and called 911. Before the intruder had discovered her, the police arrived and arrested him. He was an ex-boyfriend stalking her.

OK, fine. This article gives us the bare bones of the story. Told from a basic journalist's playbook it gives the who, what, where, when, and why of the story. But it doesn't give us any point of view beyond the basic facts. As a consequence we read this news item quickly and then move on to retweet our tweets. We have little or any feeling for the girl, or the boyfriend.

It would be very easy for a lazy director to shoot the event as written above and it would be very likely to fall totally flat because there is no point of view. We see this in TV documentaries all the time when they reenact stories from the past. We become spectators standing outside the story not part of it. But even a documentary or a news broadcast can push strong points of view, sometimes known as propaganda or more politely, bias. The great appeal of the Civil War documentaries directed by Ken Burns was that he took an approach that made us sympathize greatly with long-dead characters that we only knew from letters and old photographs.

In the article about the girl who was attacked at night the audience hasn't been given anyone to care about. Of course that doesn't have to be. We can ask them to care about the girl. We can ask them to care about the boyfriend. In some really interesting situations we can ask them to care about both characters, or switch points of view back and forth between the characters as the scene progresses. Look at two examples of how this story might work this way.

A girl is asleep in bed. We have never seen her before, don't know a thing about her. Suddenly there is a noise down the hall that awakens the girl. She looks around in the dark and listens intently. Hearing another noise she quickly gets out of bed, grabs her cell phone, and retreats to her closet and closes the door. Inside she can hear the intruder opening and shutting doors down the hall. She takes her phone and tries to dial 911. The 911 system answers and the girl speaks in a whisper trying to convey the urgency of the situation. The intruder comes closer and closer to her room. Suddenly the girl realizes she is not talking to a 911 operator but to a recording that tells her all the operators are busy handling other calls and she'll have to wait her turn. The door to her room opens and the intruder walks in. He calls her name softly. She can see through the slats of the closet door that it is someone she knows, perhaps an old boyfriend. He opens the closet door and she charges him head first, knocking him backward onto the floor. As he falls he hits his head on the foot of the bed and is knocked unconscious. At that point the 911 operator is heard from the phone asking, "What is your emergency?"

That is one point of view, the girl's. We could just as easily shoot this from the point of view of the boyfriend. He pulls up in front of the house at night and stealthily advances on the house that is totally dark. He forces a window open, all the while looking around for neighbors or police. As he climbs in the window he knocks over a lamp, making a noise that will probably wake up whoever is in the house. Now he heads for the hallway and starts to look into rooms along the hall. We can hear him whispering a name, "Julia," as he looks into each room. He goes into her bedroom and looks around then moves to open the closet door. Suddenly he is rushed by the girl and falls backward, hitting his head. Lights out. The next thing he sees is two policemen hauling him to his feet.

Clearly how the director shoots the scene will skew our sympathies one way or the other. We either root for the girl to be safe or for the boyfriend not to be caught. In *No Country for Old Men* there is a scene where Josh Brolin's character, Moss, hides in his hotel room as the assassin paces the hall searching for him. We see it totally from Moss's point of view. All we see of Chigurh is the shadow of his feet passing the door. We feel for Moss as we would feel for the girl in the earlier example. We don't see Chigurh so we don't know what he knows or what he is thinking, but we know enough about him to assume it's not good.

If we wanted to make the scene more ambivalent we could also show Chigurgh after he's entered the hotel and is searching for Moss. We could see him scheming to outwit his prey. Though we might not be sympathetic to him we can see the event from his point of view. Depending on how the scene is written we may be more scared for Moss or more interestingly actually switch our allegiance back and forth between the two characters.

But the big point here is that once we start to designate points of view the possibilities for interesting storytelling open up dramatically.

Take another scene from *No Country for Old Men*: the one in the gas station where Chigurh toys with the Proprietor. Whose point of view is this? Well we can see that Chigurh drives the scene, making it happen. Is it from Chigurh's point of view? Probably not. The opening of the scene has him paying for his gas and buying some nuts. Very simple storytelling. We're just learning some facts: "man buys gas and bag of nuts." Then Chigurh starts to ask the Proprietor questions that sound innocent on the surface but are bewildering to the owner, confusing and odd. The Proprietor tries to be polite but he is baffled by every new turn of thought. There is something clearly threatening in an unspoken way about Chigurh. Even though the Proprietor doesn't know Chigurh like the audience does, he clearly senses the danger coming from this man and is frightened by him. He tries to keep the peace. He has nowhere to escape to, no one to come to his aid. He is the pro-verbial trapped rabbit. The Coen Brothers kept everything very simple. There is no camera movement, no big close-ups. The actor playing the Proprietor, Gene Jones, was directed to be very still, not to move around. But there is no question that his fear jumps off the screen. Afraid that he will be killed, we are seeing the scene from the Proprietor's point of view. We are not on Chigurh's side and don't enjoy torturing the Proprietor. The power is in the writing initially, and then the acting secondarily. The directors, in this case also the writers, knew that the drama would speak for itself without having to hype it with camera moves or overacting.

The director can pick a point of view or even multiple points of view. There can be several points of view. Some may be much stronger than others depending on the scene. But without any clearly defined point of view the scene is likely to be flat. Choose one. If it doesn't work, try another.

Before leaving this subject there is a different kind of POV that should be mentioned. That is the point of view of the director or the writer... or both. This is an overall view of not only the scene but the entire film. The POV we've been discussing is related to individual scenes and as such are one part of the overall film.

Brett Ratner: What it takes to make a great film or to be a good filmmaker is to have a point of view. And each point of view is different. When I see a Coen Brothers movie, I don't have to see "Directed by the Coen Brothers." I know it's a Coen Brothers film. Knowing them and talking to them and seeing they are in that film... Oliver Stone is in his movies, you know, Scorsese obviously. And Michael Bay is in his films. He's so much a part of his storytelling and he has a point of view. It's not a signature; it's not a shot. It's not like Spike Lee with the shot floating down the street. It's the overall vibe of the movie. And I can't describe what mine is except maybe energetic pace, fun. That's what I bring to it: the same story directed by somebody else might've been earnest, might've been serious, not as much fun, more dramatic. People say that I took the seriousness out of *X-Men*. Maybe I wasn't as serious about it as some would have liked. But that was my point of view.

5. Where are the beats?

In his excellent book *Tips: Ideas for Actors*,[1] Jon Jory, the former producing director at the Actors Theatre of Louisville, defines a beat this way: "The beat is to acting as the paragraph is to writing. The beat changes when the subject (textual or subtextual) changes." That means that every time a character tries a different tactic to get to his goal the scene has started a new beat. In Robert Benton's Oscar triumph *Kramer vs. Kramer*, for example, when Joanna tells Ted that she's leaving him, he first thinks he is being blamed for some trivial thing and demeans her announcement. Follow the changes of subjects as the scene progresses.

BEAT 1: Joanna: *Fire* her escape plan. Ted: *Calm* her down.

```
                TED
I'm sorry I'm late, all right?
I'm sorry I didn't call..I was
busy making a living.

              JOANNA
I took two thousand out of the
savings account. That's what I
had in the bank when we got married

                TED
Joanna, whatever it is, believe
me, I'm sorry.

              JOANNA
Here are the slips for the laundry
and the cleaning. They'll be ready
on Saturday.

                TED
Now listen, before you do something
you'll really regret, you better
stop and think.²
```

---

[1] Jon Jory, *Tips* (New York: Smith and Kraus, 2000).
[2] Robert Benton, *Kramer vs. Kramer* based on the novel by Avery Corman, Columbia Pictures, 1979.

> JOANNA
> (not bothering to look up)
> I've paid the rent, the Con-Ed
> and the phone bill, so you don't
> have to worry about them.

She checks off the last item on her list as her husband watches, dumbfounded.

> JOANNA
> There, that's everything.

Joanna gets to her feet and starts toward the front door. In an instant Ted is after her.

BEAT 2: Joanna: *Dump* him. Ted: *Beg* to salvage the marriage.

> TED
> For God's sake, Joanna, would
> you at least tell me what I did
> that's so terrible! Would you do
> me that little favor?

> JOANNA
> Look, it's not your fault, okay?
> It's me. It's my fault--you just
> married the wrong person.

> TED
> (placating her)
> So we've got problems. Everybody's
> got problems--that's normal--

Joanna opens the door and they step out into the hallway.

INT. HALLWAY OUTSIDE KRAMER APT. - EVENING

> JOANNA
> Ted, you're not listening to me.
> It's over, finished.

> TED
> I'm listening, Joanna--believe me,
> I'm listening. My wife is walking
> out on me after eight years of--

                    JOANNA
              (bitter)
You just don't get it, do you?
              (as though to a child)
I - am - really - and - truly -
leaving - you.

                    TED
I heard you, Joanna.
I promise I heard you.

                    JOANNA
No you didn't.

BEAT 3: Joanna: *Abandon* Billy. Ted: *Reassure* her to get her to stay

You didn't even ask about Billy.

                    TED
              (stiffening)
What about Billy?

                    JOANNA
I'm not taking him with me.

                    TED
What?

                    JOANNA
              (tears start)
Ted, I can't...I tried...I
really tried but...I just can't
hack it anymore...

                    TED
C'mon, Joanna, you don't mean
that. You're a terrific mother--

                    JOANNA
              (from her gut)
I am not! I'm a terrible mother!
I'm an awful mother. I yell at
him all the time. I have no patience.
No...No. He's better off without me.

```
                    (unable to look at Ted)
          Ted, I've got to go...I've got
          to go.
```

BEAT 4: Joanna: *Threaten* suicide to escape. Ted: *Implore, coax* her to talk it through.

```
                         TED
                    (desperate)
          Okay, I understand and I promise
          I won't try and stop you, but you
          can't just go...Look, come inside
          and talk...Just for a few minutes.

                       JOANNA
                    (pleading)
          NO!...Please...Please don't make me
          stay...I swear...If you do, sooner
          or later...maybe tomorrow, maybe next
          week...maybe a year from now...
                    (looking directly at him)
          I'll go right out the window.
```

TIPPING POINT: WILL TED LET HER GO?

```
CROSS-CUTTING BETWEEN THEM--There is nothing
more that can be done, this is the last moment
of intimacy.

                         TED
                    (quiet)
          Where are you going?

                       JOANNA
          I don't know...

The elevator door opens, Joanna steps inside.

                         TED
          Do you want me to help you get a cab?

Joanna shakes her head. The elevator door closes
behind her and it starts to descend.

ON TED KRAMER -- He stands for a moment,
stunned, unable to move. Then he turns and races
back into the apartment.
```

Joanna pursues her goal "to escape this marriage painlessly." Then, Ted tries to apologize with more sincerity but still demeans her. She doesn't waver from her goal so Ted is forced to come up with a different approach in a new beat: *Get tough*, which occurs when he says "Now listen..."

The scene continues with Ted and Joanna each trying new ways to get what they want. This has been named the "Pinch-Ouch" acting approach. I "pinch" your arm... you go "ouch." That applies to each dialogue exchange between actors. But you can only go "Pinch-Ouch" so many times in one beat before you've worn it out and need to find a different "Pinch-Ouch." It would be like little kids facing off going "Is Not," "Is SO," "Is NOT," "Is SO" etc. With beats, a character senses when he's exhausted one tactic and has to try another.

It's very important to go through the script and mark the beats in the text as in the example above. Well-trained actors should know to mark them on their own. They look for the point where one beat ends and another one starts, indicated by a change in approach or subject matter, just like in a paragraph.

> **"Jack Nicholson** takes up the *Witches of Eastwick* screenplay to show how he breaks down a script... Nicholson has affixed numbers from 1 to 4 along the margins of this particular page; each number represents a single 'beat.' He explains that the first thing he does with a script is divide it up into 'beats' or moments of response, and 'measures' — a measure being a sequence of beats in a scene — to get to the fundamental rhythm of the part before playing it in rehearsals."[3]

> **Elia Kazan:** "The third read-through was a critical one for me. I began to watch it and think of how I would stage scenes.... I would have the climaxes, the reversals, and the stages marked in my mind pretty well. Again, I would try to have those come out of causes, out of what happened in the scene, but I would have the beats marked in my mind...."[4]

---

[3]   Janet Maslin, "The Devil," *New York Times Magazine*, July 1987.
[4]   Young, *Kazan*, 240.

Often new or weak directors don't know how to use beats. A common error is to think that everyone should pick up their cues quickly and fly through the dialogue as fast as possible. However, it's a good idea to pause a second or a beat (thus the name) while looking for a new tactic before shifting acting gears to a new action. The more important the change is to the scene the more time is taken. If the actors either forget or never did homework in the first place the director is there to guide them. Having marked the beats the director will make sure that the actors don't "drive through" them. In an effort to get a scene going quicker some directors take out all the pauses. The result, ironically, is that the scene often gets even flatter as it goes faster just like the drug commercials that have to list fifty side effects of a drug in ten seconds. It's just a flood of words drenching the audience. Any humanity is lost.

An actress, Fiona, who studied at RADA in the UK, told me the school's unwritten mantra was "say it faster and it will be all right." But every scene needs pauses here and there. Every scene needs to breathe if only for a millisecond. If there's no pausing, no time taken, no letting the scene breathe, there's no time for the audience to absorb what is going on. Clearly in an action scene or a highly emotional one the moments between beats will be extremely short... but they are there. Without beats the scene will feel like a little kid is kicking the back of your seat nonstop on an airplane flight. After the third kick you are ready to strangle someone.

A director has several tools at his disposal to separate the beats.

Tool #1: Physicalizing

Using physical movement of the characters can allow the scene to breathe and let the audience take in what's just happened. Perhaps two characters have been face to face in an argument. The one who is losing may take a moment by walking away to the window to collect her thoughts. This will be a physical way to express the dynamics of the scene. Two people, Frank and Marlee, could be sitting on a park bench arguing and Marlee stands up and angrily moves away from Frank, who is forced to follow her. This physical movement accentuates the beat and gives us time to absorb what's just happened. The strong value of using staging to identify the beat is that it shows us visually what is happening and not just verbally. Physicalizing the scene in this manner is one of the director's most powerful tools. If the director just depends on the dialogue to carry the scene it is likely to have little spark or dynamism. It can easily go flat and become just a torrent of words. After a very short time that torrent of words becomes too hard for the audience to process and they can easily stop listening. Steven Spielberg's film *Lincoln* has the very difficult job of explaining complicated political maneuvers to us which requires a lot of long speeches. At the same time he wants us to empathize with Lincoln's dilemma as he wrestles with Congress over the hotbed issue of slavery. Frankly, the audience has to work hard to keep up with the drama. Though many will focus their attention to follow, a large segment of the audience has limited patience for this and can give up on a lesser film than *Lincoln*. Only a master film-maker like Spielberg aided by a great script by Tony Kushner and brilliant performances from its all star cast could navigate these treacherous waters that have sunk so many other political films.

Tool #2: Characters Think Ahead

It doesn't have to be a long pause but we do want to see each character thinking about where to go next. That kind of thinking usually starts while the other character is still speaking. It happens while listening, which is why listening and reacting are such crucial skills. We frequently know where a conversation is going before the other person has finished speaking. By then we already have a reply ready. If we are very excited and the argument is getting heated we will jump in and interrupt the other person, screw politeness. However, even in this situation the character's brain is working and we want to be able to see that. The director who wants to see this thinking process will shoot close-ups of each key character to be able to accentuate a character's reaction to the situation.

This coverage of a scene is extremely important to have in the edit bins. It not only helps delineate the beats, it also can be a bailout when a scene needs to be shortened at any point or when the actor gives a better performance in one take versus another. Thankfully with the digital revolution and cheap media it is easier to get sufficient coverage. A director doesn't have to worry about running out of film if everything is being recorded on a memory chip. There are millions of instances in the history of film of directors standing in the cutting room cursing themselves for not taking that extra minute to get the coverage needed to create the dramatic moment that doesn't work. "I was right there, I could have done it so easily!" is the cry heard in the confessional booth of the cutting room. Any director who ever turned a camera is guilty of it. Any directors who say they've never shortchanged themselves are either denying or lying. At least, like sticking your finger in a light socket, you're not likely to make the same mistake twice.

Tool #3: Use the Camera to Show a Character's Thought Process

This can be extremely effective or extremely annoying depending on how the camera is used. Many modern films and television episodes are so enamored of the moving camera that they don't help the scene but actually obfuscate what the characters are feeling. Camera moves should support and elucidate what's going on dramatically. They should be organic to the scene, and not arbitrary. If we use the camera as though we are shooting a music video where every angle is continually moving just to be moving, we are showing off. If camera moves are not organic to the scene they are arbitrary and stick out like a hunchback in a limbo contest. What's a "cool camera move"? Like the man said, "I don't know much about art, but I know it when I see it" applies to good shots. Think of any film that has a "really cool shot" in it. It is likely that the reason you remember it is not because the camera moved all over the place but because it elevated the dramatic moment and illuminated what the character was feeling then. It was an organic part of the drama, which is the kind of camera move that every director should strive for.

The easiest and perhaps laziest cliché example of using a moving camera to help accentuate a beat is the "move in." The camera closes in slowly or quickly on a character at a critical point in the scene. It can indicate many things: the character is thinking about what's being said, is being moved by it, is planning a response, etc. This kind of move even has a special tool, with the highly technical name "the Dramanator," known to the layperson as the zoom control. At the appropriate beat in the scene the camera operator activates his Dramanator and the lens zooms in ominously, letting us airheads know that something important is happening. Cheap and cheesy? Sure, what did you expect? However it can be effective if not overused... which it usually is. When used discreetly it can be an easy way to emphasize what's going on inside a character's mind.

A better version of the same thing is to use the dolly or steadicam to physically move in or around a character at a critical moment. This kind of move feels more organic and less artificial than a zoom in. It feels as though we are being moved through space toward or away from the character. The zoom on the other hand feels more mechanical. It is possible however, to use a combination of the two tools, zoom and dolly, at the same time. A zoom move can be hidden in a dolly move very easily, allowing us to cover more ground quickly. Subtlety however, is always a concern. A camera that zooms in and out, whip panning around, is like a madman with a garden hose. They call attention to themselves and are annoying. The only time they work is in a character's terrified point of view or the re-creation of a documentary event where the cameramen had to capture things that in reality would only happen one time. The opening of *Saving Private Ryan* on the beaches at Normandy is a brilliant example of this kind of camera work.

Even if the actor has a completely blank expression on his face the illusion can be created that something is going on inside. After all, the line between subtle acting and non-acting can be thin.

Paul Newman, the absolute master of the close-up, often seemed to be doing nothing during a shot. But he had such a powerful charisma that we could read many things into what his character was thinking. We won't necessarily get that from a lesser actor but we can fake it with some kind of move-ins, move-arounds, pullbacks, crane-ups, or any sort of movement that helps power the drama. *Caveat Emptor.* Use these moves carelessly, inorganically, they become "Look Ma, I'm directing!" showoffs. Two good books, Christopher Kenworthy's *Master Shots: Volumes 1 and 2*, illustrate 200 shots from great films that will spur any director's imagination.

6. Where is the Tipping Point?

Say what?

What's a tipping point?

Almost every dramatic or comedic scene has a moment where things could go either way. Courtney could decide to go for coffee with Milo or she might blow him off. Whatever she decides to do will be preceded by a moment toward the end of the scene where she wavers about a decision. That moment of wavering has many names: tipping point, turning point, fulcrum. It's not relevant in this discussion what Courtney decides to do with Milo; it is important that she thinks about what course of action to take. Otherwise she is just "driving through the scene" probably the same way she drove through the earlier beats. Most importantly, the director misses a very key dramatic or comedic moment in the scene. And that is directorial malpractice in any jurisdiction.

> **Elia Kazan:** [Y]ou bring out the emotional underpinnings by the form you give the scene. One thing I always do, and I think that it's important for films, is stretch climaxes. [5]

Directors have to identify this tipping point in every scene to make sure the character's decision can be seen on camera. In

---

[5] Young, *Kazan*, 72.

our example we see that Milo is pushing for a yes answer and Courtney is either not interested or on the fence. The drama of the scene is watching the back and forth between the two of them. If it's a well-written scene there will be some good dialogue as the two characters spar. When Courtney resists, Milo has to come up with a new tactic for asking her out and she has to think of a new comeback. These are the beats of the scene. But at a certain point, hopefully before the scene has worn out its welcome, one or the other of them is going to decide something. It could be Courtney, it could be Milo, it could be both of them. Depends on the scene. But whoever it is we are definitely going to want to see what both characters are thinking. This is the tipping point. It doesn't come up at the front of the scene or in the middle, it's always toward the very end.

Why? Because after the tipping point... the scene is almost over. Done. Finished. The climax of the scene is the result of what happens at the tipping point. Anything that comes afterward will be as boring as reruns of the weather report and will get cut. Suppose Courtney says "yes," she will go for coffee, what happens then? Milo may smile, they may walk off together, but the scene is over. Something new has to happen now. One thing is sure, we are not going to hang around. Either there will be a new scene or a totally new beat. For example, they could walk off together and run into Milo's old girlfriend and have a very awkward conversation.

If a tipping point were to come early in the scene something new would have to follow it. There would have to be a new goal, and a new conflict to keep the scene alive. If a scene is shot where it dribbles on much beyond the tipping point and there is no dramatic or comedic value to the scene then it is very likely to be axed at the first convenient place that feels climactic.

Don't mistake a change in beats for a tipping point. Remember that the change in beats is when our characters are still pursuing their main goal but have to try to get there differently because the old tactic isn't working. At the tipping point the character has either run out of arguments or wants to resolve the conflict somehow.

Go back to Question #5, and the *Kramer vs. Kramer* scene where we delineated the beats. See where the tipping point occurs and why it has to be at that place.

It is common though, especially in comedies, for the climax of the scene to happen off-screen. Skip it altogether and just cut the scene at the tipping point. Courtney and Milo argue back and forth about going for coffee, we hang on the tipping point (Courtney thinking about what to do) for as long as it deserves and then cut to the result: their picking up skinny vanilla lattes from the barista. Or maybe we see Courtney on her skateboard riding away from Milo. Doesn't matter what the result is. It's a storytelling technique where the director knows the audience will be way ahead of the story so it's wise to outsmart them and jump ahead to the result. We've all seen the comedic version where Courtney announces, "No way am I going to that stupid dance with you!", and we cut to Milo boogying his brains out opposite Courtney, who is rolling her eyes and barely moving.

There is also the "standoff" version of the tipping point. Both characters stubbornly hold on to their goal and no one is sure who will give in first, or if either one will give in or give up. Sergio Leone made great use of this technique in his spaghetti Westerns like *Fistful of Dollars* and *The Good, The Bad and the Ugly*. In television Larry David's *Curb Your Enthusiasm* uses the standoff to great comic effect.

Another variation on this happens when a conflict is drawn out over a long time in a film. At the end of a scene there is no resolution and the characters have nowhere else to go. At that point we have to cut out of the scene, leaving the whole dramatic situation in turmoil. This is very good storytelling since it keeps the audience on edge... what's going to happen? This can go on for an entire film only resolving toward the end. *When Harry Met Sally...* tracks the rocky relationship between Harry and Sally for the entire film. We watch their relationship shifting like molten lava. "Can men and women ever just be friends?" is the question continually raised. *Nick of Time* follows the intense conflict between Johnny Depp and Christopher Walken's characters for ninety real-time minutes. The characters maneuver back and forth, each trying to gain the upper hand and nothing is resolved until the last minute.

In most action films the fights between the good guys and the bad guys are almost never resolved until the end. The passions are so high that when they are resolved the film is over; save the sappy obligatory wrap-up scene that only serves to remind people to get their parking validated.

SUMMARY

1. Choosing whose point of view a scene is gives clues to directing it.

2. There can be one or multiple points of view in a single scene. E.g. *Juno, Rashomon.*

3. The entire film has a point of view, and so does each individual character.

4. The beats of a scene identify when the character's tactics change.

5. Ignore the beats and undercut the scene.

6. Use staging, character reactions, and camera movement to illustrate beats.

7. The tipping point is the moment of decision in which the major conflict of the scene is resolved.

8. Sometimes a scene ends at the tipping point rather than playing through to the climax. The resolution of the conflict is shown in a later scene.

Chapter 13

Characters Enter the Scene

7. What do they want?

8. What do they expect?

9. What's at stake for each character?

In considering the grand design of the entire story and the scene, we can sometimes lose the trees for the forest. Knowing where each character stands as the scene begins illuminates proper structure and your approach to guiding the performances. Your approach to examining a scene isn't best done by going down a list, item by item, but rather a fluid and circular process. All the thought you put into considering scenes now will pay rich dividends when you are on set with everyone looking to you for the answers.

7. What do they want?

This question is easily recognized by its many identifying synonyms: the objective, the want, the desire, the action, the purpose, etc. Here we'll just call it the goal. In many ways it's the quickest way to give guidance to any actor and penetrate to the heart of the scene. It's the Holy Grail of shortcuts to getting an actor on track. William Ball calls it the "crowbar."[1] For decades directors have been using this question to focus the actors on what they should be doing in the play, the scene, the moment. "What are you trying to get from the other character? What are you trying to make him give you or what are you trying to do to him?"

> **Elia Kazan:** What I try to do is tell them what they want and what they do about what they want, just like in acting in the theater. And what they want often comes from what the other person wants. Usually, emotion is a result of action.[2]

Rule #1: We *Always* Have a Goal

Even when we are dreaming we are dealing with that dream and reacting to what is happening in our own mind. We don't need Christopher Nolan's brilliant film *Inception* to tell us that our life while asleep can frequently be more exciting, more frightening, and more fun than what's going on in our waking hours. Similarly when we are awake we always have a goal. Try to think of an example where we don't have a goal. I love the little sign that I've seen in some offices where the work is insanely boring: "Those who think the dead don't come back to life haven't been here at quitting time!" What is the goal of someone at a deadly desk job? What is the goal of the traffic cop assigned to stand at an intersection where there is no traffic? What is the goal of someone lying sick in bed? What is the homeless person doing lying in a doorway during the day? Just think for a few seconds and you'll realize that our brain is always trying to achieve something, even if it's only trying to get some rest or diverting ourselves by fantasizing.

If we are alive we have goals.

---

[1] William Ball, *A Sense of Direction* (New York: Drama Book Publishers, 1984), 90.
[2] Young, *Kazan*, 72.

Rule #2: No Goal, No Acting

It's called "acting" for a reason. It doesn't mean pretending, it doesn't mean faking emotion, it doesn't mean posing, it means DOING something.

If you're not DOING, you're not acting. Period. End of rule.

If the actor doesn't have a goal in mind, he is lost. Pushed around by the dialogue, the other characters, and the director, he resorts to trying to look good, posing, using all his old tricks that have served him in the past. The actor must have a goal.

Recently, I was directing an episode of the USA show *Psych*. We had a wonderful guest star, Diedrich Bader, terrific at comedy and a really good actor. *Psych* is like a comedic version of the Hercule Poirot mysteries. At the end of every episode the lead character, played by James Roday, has the difficult task of wrapping up the mystery in a multi-minute monologue that explains how he knows who the killer is. In this particular episode Roday is standing next to Bader, whose character's name is Joshua, explaining to Joshua's loyal followers that Joshua is the killer. Because Roday had to do 90% of the work in the scene explaining his complicated reasoning I was paying 90% of my attention to him and 10% or less to Bader, who only had a few lines. During the second take I shifted focus to Bader and was alarmed. Bader had a frozen smile on his face. He was paying attention to Roday but there was nothing going on inside his character. At the end of the take I ran up to him and asked, "What is your goal here?" He hesitated and then laughed as he said, "I was trying to remember my next line."

In fairness, it's really tough to remember a few short lines in the middle of someone else's long monologue. But still, what was his character trying to do? After all, he was being accused of murder in front of his loyal followers. Bader immediately brightened up and said, "I've got to convince my disciples that this is all crap. There's no way they should believe Roday, who is a phony psychic, or that I am a murderer."

"Sounds like a plan," I said, and we went for take three.

What a difference there was. Now Bader had something to play. He has a goal. Joshua came alive as he signaled to his followers in a dozen ways that he was being victimized by this phony psychic standing next to him. Once Bader had a goal beyond remembering his lines, his actor imagination came alive. Not only that but now Roday, who was in the same shot, had an obstacle to work against. He had to work harder to convince Joshua's brainwashed followers of the truth. Finding a good goal is not just a one-sided thing that helps one actor; it works to strengthen every element in the scene. When other actors encounter resistance to their goals they have to find ways to overcome it. The scene starts to have more vitality as the characters battle out their different goals.

We'll discuss later the ways to create various tactics of playing goals so that they don't become monotonous. We are talking of course about beats. In the example above, Bader was so skilled that he instinctively knew how to vary his approach to the goal so that when one tactic had been used up he would find another. In well-written screenplays different tactics are written into the scenes. In lesser screenplays, different tactics frequently have to be devised by the actor and the director in rehearsal.

Rule #3: Every Character Has His or Her Own Goal.

If every character has the same goal there is no drama, the scene will lack conflict, and worst of all, the scene will be boring.

It's not enough to talk to only a scene's lead characters about their goals. Every minor character and every extra needs a goal too. In a courtroom scene the bailiff who stands in the corner saying nothing needs a goal. As the major characters walk down a crowded street the people passing by need goals. Assistant directors usually have the job of working with the extras in scenes. The best of them know how to assign individual goals to each extra. The goals will be varied in urgency and nature so that a feeling of verisimilitude exists. All the extras aren't doing the same thing at the same time. Even an angry mob needs different ways of expressing their anger. The next time you watch a film or a documentary look at what's going on with people in the background. If they are all doing the same thing at the same time, they need either a good reason or a better AD.

In the opening of the last *Harry Potter* film we see a high-angle shot of the students at Hogwarts being marched into the school. They look like nothing more than zombies who march in lockstep with the same blank expression on their faces. Later in the film when Hogwarts is invaded by the Death Eaters and many students are wounded, we see the same students tending to one another as individuals not zombies.

Clearly the students have a good reason for their behavior in each of the two scenes. At the beginning of the film they are all under the control of the masters and their morale and individual spirit has been lost. Later when Harry Potter returns to the school they are revitalized and become again the spirited kids they once were. At the beginning of the film because they behaved like zombies the conflict in the scene came from two sources: their masters who drove them, and from our clear perception that something was terribly wrong with them.

Rule #4: One Beat, One Goal

Many might think that we have multiple goals all the time. What if we're a con artist and we want to gain the trust of the mark to rip him off at the same time? Aren't those multiple goals? Imagine our boss is angry about something we did and we are going to get raked over the coals by him. We want to defend our actions and we want to keep our job at the same time. Or we answer the phone at dinnertime only to hear our mother-in-law calling to complain about something trivial. We want to be polite but we really want to get rid of her so we can eat our dinner. Aren't these multiple goals and don't they conflict with each other? Maybe they are but probably not.

Let's look at these examples more closely. Often what we find is that the two goals that seem different are really very closely related. The main goal of the con artist is to rip off the mark. To do that he has to gain the mark's trust. He can't succeed at the con unless he gains the sucker's trust. What may seem like two goals are really part of the same goal.

The truth is that an actor can only play one thing at a time. This is one reason why a scene gets divided into beats so the actor has different places in a scene to play different goals. A scene does not necessarily have only one goal. If it is long and complicated there could be several. But they have to happen one at a time. When we discuss beats we'll talk about helping the actor separate the goals from each other.

Take the example of being called before the boss to discuss a problem that he thinks is your fault. You want to keep your job and want to defend your actions at the same time. These are not mutually exclusive goals. They are very closely related so that one goal springs out of the other. You have to defend your job in such a way that you don't lose it. That means you will be defending your job by *attacking*, or *explaining*, or *justifying*, or *persuading* or *defending* or *apologizing*, to pick a few active verbs. How much you want to keep the job is going to affect which one of these verbs you will pick. If you don't care too much about the job or are not thinking clearly you might verbally *attack* the boss. If you really need the job you might choose to *apologize*. It is a matter of choosing an active verb that encompasses both aspects.

If you believe that there are really two goals in a scene that don't relate to each other you will have to play one goal at a time. What if in the middle of explaining to your boss why you did nothing wrong you start to lose your temper because he's being unreasonable? Suddenly your emotions take over and tell you it's time to quit! Now your goal changes radically. Will you give in to this urge or curb your emotions? You're wrestling with yourself. One thing at a time.

When media tycoons Rupert and James Murdoch were summoned before the English Parliament they wanted to avoid going to jail and apologize for their newspaper's behavior at the same time. One goal exists to serve the other. Clearly they were not going to pick an action like *attack Parliament*. Many pundits cynically opined that the Murdochs were not really sorry for what happened, they just didn't want their media empire destroyed or have to go to jail. Sounds good to me.

Given this interpretation, when a movie is inevitably made of this debacle (not by 20th Century-Fox for sure) the action we would give the actors is to *appear to be remorseful*. Very different, obviously, from being truly remorseful.

On that day in Parliament when Rupert Murdoch was playing his tiny violin, speaking sentimentally about his father's gift to him of a newspaper, he was definitely trying to make himself appear to be a public-spirited citizen who was only seeking the truth.

Then an incident happened that changed everything.

Suddenly, his son James Murdoch looked to his left and leapt to his feet as an intruder who had outfoxed security ran at the elder Murdoch with a blue shaving cream pie destined for his face. All goals in the room stopped. Everything was instantly put aside as the new goal became *repel the intruder*. Mrs. Murdoch, a former athlete, leapt to her feet and clocked the pie pusher with a right cross to his noggin. London bobbies rushed in to extricate and arrest him. The TV cameras were panned off the mêlée onto some exquisitely ugly wallpaper. Everyone in that hearing room had abandoned their individual goals and focused on what was happening to Mr. Murdoch. Though it would have been funny if some clerk never looked up from what he was writing and totally ignored the pie pusher. That would be someone pursuing his own goal to the exclusion of all else.

Several minutes passed before order was regained and the hearing resumed. The goals changed back to the original ones. So it goes. The takeaway is that if there are truly multiple goals then there have to be very specific places in the scene where they occur and can be played. Simultaneous multiple goals are unplayable by either ordinary humans or extraordinary actors.

> **D. J.** Caruso: Whenever you're most at peace with the simple elements of what does the character want, how is he or she going to get it, and everyone agrees on the theme of the movie, then all of a sudden you're able to navigate and maneuver much better. I hear that some directors like Tony Richardson like to operate out of chaos but I don't know how they do it. I mean, maybe they thrive on that. Change the location at the last second, let's go to a totally different place. I don't know how to operate that way. It's not in my DNA.

8. What do they expect?

When we walk into a grocery store to buy food for the week we expect to find what we want, pay for it, and take it home. Simple expectations. We walk in with confidence and may be preoccupied with other errands, talking on the cell phone to a friend, etc. All this affects how we behave during our goal of buying food.

Now change the expectations somewhat: We are splurging for very expensive Kobe beef from the butcher. And we are late getting to the butcher shop. Sometimes Joe has it and sometimes he doesn't. There are no other markets around that carry it either. Won't this change our expectations and our behavior when we walk into the market? Won't this change how the scene with the butcher is played? Just imagine two different scenarios:

> A. We hurry in, expecting Joe the butcher to have Kobe beef, he wraps it up, and we leave.

> B. We come in thinking Joe is probably out of the Kobe beef but we have to check.

Clearly we are going to play these two versions completely differently just based on our expectation at the top.

Another example: In the high school hallway, Milo approaches a girl he likes, to ask her out for Friday night. If he is a star athlete on one of the school teams he will probably be confident and expect a yes. But he's not the star quarterback, just an average guy dared by his posse to ask out the hottest girl in school. As she's talking to her BFFs he walks up. What are his expectations now? "Well, maybe she'll go with me," or "Please don't humiliate me in front of all these girls." Certainly it won't be Mr. Football's attitude. Milo can put a brave face on and approach with bravado but it's certainly not the same. Is he trying to appear confident? Is he so defending himself against rejection that he can speak without his voice quavering? Milo's goal is the same: to get a date, but his expectation causes different behavior.

When you see an actor in rehearsal playing something that doesn't ring true, is too on-the-nose obvious, or is just boring, you know that he's either made a bad choice or a lazy one, or been misled by a stage direction. Maybe he hasn't thought about it at all. This is the time that the director needs to come up with an adjustment of that character's expectations. In the case of asking the girl for a date, say the stage direction is "He's very nervous as he approaches the gaggle of girls." The actor playing Milo may seize upon this stage direction and just pretend to be frightened. It's likely to be a very generalized "frightened" and somewhat clichéd or overacted.

But it's going to be much more interesting and fun if we can see Milo come into the scene pumped with confidence. Then when he sees the group of girls he visualizes them mocking him. Then he tries to cover up his fear and pretend to be confident. The difference is that he won't be just playing "frightened." We'll be able to see him on a mission to get a date, then taking a moment to deal with a potentially humiliating moment, then trying to hide his wilting confidence. You will definitely get a more interesting result. It may be what you want or not but it will definitely change what's going on in the scene. It will change how the girls in the scene play this as well, probably for the better.

The most common misuse of expectations by a character is to come into the scene knowing what happens at the very end of the scene and already be playing that ending. Playing the end of the scene at the beginning ruins a scene right away. We already can see what is going to happen before it happens. This is a common mistake of beginning actors and directors. The director needs to help the actor find a totally opposite expectation when the scene begins. Then as the scene progresses that expectation can change. And the scene will get interesting.

> **D. J.** Caruso: Actors can get ahead of themselves. The best character direction I gave on *The Shield* to Michael Chiklis was, "You're way ahead of yourself. You've already made your decision that you're going to alienate this guy before the scene starts. Isn't the scene more interesting if you're making that decision during the scene?" And Michael said, "Yeah, you're right." Actors have read the whole script, and know that this guy is a dick and going to screw him over, so they've already made the decision to alienate the guy when the scene starts. I said, "No, isn't it going to be great if we can see you make that decision?"

In Tony Scott and Quentin Tarantino's *True Romance* the brilliant face-off between Christopher Walken and Dennis Hopper would totally go flat or score nine on the Cringing Scale if either character played the end at the beginning. The scene would be totally predictable.

9. What's at stake for each character?

Understanding the stakes of a scene will make clear the intensity and pace with which characters pursue their goals. How much do they care about what is at issue? In *True Grit* if Mattie doesn't get Rooster Cogburn to stop drinking and focus on capturing the killers they will go unpunished and she will have failed to get justice. These are big stakes. Rooster Cogburn's stakes are much less. He just wants the easy way out. He swats at Mattie like a fly that annoys him. If he fails, he'll just drink some more. No big deal for him. Obviously each character is going to play scenes very differently because the stakes are so different.

In *The Social Network*, the Winklevoss twins do the impossible: they wangle an interview with the president of Harvard to get his help because they believe they have been defrauded by Mark Zuckerberg. At stake for them is a huge fortune that will be made from their version of what became Facebook, which they claim was stolen. Across the table is Lawrence Summers, the president of Harvard, who has nothing at stake but his time. He doesn't need more adolescent angst. The Winklevoss twins pursue their goal with passion and energy, while Summers just waits for them to run out of steam. The twins stand to lose a fortune and Summers will only lose a few minutes of his time. So in the scene there will be two very eager and aggressive young men and one old gasbag who couldn't care less.

On the other hand, in *Kramer vs. Kramer* both Ted and Joanna have a lot at stake. Ted will have to change his whole lifestyle to take care of his little son; his work will be affected if Joanna leaves him. Joanna feels so trapped in this marriage that she believes she will jump out a window if she doesn't escape. The actors playing them must pursue their goals with passion and energy. Later in the film Joanna invites Ted to dinner. He arrives expecting to hear that Joanna wants to come home. This is a good thing and he has little at stake; if anything, in his mind, life will go back to the way it should be. Joanna comes wanting to take custody of Billy, their son. At stake is her intense desire as a mother to care for Billy. She approaches the subject carefully and reasonably but is intent on taking Billy with her. Suddenly Ted has an enormous amount at stake. He is no longer Billy's absentee father but has totally bonded with the boy. He will lose the one thing in the world that he deeply cares for. When these stakes change his whole goal changes: it is now to keep Billy at all costs. Thus is set in motion the title of the film as both Ted and Joanna battle each other for their son.

How important the stakes are in any scene will be one of the major factors that affect the way characters approach their goals. This is not an excuse for overacting. Just because characters have a lot at stake does not mean they should necessarily shout and emotionally push in a scene. All the other questions in this chapter define for us the makeup of a character's behavior.

SUMMARY

1. Every character always has a goal.

2. Without a goal, the actor is not acting.

3. Different goals conflicting creates drama and tension in a scene.

4. Each beat has a tactic in service of the character's larger goal in the scene.

5. Expectations inform how the actor begins the scene. There is a difference between what a character wants and what he expects to get. For example, a homeless person asking for a handout expecting to get it, vs. expecting to be ignored.

6. If a scene isn't working, try changing the characters' expectations.

7. The stakes of the scene affect the pace and intensity of the performances. If little is at stake a character will play it totally differently than if much is to be lost.

8. Different stakes for opposing characters creates interesting conflicts. E.g., *The Social Network, True Grit.*

Chapter 14

Interacting
Characters

10. What's stopping them?

11. How do they try to get what they want?

12. How does each character look at the other?

Once you know what the characters want, and the beats that are to be hit during the scene, the fun begins. When two (or more) characters have strong opposing goals they will create fireworks trying to get what they want. Putting the characters into the scene like this is like playing pinball when extra balls are thrown onto the table — they bounce off the obstacles as well as one another!

The three questions in this chapter look at how characters bounce off one another in a dramatic way. The answers to these questions will help navigate your actors through the obstacles of a scene, and provide ideas for focusing each on his character's objective, as it relates to other characters in the scene.

10. What's stopping them?

Don't say there are no obstacles in your scene. If that's true, you're in paddleless poo. That's a real obstacle to what you, the director, want: making a scene work well, making it interesting, unexpected. If you can't find any obstacles to a character's goal something is definitely wrong with the scene. If you can't find any or can't invent any then it's time to go to the writer and say, "Until we have an obstacle in the scene, we don't have a scene." If in *True Grit* Mattie walks into the auctioneer's office and asks for a refund on the horses her father bought and the auctioneer agrees to give it to her, there is no scene. The whole thing is over. It's an errand, the same as if we watch someone go to the grocery store and buy food for the week. Errands are not dramatic and if it's not dramatic we don't want to hear about it.

There has to be an obstacle to what Mattie wants for it to be worth our time to include it in the story. The auctioneer, appropriately named Stonehill, is a cold businessman dealing with a fourteen-year-old girl whom he doesn't know, respect, or care about. She is determined to get a refund on horses she doesn't want and he is just as determined that sold means sold, no refunds or store credit allowed. So the battle is set and the scene is more powerful than most action scenes in films because we learn to care so much for this young girl who refuses to let herself be pushed around by arrogant adults. Because Mattie has such a powerful motivation to get back what she deserves and because the auctioneer is determined not to give in to this "unnatural child" we have one of the strongest dramatic scenes imaginable. The goals of each character are so opposed and so strong, and their expectations are so high, that we can witness fireworks in this sleepy little Western town.

```
                    MATTIE
    I will take two hundred dollars for
    Judy, plus one hundred for the
    ponies and twenty-five dollars for
    the gray horse that Tom Chaney
    left. He is easily worth forty.
```

```
That is three hundred twenty-five
dollars total.

          STONEHILL
The ponies have no part of this. I
will not buy them.

          MATTIE
Then the price for Judy is three
hundred twenty-five dollars.

          STONEHILL
I would not pay three hundred and
twenty-five dollars for winged
Pegasus! As for the gray horse, it
does not belong to you! And you
are a snip![1]
```

Writer/producer David Levinson describes these dramatics as "lines of tension." Tension caused by opposing goals in the scene. The more opposing goals there are, the more lines of tension. In a dramatic scene there may only be one or two. Any really good action sequence may have several lines of tension. Up to an indeterminate point the more lines of tension the better. This may only work to a certain point when the audience has had enough tension and they can't take any more. In suspense or horror movies sometimes the audience will break out laughing when it gets too much. In action movies their brains may go on collective overload and just stop paying attention or following what's happening.

A good example of lines of tension is from Shakespeare's *Henry V*, in what may appear out of context to be an innocent scene. In the last act, Henry, the English king, meets the Princess of France with the intention of marrying her to form an alliance with France. This could be the most boring scene ever watched, even if we know that they've never met before and don't really speak each other's language. That's if we see the scene out of context. But what we will know if we have seen the play up to that point is

---

[1] Joel and Ethan Coen, *True Grit,* screenplay based on the novel by Charles Portis, Paramount Pictures, 2009.

that King Henry's forces have severely trounced the French army. Now he intends to woo and marry the French princess who hates him for what he has done to her country.

> KATHERINE: The tongues of men are full of deceits…. Is it possible that I should love the enemy of France?[2]

At the very least Katherine thinks King Henry is just flattering her. Knowing the context we can watch the king and the princess exchange dialogue that seemed innocent at first blush but is now loaded with tension as they maintain a polite façade but are really throwing down. It is spectacular to watch this scene performed and see the king squirming and struggling to find a way into this woman's heart. We feel the tension as their opposite goals collide. Their obstacles are each other, which may be the strongest kind of drama.

One of the best scenes in *Juno* is when Juno, who is sixteen, goes over to the house of the couple that will adopt her baby. She has come to visit with the husband, Mark, who though thirty-five years old seems hip and on her wavelength. If we just read the scene out of context it could be a dull scene of two people hanging out in the basement. In fact, it starts out that way as Juno and Mark enter the basement and start to check out his old LP collection. They are laughing and joking as he shows her some Japanese comics he's collected that have a drawing of a pregnant superheroine, Super Yuki. He thinks it looks like the pregnant Juno. Juno's brought a CD of some music with her and puts it in the player.

```
The Sound of "All the Young Dudes" fills the
room. Mark laughs.

                    JUNO
        What?

                    MARK
        I actually know this one.
```

---

[2] William Shakespeare, *Henry V*, Act V, Scene 2.

                    JUNO
    You do?

                    MARK
    Yeah, this song's older than me, if
    you can believe that. I danced to
    it at my senior prom.

                    JUNO
    Oh man, I can just picture you slow
    dancing like a dork!

She mockingly places her hands on Mark's waist
and moves back and forth stiffly.

                    MARK
    No, I put my hands on your waist.
    Then you put your arms around my neck.
    That's how we did it in '88.

Mark puts his hands on what remains of Juno's
waist. She drapes her arms around his neck self-
consciously.[3]

Immediately, red flags fly up. Inappropriate! Juno resists dancing, but Mark pushes it and as they move to a slow beat he does something worse. He confesses that he is leaving his wife. The top blows off the scene as Juno fights to repair what is now a totally broken situation. Because Mark is an idiot and a closet pig he doesn't get what he's done wrong at first; by the time he crunches the numbers, it's too late and Juno storms out. The brilliance of the scene is how cleverly the lines of tension subtly build to create obstacles to everyone's goals. There is a sneaking sense of unease as we watch these two interact and the "nice guy" mutates to "creep" before our eyes.

Now imagine a situation where there are *no* lines of tension in the scene. This can happen often with expository scenes toward the beginning where the writers have to lay pipe so the audience can follow the details of what's to come. This is essentially undramatic material but usually very necessary to the understanding of the film or the play. This is one of the problems with *The Da*

---

[3] Diablo Cody, *Juno*, Fox Searchlight Pictures, 2008.

Vinci Code. There is so much art history information and religious information that has to be conveyed to the audience that the film becomes very talky and possibly boring. Though the novel was a giant best-seller and the film was commercially successful it didn't hold audiences' attention well and was difficult to follow. What it needed were stronger obstacles to the scene and character goals.

Audiences are in the theater for two or more hours and their attention can be severely tried long before that. Intermissions at plays are for more than selling drinks in the lobby. We read novels in many sittings, a few chapters at a time. We consequently have more patience for expository material. But all the great novelists know they need lots of conflict and obstacles in their storytelling if they are to succeed.

If you the director can't find conflict in the scene you have to try to create conflict. The best conflict is organic, causing something to happen during the scene, showing conflict where there didn't appear to be much before. In the Mattie/Rooster scene from *True Grit* discussed earlier, it could have been set in many places — on the street, in a bar, a hotel room. But the Coens cleverly put Rooster in an outhouse. The idea of a young girl trying to hire a drunk inside a smelly box shows more of her determination and how desperate she is to get anybody to help her.

Often this can be a solution the director imposes upon the scene, which brings to the surface something that was only internal to the characters. For example, two businessmen are discussing a business deal in a scene. This deal is important to the story but the businessmen are concealing their real feelings and it is hard for us to see where the conflict lies. What if we have them playing a game while they discuss the deal? They could be playing handball or squash or one-on-one basketball in a driveway. We can use the built-in competition in these games to help the audience see conflict that was very internal before. How aggressively do they play, is one more fit than the other, one more sneaky than the other? Any of this can help bring that dull scene to life.

In my HBO film *The Jack Bull* there was a scene with the governor of Wyoming when it was still a territory. He desperately wants Wyoming to be awarded statehood by Congress. But there has recently been huge civil unrest, riots and barn burnings in the territory. If Congress thinks Wyoming is just a wild and crazy place out of control, they'll never grant statehood. On paper this scene has "dull, tedious, boring" stamped all over the page as the governor and his aides stand around and complain about how bad things are. How to show the dramatics was the challenge. The costume designer, Ha Nguyen, suggested that the governor could be being fitted for a new suit that he wants to wear at a possible statehood ceremony. As the scene progresses and he learns how things are going to hell in the territory, the tailor is pulling the suit apart. First the sleeves, then the jacket, then finally the trousers are ripped from the governor's body. The end of the scene leaves the governor (Scott Wilson) standing in his underwear. It was a theatrical, organic, and funny solution showing visibly and amusingly how his dream was collapsing around him.

In Donald Petrie's comedy *Miss Congeniality* with Sandra Bullock and Benjamin Bratt, there is a crucial scene where he has to convince her to enter a beauty pageant that her very tomboyish character wants no part of. It was originally a straightforward dialogue scene set in a living room. Petrie cleverly moved it to her gym where they staged the scene as a wrestling match complete with body slams and flying kicks. The dialogue never changed. One of the funniest moments is when Bratt has her head in a leg lock and her face is all squished up and she asks him, "You mean I have to wear the bathing suit and be all beautiful?"

One clichéd situation that has been overused in films features a salesman calling a very important potential client on the phone trying desperately to sell him something. The big client is speaking to the salesman and very politely strings him along. However the audience is allowed to see that the client is practicing his golf putting while he talks on the phone, or is making out with his secretary. The clear message to the audience is that the client doesn't give two hoots in hell about what the salesman wants. What reads on the script page as a polite conversation between two people is transformed into a scene where the previously hidden conflict is pushed front and center.

The other big clichéd attempt to insert tension in a scene is where the boy and the girl are in front of her house trying to say good night or are about to make out when her Dad calls to her from the front door to come inside.

A desperate example of a director trying to wedge some conflict into a scene that had none before would be two people walking along discussing their feelings about a third character who isn't present. That's it. For lack of anything else a director could try to create conflict by having one of the characters have a stone in his shoe. As they walk, the character tries to ignore it but eventually has to find a place to sit, to take off his shoe, remove the rock, put the shoe back on, then test his walk gingerly to see if it's better. All the while, continuing the dialogue. This brings a small degree of tension to the scene even though it's shoehorned in. (Note: Bad pun intended.) But weak scenes often call for desperate measures. Of course it's better if the new action is organically connected to the content of the scene as in the example of the salesman and the client.

11. How do they get what they want?

Up till now we have been asking easy questions: who are the characters, what do they want, what's stopping them, etc. The hard question is: *How* do they try to get to their goal? What tactics do they use? This means that all the questions we've asked up till now will be called into play as the actor and the director collaborate on what tactics the characters will use to get what they want. Do they plead, or beg or demand? Do they harangue, attack, bribe, cajole? Just as we always have something we want or are trying to do, we always have a way that we are trying to do it. Let's say that our young man Milo is still trying to get Courtney to go out with him. That's his goal. He only has one line, and a truly lame one at that:

```
                    MILO
        Courtney, how 'bout a Starbucks?
```

So how is the actor supposed to read this line? There have to be hundreds of choices. *How* does he invite her? Does he ask her cheerfully or sadly? Does he act smilingly, or with hostility? All of these adverbs could be an accurate description of how he invites her. But, read carefully: neither the writer, the director nor the actor should think in adverbs.

When directing actors never speak in adverbs. Repeat, never speak in adverbs. Adverbs in the stage directions of a screenplay should be crossed out. Adverbs lead you down the path to bad acting... every time. If we tell our actor Tom to ask Courtney "cheerfully" we are going to get his *impression* of cheerful. He will paste it on his face like a mask. It will be a general, stereotyped version. He is trying to give us the result that we've asked for but ironically that's not what we want. This is the path to generic, clichéd, indicated, dishonest McActing.

What we want is something deeper, something that comes from inside his character. What we want is the way that his character would approach this situation, the tactics that he uses. So how do we get there? What words can we use to guide our actor?

Only Verbs... Active Verbs!

The clearest and most effective way to perform any action is to first boil the action down to a verb. Not just any verb however, but one that is active, one that moves the character forward.

Passive verbs like "to be," "to think," "to have," and "to hold" are not helpful except in some Zen-like context. We want action. Actions need active verbs to get started. Active or dynamic verbs are words like *to charm, demand, beg, harass, spank, run, hit*, and *go*. All of these involve action. Avoid the adverbial version of these words such as "charmingly," or "demandingly." When we use the active verb form the actor can create choices that are fresh and organic to their character.

Jeanne Tripplehorn: Give me a verb. I love to be given verbs. Those to me are the most helpful. Communicate with me in the most direct way.

Let's return to our hapless character Milo. He has many choices how to approach Courtney. To charm her is an obvious one. Beg her is another; harass, threaten her and so on. Whatever verb the actor chooses gives him a specific way to get to his goal. It doesn't mean he will be successful, it doesn't mean it's the right way to go about getting her to go with him. That's OK though, it's nearly always more interesting dramatically when a character has trouble succeeding.

How do we know what's the right choice? Well, that's the fun part.

Remember in directing and acting there are no answers in the back of the script. There are always choices that have to be made and they may be strong choices, weak ones, clichéd ones, or flat-out bad ones. It would be easy to say this is where we descend into the black hole called talent, that ineffable quality that many say can't be taught. If this were true we might as well throw up our hands and walk away. After all if it can't be taught, as Nicholas Proferes once observed, one either has talent or one doesn't and there's nothing to be done about it.

Thankfully, this is not strictly the case; some people are inherently better at certain things than others. Kobe Bryant has a great athletic talent, Martin Scorsese has a great talent for directing, Pablo Picasso had a great painting talent and so on. But that doesn't exclude the rest of us. We all have some degree of talent. It may not be as strong or as intuitive as others but we are not lost. What we can do is work to improve our abilities in our chosen fields. The basketball player practices free throws and jump shots for hours. Artists continue to take classes and create pieces. Filmmakers know to keep asking questions of their scripts, their scenes, and their actors. Everyone knows that just as the athlete has to go to the gym to stay strong and sharp, the filmmaker has to continue making films to keep his creative engine going. Remember the old musician's joke: "How do I get to Carnegie Hall? Practice, practice, practice."

In the case of Milo and Courtney we still haven't answered the question *"How* does he ask her?" And the maddening answer is... wait for it... it depends. Depends on what? Let's see. OK, stay with me on this one.

A. *Why* does he want to date Courtney? Is it because she is hot? Did his mother tell him she is a good match? Does he have a bet with his friends that he can get a date with her? Does he want information from her? What does the writer give us as prior circumstances? All of these situations are very different and each one will cause Milo to approach her differently. The situation of the story is going to make Milo frame his approach individually.

B. What kind of character is Milo? A shy Milo (Napoleon Dynamite?), who has a bet with his friends, will talk to Courtney one way. An aggressive Milo (Vince Vaughn?) will talk to her another way. The writer should offer helpful clues about Milo's character. A good writer will throw curve balls at the character, which makes the actor's choices more complicated. Imagine that the aggressive Milo is intimidated by smart women like Courtney. We know that because the writer tells us he's tongue-tied in their presence. How will that affect how he approaches her?

C. What does Milo expect when he approaches Courtney? As we discussed before it also depends on how he sees her. Does he see her as a pushover, or an intimidating woman, or someone on his wavelength? Does he expect to get rejected or accepted; mocked or flattered?

So the more we know about both Milo and Courtney in all these aspects, the more intelligent and creative questions we can ask about them and the more choices of active verbs we can try out with the actor.

A great active verb tool for every director and actor is a thesaurus. Thankfully authors like Judith Weston[4] and William Ball have compiled very handy lists of active verbs in their books on directing actors. There is also a terrific book called *Actions: The Actor's Thesaurus* [5] that is a treasure-trove of active verbs. I never prepare a film without having one of these sources close at hand.

An excellent way to proceed with the scene or screenplay you are preparing is to write actions in the right-hand margin next to each line of dialogue. Big job? But imagine the alternative: we read the scene a few times and say to ourselves, "Milo wants to date Courtney and Courtney wants to ensure he is an OK guy." That in itself is probably correct. The trouble is it doesn't go far enough. The actors could start acting at the beginning of the scene knowing only that is their goal. They would be all right for a few lines, but if the scene goes on much longer they will need variations in how they approach the goal. It will be boring otherwise.

Courtney is standing at the copy machine checking a job she's running. Milo saunters up carrying some files.

```
                    MILO
        Courtney, what's up?

                    COURTNEY
                (eyeing him carefully)
        You're... from accounting, right?

                    MILO
        How'd you know that? I stopped wearing
        pocket protectors a long time ago. I'm
        Milo.

                    COURTNEY
                (looking for an exit)
        How long have you worked here?
```

---

[4] Judith Weston, *Directing Actors* (Studio City, CA: Michael Wiese Productions, 1996).
[5] Caldarone and Williams, *Actions: The Actor's Thesaurus* (New York: Drama Publishers, 2004).

Pretty boring, right? Forget that the dialogue is terrible. Even if the writer gave them more interesting things to say they are stuck in a rut. We have to have variation. And the variation nearly always happens when the beat changes.

12. How does a character regard the other?

Columbia professor Nicholas Proferes in his excellent book *Film Directing Fundamentals* poses this very interesting question. He refers to "dynamic relationships."[6] The idea is that there are two kinds of relationships in life: static and dynamic. A static relationship would be between you and your mother or father, your sibling or your cousin. These are generic relationships that don't change. Your mother will always be your mother and your brother will always be your brother. Even you and your boss comprise a static relationship. He might be a different person from time to time but he is still your boss or someone who oversees the work that you do. That part doesn't change just as your mother will always be the person who gave birth to you. What does change is how you see that person. Teenage girls often see their mothers as "witches" on Friday night and "BFFs" on Saturday when they need something. That's the dynamic part.

Another way to look at it is to imagine what one character would say about the other when they are not around. "How's Bill?" says one. "What a jerk!" replies the other. He may not say this to Bill's face, but that's what he's thinking.

When you first come to work at a job the boss may greet you effusively, show you around, explain the job carefully, and make sure you have everything you need. You think to yourself, "He's a nice guy, or a really supportive person." After a few weeks on the job you hear that he makes negative comments about you behind your back. You can now see that he is probably a back-stabbing SOB. Then you learn that his wife is very ill and this has made him be

---

[6] Nicholas Proferes, *Film Directing Fundamentals* (New York: Focal Press, 2008), 17.

ill-tempered. You still think he is a back-stabber but perhaps you don't judge him as harshly as before. He is still your boss, that doesn't change. But your views of him change dynamically with the situation you are in.

In *Juno*, when Juno comes to hang out with Mark in the basement she sees him as a cool older guy. After she learns that Mark is leaving his wife the relationship dynamics change and she sees him as a creep. Similarly Mark may see Juno at the beginning of the scene as a cute escape from his wife. At the end of the scene he sees her as a naïve child. So when we ask the earlier question about what is different at the end of the scene from the beginning, we should also ask what's the dynamic relationship between the characters at the beginning and at the end of the scene? How characters view each other determines how they deal with one another. And because that relationship is not fixed but dynamic it is more interesting and exciting dramatically. Our example from *True Grit* with Mattie and the auctioneer is an excellent one to illustrate the point further. At the beginning the auctioneer sees Mattie as a naïve girl he can push around; by the end he sees her as his worst nightmare. Mattie on the other hand sees the auctioneer as a bothersome obstacle to what she wants. By the end he is roadkill.

Why is this concept of dynamic relationship helpful to actors and directors? Simply because it helps them understand how characters relate to other characters in the scene and helps them make more interesting and truthful acting choices. The really good actor does this instinctively so that we can see how he views the other character or characters in the scene. A lazy or unskilled actor and/ or director will not take any of this into account and that's why scenes can often seem one-dimensional, flat, or clichéd. Always ask, "How does Character A feel about Character B at the beginning, the middle, and the end of a scene?"

SUMMARY

1. Goals are meaningless dramatically without obstacles to challenge them.

2. When two characters have opposing goals, one's goal becomes the other's obstacle and vice versa.

3. If a scene lacks sufficient obstacles in the script, create some, using staging, character business, and other directorial choices.

4. Tactics are how characters go about achieving their goals.

5. Active verbs are the best way to convey how actors should behave in achieving their goals.

6. Do your homework and make notes of active verbs for each beat of the scene in your script.

7. Static relationships are fixed, like a mother and her child. This is not very interesting dramatically.

8. What is interesting is how each character dynamically views another. A daughter may think her mother is a "witch" today, but a "BFF" tomorrow.

9. Dynamic relationships change with time and circumstance.

10. The idea of dynamic relationships in a scene can help the actors make more interesting acting choices during the course of a scene.

Epilogue

We are well served to remember Alfred Hitchcock's analogy about preparation. He told Truffaut that the unprepared director was like an orchestra conductor who wanders out to the podium, picks up the baton, and asks his players, "How about a B flat?" That's different from the conductor who knows every note of his score, who has studied the dynamics of the music, the themes and subthemes, and yes, the soul of the composition. He has a clear audio vision of what he thinks the piece should sound like.

Films unfortunately often get directed in a more haphazard manner. Some directors take pride in their ability to walk onto a set and just start to make things up on the spot. I actually heard an Academy Award–winning director say to his AD early one morning, "So Jerry, what are we shooting today?" Other directors, who may be a bit overprepared, come to work with armloads of storyboards, elaborate diagrams, and detailed notes.

So which is the right approach?

Doesn't matter.

Seriously?

What matters is how well the film works. If the director sleeps in his chair all day long but the film is great, nobody cares what kind of preparation he did. (Has this ever happened?) The opposite is also true: a film can be prepped to the nth degree, and yet, to use a technical term, still suck. But there is a way that is more dependable than hoping inspiration will strike, which may or may not work depending on the alignment of the planets, the goats' entrails, or how much sleep the director had last night. There is a way that doesn't require one to be a micro-manager who looks to control all aspects of the film.

The ways that the great majority of talented and skilled professional directors prepare will vary from director to director but show many common characteristics. A good director will think out how a film will play, how the story will be told, what the characters are like, how it looks, even down to what individual cuts need to be shot in sequences. He will plan as much as he has time and inclination for. When it comes to the first day of shooting he is confident that his preparation will serve him well. And...

He is ready to throw it all away.

Why?

What if somebody has a better idea? When five, ten, or fifty people are working on a film? There will be five, ten, or fifty ideas about how something should go. The smart director is set on a strong path but is always looking out for that alternative route that might be more interesting, more fun, more edgy, whatever. Directors develop a sixth sense for what people around them are thinking. They are not afraid to ask their actors, their DP, or AD, "What do you think?" That's not so they can see if someone will kiss up to them, that's to see if there are fresh ideas, something that hasn't been thought of. If there are new ideas, as very often happens, a good director won't be threatened but, rather, will analyze the new possiblities in the context of the whole film, which he probably knows better than anyone at this point. He is free to accept or reject the idea since the film rests on his shoulders, not on those of whoever had the idea. At the same time the director is grateful to the suggester for the idea in the first place — even if the idea is rejected — because he wants to encourage ideas, not stifle them, which is the easiest and laziest thing to do.

Just say no once or twice to a crew member or an actor and they'll never trouble you again. And it probably will be your loss. Keep your options open till the day the final version is locked and unchangeable. Even then there are director's versions, TV versions, airline versions, audio commentaries, etc., where directors change their minds or have new ideas about how the film should go. One doesn't have to be George Lucas, who continues to tweak his *Star Wars* films, to be able to revisit one's work. Long after the death of Orson Welles, he finally got a version of *Touch of Evil* closer to what he wanted when Universal Studios let Rick Schmidlin and Walter Murch make Welles' forty-eight pages of changes that had been ignored for decades.

Films are like your children, who may grow up, move out on their own, become successful. But one thing is for sure, they still write home for money. And you will send it to them!

Acknowledgments

This book is dedicated to my mentor and close friend, David Levinson. Without his help, encouragement, and wise counsel for more years than dogs have fleas, I would still be stuck in the basement of the Universal Studios casting department. Better than any shrink and a hell of a lot cheaper, he has shepherded me through personal crises and a career path with the ups and downs of a sine wave on steroids.

Trusting me with my first directing job, he wrote and produced the episode of *The Senator* with Hal Holbrook that got me my first Emmy nomination and his first Emmy award. With an uncanny ear for great writing and a sharp eye for good directing he has mentored many of the best producers and directors now working in television.

His sharp, sarcastic tongue and take-no-prisoners approach to storytelling has quailed many a timid talent while earning their respect through his harsh lessons in excellence. We who know, love, and respect him intend to compile a handbook of his pith.

Shit Levinson Says will be the manual for all young writers and directors who will never find a better rabbi.

Without a lot of support and help from many friends and colleagues a book like this is not possible. My dear wife, Julia, has always been highly supportive the whole time that I'm trapped behind a MacBook Pro, even when we're supposed to be out in a boat fly-fishing in Montana.

My tireless assistant, filmmaker Ted Wilkinson, whose OCD has prevented endless goofs and gaffes, has been a great sounding board and source of ideas for organizing the text.

My daughter, Kelley Huffines, has always been my best editor. Somehow finding time between innumerable "Mommy" chores to bust me on any mistakes, inaccuracies, or prevarications, she combs and repairs the text with eagle eyes.

Senior copy editor Gary Sunshine, who can spot illogical, even illegal copy from a thousand yards.

My brother and Alabama historian, Tom Badham, whose wicked sense of humor and Southern sarcasm help save me from the quicksand of pomposity.

I owe a big debt of thanks to all the film distribution companies that provided international posters of my films. They're great fun to see and share.

Finally my two best Westie friends, Fanny and Oliver, have kept me barely sane by enforcing a rigorous walking schedule and pulling me away from the computer.

As this book was already at the printer, I learned of the passing of my longtime friend and brilliant film editor Frank Morriss, who edited twenty-two feature films for me. More than a great artist, he was the kindest and most generous man who trained many young aspirants in the black art of editing. Nominated for Academy Awards for *Blue Thunder* and *Romancing the Stone*, he won two Emmys and an ACE award for *Duel* and *The Execution of Private Slovik*. He made many contributions to the sections of this book on shooting action. Frank, I will miss your friendship, your talent, your sage advice, and your never-failing support and enthusiasm. Godspeed, dear friend.

Further Reading

I'll Be In My Trailer: The Creative Wars Between Directors and Actors by John Badham and Craig Modderno. Studio City, CA: Michael Wiese Productions, 2005.

http://shop.mwp.com/products/ill-be-in-my-trailer

Directing Actors: Creating Memorable Performances for Film and Television by Judith Weston. Studio City, CA: Michael Wiese Productions, 1999.

http://shop.mwp.com/search?q=directing+actors

Judith Weston's book effectively encapsulates many of the concepts that great directors and acting teachers have used and taught for decades.

Actions: The Actors' Thesaurus by Marina Caldarone and Maggie Lloyd Williams. New York: Drama Publishers, 2004.

This excellent handbook is a never-leave-behind item that is always stuffed in my bag when I go into rehearsals. Filled with action verbs of every kind, organized in an easy-to-use thesaurus format, it is a wonderful source of directions.

A Practical Handbook for the Actor by Bruder, Cohn, Olnek, Pollack, Previto, Zigler. New York: Vintage Books, 1986.

http://www.amazon.com/Practical-Handbook-Actor-Melissa-Bruder/dp/0394744128/ref=sr_1_1?ie=UTF8&qid=1351548837&sr=8-1&keywords=practical+handbook+for+the+actor

Written by workshop students of David Mamet and William H. Macy, this book is as helpful to the director as it is to the actor. Its chapter on physical action alone is worth the price of the whole book.

Master Shots Volumes 1 and 2 by Christopher Kenworthy. Studio City, CA: Michael Wiese Productions, 2010 and 2011.

http://shop.mwp.com/search?q=Master+Shots

Hundreds of camera setups for different situations. Frame grabs from many famous films illustrate the text.

Leader Effectiveness Training (LET) by Thomas Gordon. New York: Perigree, 2001.

http://www.amazon.com/s/ref=nb_sb_ss_i_0_20?url=search-alias%3Dstripbooks&field-keywords=leader+effectiveness+training

What does this have to do with directing? The principles of communicating with people effectively and resolving conflict works the same in business, marriages, parenting, and even filmmaking. An invaluable tool for learning and sharpening people skills.

The One Minute Manager by Kenneth Blanchard, PhD, and Spencer Johnson, MD. New York: Berkley, 1983.

http://www.amazon.com/s/ref=nb_sb_ss_i_0_18?url=search-alias%3Dstripbooks&field-keywords=one+minute+manager&sprefix

This thin little book disguises a wealth of information about managing people. More stress and conflict can be resolved with the simple techniques here than by reading tomes of psychology.

Friendly Enemies by Delia Salvi. New York: Billboard Books, 2003.

http://www.amazon.com/Friendly-Enemies-Director-Actor-Delia-Salvi/dp/0823079449/

The subtitle "Maximizing the Director-Actor Relationship" tells all you need to know about this very informative book, often written from the actor's point of view. There are excellent insights into the minds of both directors and actors.

The No Asshole Rule by Robert I Sutton. New York: Warner Business Books, 2007.

http://www.amazon.com/The-Asshole-Rule-Civilized-Workplace/dp/0446698202/

Its subtitle is "Building a Civilized Workplace and Surviving One that Isn't." Winner of the Quill Award as the Best Business Book of 2007. First published in the staid *Harvard Business Review* based on the notion that employees with malicious intents or negative attitudes destroy productive and pleasant work environments and hinder their success. (Amazon description)

Photo Credits

Using This Book

Steven Soderbergh (courtesy Steven Soderbergh)

Introduction

Taylor Hackford (courtesy Marc Bryan-Brown)

Gilbert Cates (courtesy Geffen Playhouse)

Jodie Foster (courtesy Jodie Foster)

Stephen Collins (courtesy Stephen Collins)

Michael Zinberg (courtesy Paramount Pictures)

D. J. Caruso (courtesy D. J. Caruso)

Michael McMurray (courtesy Michael McMurray)

Chapter 1

Martin Sheen (courtesy Martin Sheen)

Gary Busey (courtesy Gary Busey)

Eriq La Salle (courtesy Eriq LaSalle)

Martha Coolidge (courtesy Martha Coolidge)

Donald Petrie (courtesy Donald Petrie)

Allan Arkush (courtesy Allan Arkush)

John Rich (Elisa Haber, courtesy DGA)

Patty Jenkins (courtesy Patty Jenkins)

Brad Silberling (courtesy Paramount Pictures)

Chapter 2

Bingo Long poster (courtesy Universal Pictures)

Paris Barclay (courtesy Paris Barclay)

Chapter 3

James Woods (courtesy Universal Pictures)

Tom Mankiewicz (courtesy Tom Mankiewicz)

Sydney Pollack (courtesy Sydney Pollack)

Chapter 4

Oliver Stone (courtesy Oliver Stone)

David S. Ward (courtesy David S. Ward)

Penelope Ann Miller (courtesy Penelope Ann Miller)

Richard Donner (courtesy Richard Donner)

Peter Hyams (courtesy Peter Hyams)

Betty Thomas (courtesy Betty Thomas)

Richard Dreyfuss (courtesy Richard Dreyfuss)

Brett Ratner (courtesy Brett Ratner)

Saturday Night Fever Japanese poster (courtesy Paramount Pictures)

Chapter 5

John Frankenheimer (courtesy John Frankenheimer)

Judge Reinhold (courtesy Judge Reinhold)

Bird on a Wire Norwegian poster (courtesy Universal Pictures)

Goldie Hawn (photo by Joe Lederer)

Mel Gibson, Dawn Stofer-Rupp (photo by Joe Lederer)

Mary Badham (photo by Leo Fuchs)

Chapter 6

Blue Thunder DVD cover (courtesy Columbia Pictures)

Blue Thunder stills (photos by Bruce Talamon)

Tanzania photographs (photos by John Badham)

Chapter 8

Point of No Return Japanese poster (courtesy Warner Bros. Pictures)

Nikita poster (courtesy Warner Bros.)

American Flyers Italian poster (courtesy Warner Bros. Pictures)

Chapter 9

Bird on a Wire storyboards (courtesy Nikita Knatz)

Tom's Restaurant (ValeStock/Shutterstock.com)

Stakeout stills (photos by Bob Akester)

Chapter 10

Still from *No Country for Old Men* (courtesy Touchstone Pictures)

Nick of Time Japanese poster (courtesy Paramount Pictures)

About the Author

John Badham has earned the reputation of an "actor's director" through a career impressive in both range and diversity. In 1977, he guided a then-unknown Travolta to worldwide fame with *Saturday Night Fever*, a cultural milestone that launched the disco era and went on to become one of the top-grossing films of all time. Two of his early actions films, *Blue Thunder* and *WarGames*, both released in 1983, received four Academy Award nominations.

Badham's first feature film, *The Bingo Long Traveling All-Stars and Motor Kings* (1976), teamed an impressive cast including James Earl Jones, Billy Dee Williams, and Richard Pryor. The Los Angeles Film Festival honored the twenty-fifth anniversary of the film with a screening and talk with Badham moderated by leading film journalist Elvis Mitchell. Badham has also received recognition for his vivid adaptations of two Broadway plays: *Whose Life Is It Anyway?* (1981), starring Richard Dreyfuss, and the stylized *Dracula* (1979), with Frank Langella and Laurence Olivier, which swept the Grand Prizes at the Paris International Science Fiction Festival and the U.S. Science Fiction, Fantasy, and Horror Awards. He then directed Kevin Costner in the cycling action-drama *American Flyers* (1985), followed by the delightful comedy *Short Circuit* (1986), featuring Ally Sheedy, Steve Guttenberg, and robot Number 5.

In 1987, Badham directed Richard Dreyfuss and Emilio Estevez as a pair of undercover cops in the hit movie *Stakeout*. He went on to helm the action/comedy *Bird on a Wire* with Mel Gibson and Goldie Hawn in 1990. Both movies rank among the top-ten grossing movies of their respective years. Badham's film *Point of No Return* (1993) propelled Bridget Fonda to stardom, as a government-created assassin. In *Another Stakeout* (1993), Badham reunited Dreyfuss and Estevez, and then took Wesley Snipes into the high adrenaline world of skydiving to catch a group of killers in *Drop Zone* (1994). Badham's *Nick of Time* (1995) starred Johnny Depp as an ordinary father who is forced into a plot to assassinate the governor of California when his young daughter is kidnapped.

Badham is also a prominent television producer and director. He has directed episodes of the hit shows *The Shield, Heroes, Men in Trees, In Plain Sight, Standoff, Crossing Jordan, Las Vegas, Nikita,* and *Psych.* He served as an executive producer for the Steven Bochco drama *Blind Justice* and directed several episodes. He received two Emmy nominations for his work on the '70s series *The Senator* and *The Law.*

Badham has directed a number of telefeatures, beginning in the '70s with *The Impatient Heart* (1972); *Isn't It Shocking?* (1973), a black comedy starring Alan Alda; and *Reflections of Murder* (1974), based on the classic French film *Diabolique.* Badham's *Floating Away* (1998), starring Paul Hogan and Roseanna Arquette, won the Prism Award for its portrayal of alcohol abuse. Badham has also helmed *The Jack Bull* (1999) for HBO, starring John Cusack and John Goodman, and *The Last Debate* (2000) for Showtime, starring James Garner and Peter Gallagher. He focused on drama with USA's *My Brother's Keeper* starring Jeanne Tripplehorn (2002), Lifetime's *Obsessed* (2002) starring Jenna Elfman, and CBS's *Footsteps* (2003) starring Candice Bergen. He returned to big action and fun with *Evel Knievel* (2004).

Badham's book *I'll Be in My Trailer: The Creative Wars Between Directors and Actors,* exploring the intimate and delicate creative partnership between actor and director, is used as a textbook in courses teaching techniques of working with actors. It was published by Michael Wiese Productions in July 2006.

Badham was born in England, the son of actress Mary Hewitt and a U.S. Army general, who moved the family back to his home in Birmingham, Alabama. Badham's sister, Mary, became the first of the two siblings to break into the movie business and at age 10, she received an Oscar nomination for her portrayal of the young protagonist in *To Kill a Mockingbird*.

Badham is Professor of Media Arts at The Dodge School of Film and Media, Chapman University in Orange, California. Badham did undergraduate work at Yale in philosophy, and received his Master of Fine Arts degree from the Yale School of Drama. He was presented with an honorary Doctor of Humane Letters from Columbia College Hollywood in June 2008. Selections from his latest films can be seen at www.johnbadham.com.

Index

I'LL BE IN MY TRAILER
THE CREATIVE WARS BETWEEN DIRECTORS & ACTORS

JOHN BADHAM AND CRAIG MODDERNO

I'll BE IN MY TRAILER
THE CREATIVE WARS BETWEEN
DIRECTORS & ACTORS

JOHN BADHAM
[DIRECTOR OF WAR GAMES, SATURDAY NIGHT FEVER]
& CRAIG MODDERNO
[CONTRIBUTING WRITER, NEW YORK TIMES]

What do you do when actors won't do what you tell them to? Remembering his own awkwardness and terror as a beginning director working with actors who always had their own ideas, director John Badham (*Saturday Night Fever*, *WarGames*, *Stakeout*, *The Shield*) has a bookload of knowledge to pass along in this inspired and insightful must-read for directors at all levels of their craft.

Here are no-holds-barred out-of-school tales culled from celebrated top directors and actors like Sydney Pollack, Michael Mann, John Frankenheimer, Mel Gibson, James Woods, Anne Bancroft, Jenna Elfman, Roger Corman, and many more that reveal:
· The 10 worst things and the 10 best things you can say to an actor
· The nature of an actor's temperament and the true nature of his contributions
· The nature of creativity and its many pitfalls
· The processes of casting and rehearsal
· What happens in an actor's mind during a performance
· What directors do that alienates actors
· And much more

"*Most young directors are afraid of actors. They come from film school with a heavy technical background, but they don't know how to deal with an actor. Even many experienced directors barely talk to their actors.*"
> — Oliver Stone, Director, *JFK, Platoon, Wall Street, Born on the Fourth of July*

"*Directors have needed a book like this since D. W. Griffith invented the close-up. We directors have to pass along to other directors our hard-earned lessons about actors. Maybe then they won't have to start from total ignorance like I did, like you did, like we all did.*"
> — John Frankenheimer, Director, *The Manchurian Candidate, Grand Prix, Seconds*

JOHN BADHAM is the award-winning director of such classic films as *Saturday Night Fever*, *Stake Out*, and *WarGames* and such top TV shows as *Heroes*, *The Shield*, and *Crossing Jordan*. Badham currently is the DeMille Professor of Film and Media at Chapman University.

CRAIG MODDERNO is a contributing writer to the *New York Times*.

$26.95 · 243 PAGES · ORDER NUMBER 58RLS · ISBN: 9781932907148

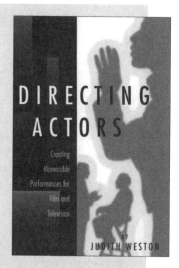

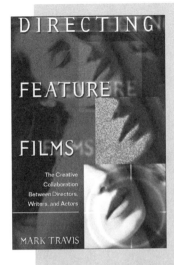

MASTER SHOTS VOL 1
2ND EDITION
100 ADVANCED CAMERA TECHNIQUES TO GET AN EXPENSIVE LOOK ON YOUR LOW-BUDGET MOVIE

CHRISTOPHER KENWORTHY

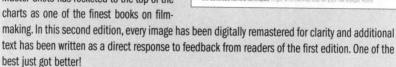

Master Shots has rocketed to the top of the charts as one of the finest books on film-making. In this second edition, every image has been digitally remastered for clarity and additional text has been written as a direct response to feedback from readers of the first edition. One of the best just got better!

"Good books on film directing are rare, specifically books focusing on challenging staging and framing sequences like action and chase scenes. Kenworthy goes a long way here toward bridging this knowledge gap. Essential for beginners or those looking for a refresher before (or during) their next film."

> — Christopher Riley, author, *The Hollywood Standard*

"A great how-to manual for anyone who must communicate with directors. Whether a director, writer, actor, designer, or producer, Master Shots *helps you think about storytelling from the camera's perspective, making you a better filmmaker and collaborator.*"

> — Chad Gervich, TV writer/producer, *Reality Binge*;
> author, *Small Screen, Big Picture: A Writer's Guide to the TV Business*

"THIS BOOK SHOULD BE BANNED! These are the best tricks and secret techniques of professional directors. Why should they be given away for a few dollars?"

> — John Badham, director, *Saturday Night Fever, WarGames*;
> author, *I'll Be in My Trailer*

CHRISTOPHER KENWORTHY has worked as a writer, director, and producer for the past ten years. He directed the feature film *The Sculptor*, which played to sold-out screenings in Australia. Recent works include sketch comedy for the BBC's *Scallywagga*, a title sequence for National Geographic Channel, visual effects for 3D World, music videos for KScope Music and Elefant Records, and an animated wall projection for The Blue Room Theater, Perth, Australia.

$26.95 · 362 PAGES · ORDER NUMBER 179RLS · ISBN: 9781615930876